Doing Phonology

Doing Phonology

Observing, Recording, Interpreting

John Kelly *and* John Local

Manchester University Press

Manchester and New York

Distributed exclusively in the USA and Canada by St. Martin's Press

Copyright © John Kelly and John Local 1989

Published by Manchester University Press
Oxford Road, Manchester M13 9PL, UK
and Room 400, 175 Fifth Avenue,
New York, NY 10010, USA

Distributed exclusively in the USA and Canada
by St. Martin's Press, Inc.,
175 Fifth Avenue, New York, NY 10010, USA

British Library cataloguing in publication data
Kelly, John
    Doing phonology: observing, recording, interpreting.
    1. Phonology
    I. Title II. Local, John
    414

Library of Congress cataloguing in publication data applied for

ISBN 0 7190 2894 9 *hardback*

Printed in Great Britain
by Biddles Ltd, Guildford and King's Lynn

Contents

Preface

We feel that a few words of explanation are needed for putting yet another book on the market with the word 'phonology' in the title. Over and above that, we feel the need to present some kind of *apologia* for the kind of approach to phonological interpretation that readers will find in this book. The two matters come to the same thing in fact: our *apologia* will be, in itself, an explanation for our venturing out with the present piece of work.

We should say at the outset that this is not a text book. It was not written exclusively for students, in the sense of those undertaking a formal academic course. But we think it could be used as a text book; we hope that some teachers and students will so use it, and we naturally hope that they will enjoy and profit from what they find.

There are elements of the text book in it. But there are elements of the diary too, and of the monograph to some extent. At first we intended to call it a 'Handbook of Phonology'. But this smacked too much of the pedagogical and dogmatic and we trust it is neither. So we do not consider it 'A Handbook'. Rather, it is about how we, as two professional academic phoneticians and phonologists, have gone about doing phonology both in the field and in our home scholastic setting. On the whole it is written for ourselves, to put our work in perspective, take stock, and see where we have got to. But anyone at all who *does* phonology should get something out of reading it, and we hope that those who are principally commentators might, too.

The first principle that underlies the way our work has been and is carried out is almost a heretical one, and so best got to grips with straight away. It is that phonetic records of spoken language material are the only serious starting point for phonological analysis and that they should be as detailed and accurate as it is possible for the investigator to make them. This is not a principle to which we pay lip-service; we take it extremely seriously. Consequently we make a point of working on language material in this way and of basing analyses only on material that we have observed and recorded ourselves. This is reflected in the book by the fact that in only very few cases do we present analyses of material that is not of this provenance. Where we present impressionistic records these are taken exactly as they stand from our own notebooks.

Over the years a schizophrenic position has emerged as regards the matter of making phonetic records, 'collecting (primary) data', 'transcribing' or whatever label is used. One half of this view says that attention to fine detail is a phonetic indulgence and apt, indeed certain, to vitiate the clean lines of the final analysis. One is urged to go straight for what is 'distinctive', getting quickly away from the 'predictable' which is to be dealt with as 'conditioned variation', 'coarticulation' or whatever. 'Distinctive' here, though, has a specific theoretical meaning and is very limited in what it refers to. Usually it has to do with the 'distinctive' elements of word-structure, and this, moreover, in some idealised style such as 'slow, colloquial' of a generalised accent such as 'educated middle-class Parisian'. What is distinctive under these very artificial conditions may not be what is distinctive in everyday noisy situations and in rapid, familiar, conversation.

In some of the sections of the book we shall present material of the 'rapid, familiar' kind and of other kinds that are not at all idealised. We do this to demonstrate that for the hurly-burly of language situations in general it is *only* a record that is painstaking in its attention to detail that can hope to come to terms with what it is that plays a part at the phonological level in effective communication. Our records are phonetically quite detailed, and we spare readers nothing in this respect, since the phonological analyses we adumbrate are based on the fine structure of this detail.

To those who are unwilling to accept that things can be attended to and notated in the kind of detail we present in this book our best reply is probably to point to the records included in Part 4 that were made independently by one of our post-graduate students. This is not an isolated case. A number of other post-graduate and undergraduate students have produced records containing an order of detail that has been conducive to the production of what we think are interesting analytical commentaries. The Spanish material in Part 4 and some of the material in Study 5 were produced in the first place by undergraduate students, though later reworked by one of the authors.

The charge might be made, also, that our records are the result of wishful thinking as it were and that we hear what we wish to hear. Our response to this is twofold. In the first place the work was done under circumstances which would militate against this. Both authors have had a busy teaching and pastoral schedule, which has meant that only rarely have we been able to work on our materials systematically as they were collected. We exhort others to do this, and in an ideal world we would like to do it ourselves. But frequently it has not fallen out like that. So, in many cases, our making of records has been little more than just that. The records have been made and put away to await later interpretation. The Dutch materials which we discuss in Part 4, for instance, were taken down in the course of three one-hour sessions; no interpretative work (except of the kind that is done intuitively during recording) was done on them until several months after the informant had left Britain. This is not necessarily a good way to work, but it goes a long way towards reducing the likelihood that the early stages of our work were skewed towards a desired final outcome. The Bakosi and Tongan materials discussed in Part 4 both fall into the same category.

In the second place we have undertaken a range of instrumental investigations, subsequent to phonological interpretation, which satisfy us that our impressionistic categories are not chimerical. An account of such instrumental work is out of place in a book which is given over to a exploration of phonolgical interpretation, for instrumental findings, though crucial to an understanding, in quantitative terms, of phonetic exponency, do not in themselves contribute to the elaboration of phonological entities.

The second strand of the schizophrenia mentioned above is the belief, quite frequently put into print, that linguists, phoneticians particularly, when working on languages unfamiliar to them, do in fact do accurate and detailed recording in order to arrive at categories of the phonemic type. The position seems to be that we take note of a great deal of what is essentially phonetic 'dross' but then have to be painstaking in filtering it out of our work so as to get to the basic phonological categories. The whole situation is, of course, brought about by the dominance of a phoneme-based account of phonological structure, with what it brings with it of segmentality, sequence, allophonic and coarticulatory variance and so on. We want to make a plea in this book for an approach that records linguistic events in as much of their complexity as they present to us, an approach which also incorporates a methodology for 'making sense' of a lot of this complexity as reflecting the manifold systematicities of spoken language. We are not going to present this approach in its entirety and this is why we do not regard this book as an instruction manual. For instance, though we discuss aspects of representation here, we postpone to a later date a detailed theoretical consideration of phonological represention. Readers will soon note for themselves that we do not have techniques either for observing or for interpreting that are developed enough to meet all the demands we make upon them. But we do have a beginning.

Those versed in the linguistic literature of the last forty years or so will not be slow to recognise a certain debt to the writings of scholars working during the fifties and sixties in an approach that came to be known, not very satisfactorily, as 'prosodic analysis'. We are happy to acknowledge this debt. The work of J.R. Firth and his associates has for some time seemed to us to be one most conducive to progress in the field of phonology. We do not present here a reworking of Firthian prosodic analysis, rather we exploit in our work those parts of the approach that seem to us to provide powerful ways of dealing with the complexity of language structure in the phonological domain. For instance, Firth's insistence on language as an activity, on context and on polysystematicity appear to us to be unassailable as basic components of an approach to phonological description.

There are several things that will be looked for in a book like this and that will not be found. We decided not to include exercises or problems, for a number of reasons. One was that to print them in a way which would make them workable, with all the detail, ranges of variability and so on that we have insisted should characterise our own illustrative material, would increase the size and cost of the book to unwelcome proportions. In addition, as we are reluctant ourselves to work with material that we have not seen and heard produced, it would be out of keeping with the spirit of what we have written to encourage others to do what we ourselves are not prepared to do. Moreover, a lot of the material in the book is already presented after the fashion of worked problems.

Perhaps more seriously, we have, knowingly, given less than adequate coverage to certain areas of phonology. We have already said that we do not deal in any comprehensive way with formal phonological representation. Nor, for instance, do we deal with tonal matters in anything like the depth that they warrant. The reason for this is that tonal systems are, in our experience, complex and often entail a good deal of expository matter to present, say, the grammatical relationships involved. It seemed to us that to extend our approach to the study of pitch, accent and related matters would require almost as much space again as we use here, and we decided to focus attention almost, though not quite, exclusively on 'segmental' phonology, for the purposes of presentation and exposition. It will, we hope, be quite clear to readers that we make no such artificial distinction in our everyday work, and that the restriction in the present case is a matter of policy rather than of oversight. In any case, our 'segmental' phonology is far from segmental in the conventional sense.

It is appropriate here to make our position clear on other approaches to phonology. We do not discuss other approaches in the body of the book, preferring to *do* phonology rather than comment on the ways others pursue the enterprise. We forsee that, for some, what we do here will probably not amount to 'phonology' at all, in their sense, being based, as it is, on a close observation of the phonetic 'facts' rather than beginning from 'a phonological theory'. There *are* theoretical implications in the detail of the phonetic displays we present and we have tried to draw these out in the course of exposition. We may be accused of subjectivity, of errant impressionism and hair-splitting, perhaps even of fantasy. Our response to this is to say that if we wish to work on, say, an unwritten, and so far unstudied, language we know of no other means of doing this than taking it down at first hand in all its detail. We would go on to say that if a methodology is to hand for doing this, and it has to be or no new languages can ever be looked at, it can only be profitable to apply it to English, Finnish, Xhosa or Malay since it may tell us something new and interesting and cannot tell us anything that is not 'of the language'. We do not believe, then, that phonology has now all been done, even for languages like English, and that all that remains is to sort out the 'phonological representation'. In fact, as professional English-speaking phoneticians it is our view that remarkably little is known about the phonetics and phonology of English especially in its many varieties and in the conversational mode.

What we say above is not intended to be taken as a repudiation of present-day phonological theories. Some of the work carried out within metrical phonology in particular seems to us to have thrown light in a cogent way on the workings of complex phonological systems; and the distinctive feature notation in general gave rise to a lot of serious work which has cleared the ground for later progress. But phoneme theory seems to us to have nothing interesting to offer. Indeed it has done a lot more harm than good, frequently as a result of being applied in areas in which it was not intended to operate. It is, in fact, the specious simplicity of phonemic 'solutions' (which even underlie many recent non-linear approaches to phonological analysis), 'phoneme inventories' and the like that we have to thank for the impression, quite commonly encountered even amonst linguists, that the phonology of the world's better-known languages has now been 'done'.

It would be an idle undertaking to compare the approach presented here with what is found elsewhere. We are, at this stage, illustrating an approach rather than setting out a theory. Our methods of statement are *ad hoc* (though in reality this is no different from the kinds of things to be found in more formal-looking phonological approaches) and, most importantly, we start from a different place. We have no argument with those who see the ultimate goal of work in phonology as being the statement of perceptual primes or of universal feature sets: but in the task as we undertake it it is too early to talk seriously of such things.

The book has five Parts. Three of these, Parts 2 to 4, deal with various stages of the job of making phonological descriptions. We do not deal with all the stages, since we leave off in Part 4 before true formal analytic statements have been reached. Here we write only about the production of records of language events and about some steps to be taken in interpreting them. We present the activities of Parts 2 to 4 as a sequence and there is a logical progression from one to another. But we do not wish to imply that the activities involved take place exclusively of one another or in sequence. It is possible, for example, to have interpretative ideas before any records have been made. Speculation on the basis of published accounts can underlie this, a perfectly legitimate activity, provided that such speculation does not lead to overhasty record making. In Serbo-Croat, to take an example, there are two 'accents', called Falling and Rising. These are distributed such that Falling can occur on monosyllables, Rising can not. In words of more than one syllable the Falling accent can occur on any syllable, the Rising one can occur on any syllable but the final one. Words have only one accent in their structure.

These statements show that Rising accent is different from Falling in two important ways, both of which involve restrictions on Rising accent. Can we explain the restrictions, which at first sight might seem unconnected and without reason? To connect them we need a generalisation. The generalisation that suggests itself is that Rising never occurs on a final syllable, if we allow a monosyllable to count as 'final'. This further suggests that Rising accents have to do with *two-syllable* stretches, can, that is, operate only over this minimum extent. Such an explanation rules out the occurrence of Rising accent on

❏ monosyllables

❏ final syllables of polysyllables

which are precisely the cases in which we find them excluded. We might go on to hypothesise that, in historical terms, perhaps, something about the nature of the second syllable of a pair brought about a Rising accent over both of them. Whatever we hypothesise we shall want to regard Rising accent pieces as essentially different from Falling accent ones, and probably more complex in the way in which they have come into being. We have no impressionistic records of Serbo-Croat and this piece of interpretation of ours is pre-investigative, based on what we find in grammar books. Some interpretative steps can be taken, then, without recourse to impressionistic records. Others cannot. Hence the importance of such records. We can only interpret fully what we have in full.

For all that there is a logical progression from Part 2 to Part 4 it is perfectly possible to read any Part of the book as a independent section without deteriment to understanding. Part 4 is its centre and, we think rightly, much longer than any other Part. It is, in a sense, extendable *ad lib*. We have made choices about what to include and what to highlight that naturally mirror our own beliefs. So we have not said much about certain of the 'principles' which we present at the beginning of Part 4. We have paid relatively little attention to the 'parsimony principle' and have not given any worked examples of material which impinge on it. This is partly because we feel that the appeal to parsimony has had in some ways a bad effect on the study of phonology. Others of our principles which get little or no discussion in the phonology literature we have been more expansive about, hence our frequent return to the topics of parametric interpretation and phasing.

The book closes with five case-studies included because this is a book about *doing* in which we want a maximum amount of exemplification over as large a canvas as we can manage. There are no strong links between the studies in Part 5 or between these and the material of Parts 2 to 4. There is no index and no bibliography. We have tried to use relatively few technical terms and we refer to published sources only in Part 3 where details are given as they arise.

Although we have a good deal to say about the attitudes and skills that we need to bring to the job of making impressionistic records for phonological work we do not *teach* any phonetics at all in this book. It makes little sense to try to teach auditory phonetic skills *via* the printed page. In the matter of notation, a reader who knows both in the head and in the ear the values of the full IPA system should be able to follow the records presented here. They look more daunting than they actually are. In many cases they are the subject of commentaries which will help the reader to unravel them.

Some of our notational practices that diverge from those of the IPA are discussed in Part 3 and others we hope are transparent. A double diacritic, for instance, means more of the quality signified by the single one: u̟̟ is fronter than u̟ , i̞̞ is opener than i̞ . In the matter of symbol shapes we use only one that might be unfamiliar, namely ɑ̈ , for a vocoid half-way between a and ɑ . This symbol has been in informal use for some time by linguists of our acquaintance, but is not part of the IPA stock.

Acknowledgements

We would like thank John Coleman, Adrian Simpson and Bill Wells for reading large parts of 'this book and giving detailed comments. They have also provided a rich source of ideas and encouragement.
We are grateful to Kate Brown, Dave Huxtable, Adrian Simpson and Vince McNeany for giving us access to their material and tape-recordings.

We thank International Phonetic Association for premission to reprint the IPA chart and Paul Tench for permission to reproduce the second of the two parametric representations given in Part 3.

We thank the Bodleian Library, Oxford, for permission to reproduce folio 120 of Ms Ashmole 1153 which contains the fragment of Robert Robinson's transcription discussed in Part 3 and the Philological Society for permission to reproduce Francis Lodwick's *Universall Alphabet* in the same Part.

We are grateful to David Abercrombie for giving us access to a copy of a first edition of Alexander Bell's *Visible Speech.*

We also thank Ian Wand for allowing us to use the resources of the Department of Computing Science at the University of York to produce this book. The text was prepared using word-processing utilities written by Tony Fisher and printed on an Apple LaserWriter.

Lastly, we would like to thank our many informants without whose patience and co-operation this book could not have been written.

JK
JL

Experimental Phonetics Laboratory
University of York
UK

August 1988

Part 1
Preliminaries

1.1 The study of language

Many of those who read this book will be doing so because they have
an interest of one kind or another in language. Interest in language
as a human artefact and activity has been expressed by human beings
for many centuries, possibly always. Poetry and song are a manifestation of language put to creative and to emotional and emotive uses;
and an interest in the use of language is a prerequisite for writers,
lawyers, teachers, actors, salesmen and many others; medical workers, for example, have long had an interest in the nature of language
and in its modes of expression in speech and writing. There is an
undeniable link between language and thought and the categories of
the two, and so philosophers and psychologists too have taken
language into their purview. Historians may have an interest in
language since theories of language development and change, and hypotheses about how languages can affect and influence one another
when communities come into contact, may have something to tell us
about historical aspects of such contacts. Explorers and missionaries
have often engaged in work on languages, sometimes as an academic
enterprise, sometimes as one of the practicalities of their chosen occu-
pations.

The study of language, of its nature and use, and of its several
manifestations, has been going on for a long time. Some part of this
study is now in the hands of professionals. It is they who have the
responsibility, in the main, for elaborating and testing hypotheses
about linguistic structure and language behaviour. They also have the
job of establishing principles and guide-lines that ordain the proper
conduct of research into languages and the nature of language.

This theoretical work on language and languages is carried out in large part in institutes of higher education and research institutes; such formalised academic study usually goes under the name of linguistics. Academic linguistics is carried out in the first instance, for its own sake, and is done in the spirit of exploration. Alongside this, many academic linguists have been or are continually engaged in putting into practice the results of theoretical work, or of making connections from it into the daily worlds of medicine, music, technology and so on. As in other disciplines, the basic work of observation and theorising goes on alongside practical application; each flows into and feeds the other.

The use of the term 'linguist' for scholars in this field is not a particularly happy one, since the word has overtones of 'polyglot' or 'interpreter'. But the term 'linguistician', which has been suggested, has never been seriously taken up, so we shall stick to 'linguist' in this book, it being understood that 'linguist' here is 'the professional engaged in work on the nature and/or use of language'. Linguists may also be teachers of linguistics.

Since linguistics covers so very much, it is usual for most linguists to specialise in one part or another of it. Some are more concerned with the use of language as opposed to its nature, insofar as these can be held apart; some are more concerned with relationships between languages or with their history. And ultimately, reflexivity takes place whereby the history of linguistics becomes a proper and well-founded object of interest and study.

1.2 Language description

It is by means of the description of many languages that linguists can best begin to move towards some set of postulates about the nature of language: and description has to be based on observation. Even those linguists who specialise in the history of languages have much to learn from the observation of language as they see it around them. So observation of language material is of central importance within the linguistic disciplines.

A number of questions arise for academic linguists concerned with the proper conduct of the discipline both by themselves and by others. One question has to do with what is construed as 'language'; a second with how objective the business of observation can be held to be; a third with the relationship between observation and descriptive categories; and there are others. In this book we are going to restrict our discussion to the spoken medium of language: it is the descriptive categories that deal with the spoken medium alone that we shall be concerned with; and it is specifically the techniques of observation that are directed towards the spoken medium that we shall take as falling under examination.

In the conduct of first-hand observation and description of spoken languages, institutionalised, or other, writing systems have no primary role to play. This is not to say that linguists are not interested in writing systems or that these have no relevance for the study of language. But they have no *primary* role to play for various reasons. One is that many languages have no writing systems, so that if we are to apply the same descriptive apparatus to the spoken medium of all languages equally, that apparatus will be, ideally, constructed independently of any writing system. Secondly, writing systems are not designed to give an observational record of language events in their spoken medium, and they do not deal in a systematic and exhaustive fashion with specific individual speech events. For descriptive purposes we need an apparatus which can do just that.

We return to our first question which had to do with what counts as 'language'. It may seem a strange question, but the problem is soon seen if we consider the question of the utterances of a two-and-a-half year old English child. Are these utterances English? If not, what are they? Are the utterances of a very drunken English speaker? One answer is no, in that frequently other speakers of the same speech community cannot understand them. Another answer is yes in that they cannot be assigned to any other known natural language and *can* be assigned to English *via* a series of possibly complex relational statements. We might resolve this difficulty by setting up a category of marginal English to which these two types, in their different ways, belong. But any number of other types of English might be thought to be marginal. Reading the news for instance - very few people do it, and as a language event it is of a special kind, since it is by definition mediated by wireless or television; no interruptions or responses are allowed; it has a written source; its tempo and other dynamics are of a particular kind: and no gestures or other such attendant manifestations are in order. In as far as we identify these characteristics as somehow marginal we are implicitly assigning centrality to some activity that does not bear these characteristics, which is, that is to say, interrupted and responded to, which exhibits a wide range of tempo and other uttered effects, which is accompanied by a wide range of gesture, which is face-to-face and maximally interactive, which is spontaneous and has no source in written material.

A very great part of the spoken language that goes on every day of this kind is conversation: and many other speech activities derive from conversation, and are distillations from it. This is demonstrated by the fact that the range of linguistic phenomena exhibited by such activities is usually limited and less than the range exhibited by conversations. In literate communities, non-conversational activities often derive from the written medium. All these activities are to be called 'language events'; some are more central, some more marginal.

It befits any discipline to set the bounds of the area of interest as wide as seems fruitful and is practicable. Linguists will want to have, in time, full descriptions of all these types of language event for all languages; and this includes the inchoate language forms of children and the speech of drunks, since both have important things to tell us. So we are not too concerned about what constitutes 'language' for the purpose of 'linguistics'. It is important to have a classification and a hierarchy of kinds of speech activity, and equally important to know how each kind relates to the others. It is important too to see the centrality of conversation as being the arena in which most language operations are acted out. Given these considerations it is essential to have a descriptive apparatus which will deal with all the events we come across, and especially with conversation.

We have now made a requirement of a descriptive apparatus - that it should be equipped to supply an adequate observational written record of the sound fabric of uttered events, including conversation, while being independent of any institutionalised writing system. The discipline of linguistics has still some way to go before reaching this ideal provision. In fact we are rather worse off in this respect now than we were a hundred years ago. At that time, largely as the result of large-scale experiments in Europe and the United States, a number of notation systems were in use that came nearer to satisfying this ideal. The most striking of these was A.M. Bell's Visible Speech, particularly in the later recension made by Henry Sweet. However, Visible Speech fell into disuse. In an ideal world, again, we should have preferred to have used Visible Speech or an adaptation of it in the later chapters of this book. But in order to make our presentation accessible to a general linguistic readership we have chosen to use an adapted IPA notation of the kind that we have been in the habit of using with our own students.

1.3 Techniques in description and their problems

To return to the question of language material: not only is there a range of language events available to us and calling for adequate and proper description, there is also a range of ways in which we can gather the material. Some kinds of material can be elicited from informants, and this in a number of ways. Other kinds such as conversation, news-readings, sermons and the like, cannot be elicited, and other techniques have to be used. Both categories present their special problems. In elicitation linguists have to a large extent freedom as to what they choose to elicit, and this is an advantage. But responding to elicitation is not a naturally-occuring language event no matter what the language items asked for and problems can arise on the part of the informant. If the 'word' is concentrated on, as often happens, it is not a natural event for the native speaker presenting the language material, the informant, to repeat isolated words or phrases over and over again, and there is often difficulty about the absence of context. If sentence-type entities are taken, it is often difficult to record them in detail without tiring the informant very quickly. Informants also may often experience a sense of alienation if asked to produce sentences in isolation.

One way of eliciting speech is through a mediating language. An obvious problem with this that the informant may not understand the mediating language as well as s/he appears to. This may detract from the informant's value in the job. If they are not prepared to acknowledge this deficiency they may cover it by offering approximate responses. One African informant whom we worked with thought that 'tiny' (of persons) meant 'small in the side-to-side dimension' (ie thin) and produced 'tiny' as a gloss for a word in his language which (apparently!) means 'thin'. The linguist needs to be on his guard against this.

Secondly, seemingly simple English sentences can produce problems. 'she ate the soup' for instance can be met with the question 'did she eat it all?'. It is no way out to say 'it doesn't matter', since in the informant's language it does matter and no response matching 'she ate the soup' can be made. Languages with no ostensible articles (Polish, Swahili), or with one (Welsh), provide immediate problems of deixis, reference and so on when translation from English is being done. And speakers of many languages are nonplussed if presented with English 'sentences' such as 'he ran' or 'I like her singing'. This might arise in the first case because, for them, all verbs are transitive and the thing simply cannot be dealt with at all. Even if we rephrase as 'he ran it', the next question is 'what?' since what he ran (a race, a distance) might affect a compulsory object marker. In the second case, the language may have no deverbal nominatives of the 'singing' type and a paraphrase has to be resorted to such as 'I like the way she sings' or 'her songs please me'. Sometimes these switches are made by informants without notice being given, this leading to later difficulties in interpreting the written record.

Lexis is an obvious area of difficulty. Items in English may have no obvious match in the language under investigation, partly because of cultural conditions, partly because of the way the lexis is organised (kinship terms are a good example of this) or because of the way the grammar and the lexis are differently intertwined. Languages tend to 'process' these two in different ways - so in the kind of language above where 'she ate the soup' presents a problem, we might have a (compulsory) marker within the verbal form that shows it to be completive or non-completive; or the verb form itself might be of this kind, as they are in Slavonic and some Chadic languages. In English, if we want to make it quite clear that completive is what we mean we say something like 'she ate it up' where the phrasal verb 'eat up' carries this meaning (as again in 'filled up', 'used up'). Situations of this kind are commonplace. Polish ON WYŚPIEWYWAŁ SIĘ can only be got into English as something like 'he used to keep on bursting out into song'.

This being the case, we cannot apply to our work any simple-minded rule that expects 'two words' of Yoruba or Szechuanese or whatever for 'two words' of English; or anything that matches the English structures in predictable ways. For this reason, the English used for eliciting has to be referred to as a 'gloss' or a 'translation meaning', and similarities in the English cannot be taken as indicative of similarities in the language under investigation. Even when 'I like her singing' is problematic, 'I like her mother' may be straightforward, but then the two structures in the target language may have little in common - 'her' possibly. Even here, though this second utterance is culturally possible in English, in some cultures such a casual personal judgement about an elder would be improper, and an informant would not want to produce it, not because it is difficult in the formal sense or awkward to paraphrase, but because it is taboo.

When working from English into a language of a very different culture, it is important to remember that the language has many words in it, thousands probably, that no English word-list or questionnaire can elicit, simply because they do not exist in English. Flora and fauna are an obvious case of this, as are foodstuffs, raw, semi-raw and prepared, and all artefacts. Local religious customs and ceremonies come into this category too.

Mediating languages can produce more subtle problems. In areas where the mediating language has been in use over a long period as a contact language or a second language or where a creole has grown up, the speakers of the language under investigation may use English words well-established in the culture but which refer to slightly different things than an outside observer might think. 'Leopard', 'alligator' and 'hare' are in common use in West Africa to refer to creatures that are, strictly speaking, not leopards, alligators or hares at all. In addition the mediating language may contain words that are taken to be central to it but which are unknown to an innocent investigator. In West Africa again 'dash' (from Portuguese) for 'a bribe' is part of the local English and regarded as an English word.

Many problems of this kind can be avoided by working *via* a language more closely related to the language under investigation than English is, if this language is well controlled by both parties. It might be more profitable to work on a Chadic language through the medium of Hausa, for example, in a field situation. In a teaching situation this is, of course, less feasible.

Apart from the face-to-face situation it is possible, of course, to work from tape-recordings. There are advantages and disadvantages to this. The advantages are that a tape-recording can be replayed ad lib without any question of informant fatigue, that tape-recordings can be exchanged from hand to hand if we wish to submit our material to another analyst, and that tape-recordings cannot digress or provide problematic linguistic situations. In our view, though, the disadvantages outweigh these advantages. One is that we lose the benefit of live repetitions of the material, another that we lose the benefit of visual exposure to the speaker, something we regard as being of the first importance.

The best way out of these difficulties is to work at live sessions which are tape-recorded in their entirety, if this is feasible and can be managed without any disruption of a good working atmosphere. We are talking here of elicited material. In the case of non-elicited material, of course, there can be no question of anything other than tape-recording, since it is not possible to make a full written record of a live conversation, using a running transcription. The kind of material we are working on, and the methods we use are interlocked into each other to some extent. And, of course, the kind of material we gather depends on our aims. The comparativist will want, first and foremost,

to have a list of particular lexical items, not necessarily very extensive, to compare with parallel lists for other related or putatively related languages: and a linguist whose main concern is producing a
translation of the Bible will not have, perhaps, a primary interest in conversational material.

In a teaching situation, conversational material is not always appropriate or easy to use. We would hold, though, that students of
phonetics and linguistics should be exposed to it at some point in
their course, largely indeed because of the difficulties it throws up,
and the number of orthodoxies it calls into question. In the case-
studies at the end of the book we will deal with some examples from
conversations in English to illustrate the kind of benefits that accrue
from this work.

1.4 Some mental preparations

When beginning to look at material in a new language with a view to
making an analysis it is important to approach the language with as
few preconceptions as possible. We hold this to be crucial, so much
so in fact that in our teaching we do not reveal the name of the
language being worked on until towards the end of the term's work.
If students can find it out for themselves, of course, and choose to
do so using such clues as they have available, all well and good. This
task then becomes part of the term's research for them. But it is bad
practice if working on Albanian, say, to read all or any of the literature
on Albanian beforehand. All that is required before starting work in a
training situation is the knowledge that this is a natural language and
that this is a representative speaker. The second of these is, of course,
sometimes difficult to confirm. In a field-work situation things are
different: acceptability can be more easily gauged from direct observation, and the natural language question does not arise.

In a number of situations it is possible to work with only one informant. This arises especially in training sessions in academic settings. The claims made then about 'the phonetics of X' are made for
one speaker, and the phonology is the phonology of one speaker.
We make the assumption in this case that the informant is a representative speaker of an institutionalised community language. Work
done in this fashion has a lot of virtues, one being that one speaker
can be studied in depth. However, under conditions like this, informants are, in some sense, never really 'speaking' their language and it
is important to have recourse when at all possible to other comparable
speakers, and to experience the language spoken in its community set-

ting. In this way we make 'renewal of connection', to use an expression of J.R. Firth's, between the idealised categories of our earlier description and the matter of the language.

With the above considerations in mind, work can proceed. Our first, and by far our most important, job is the making of an adequate written record of the set of utterances produced by the informant(s) in terms of the phonetic productive and receptive events that relate to them. We need no prior information about the language itself in order to do this. If we had any it could lead to hasty judgements or, worse, to our judgement being denied altogether in favour of the 'correct answer'. If we are working in a teaching situation on a language which we are told 'has' ejectives, there is a kind of pressure on beginning students to hunt the ejectives and to imagine they are there when they are not. Or, similarly, when they are there, to be content with having identified these exotic items without really trying to describe them. It is quite easy for beginners if they are told they are working on Luo, to notate Luo ɗ with the symbol ɗ , though this sound in Luo is different from its relative in English. It is also, likewise, not particularly instructive for our purpose to know at the outset that 'there is vowel harmony in Fante' or 'that there are two tones in Kinyarwanda' or that 'Tongan has only one liquid', since these findings should be the result of the work, not the input to it. There is no reason at all, of course, to refrain from reading the relevant literature at a later stage. This can sometimes have interesting results but care should be taken that the literature *is* relevant, ie that the language variety is the same. It is unwise to work on the spoken Swahili of Mombasa Old Town, say, and to then read literature on the Swahili vernacular of the Mrima coast.

Informants quite frequently volunteer information about their languages or about cultural contexts for utterances or about matters sociolinguistic. These should always be listened to and noted. Sometimes this information is wrong, more especially that on formal linguistic matters. An Urhobo informant gave **iteboro** for 'table', and added the supplementary information, that it was a loan from English and that the Urhobo had their own word. On being asked for it he produced **imeʒa** which is in fact a loan from Portuguese. This is interesting in the light of the fact that **imeʒa** breaks the vowel harmony rules of Urhobo (**iteboro** does not) and that - **ʒ** - is extremely rare in the language. Conversely, a Danish informant produced, quite spontaneously, some information on the Danish pronunciation of Latin that proved genuinely helpful in working on the distribution of the Ɂ in Danish. Sometimes etymologies are offered. Frequently these are folk etymologies and of no primary importance, such as the origin one of the authors was given for Swahili MKEKA 'mat', said by an elderly sheikh to come from MKE 'wife' and KAA 'sit'. One advantage of having complete tape recordings of informant sessions is that all such information is captured without having to have recourse to lengthy notes.

The approach above is, of course, simply part and parcel of treating an informant with respect. It is particularly the case that language and linguistics students need to have this attitude instilled into them. They need also to be taught to regard variability in an utterance as regular, and not to take the informant to task for 'saying it differently' any more than they should laugh at things in utterances, in their glosses, or in the cultural context described which strike them as 'funny'. They need to learn sensitivity in handling areas that are or appear to be taboo. Naming is a frequent instance here: the names of cults for instance, or cult names for individuals, may be secret, or, at the least, the informant may feel ill at ease revealing them to outsiders. Unnecessary though this reticence may seem to the investigator, the must learn to recognise it and handle the situation with tact. The linguist should ensure too that the informant realises that the only reason for asking for such material in a purely linguistic, as opposed to cultural, piece of research, is simply to produce as large a lexis as possible with representation from all parts of the language. Personal names, and particularly loans, often have idiosyncracies of structure; and they are important for this reason.

1.5 Reference outwards

It is important, in fact, to keep making references outwards, in a general way, away from the language under study, as well as to make connections within it. This should be done whilst observing and recording, too, as it frequently suggests new areas into which to push the investigation. We mean here that the linguist should keep his or her linguistic wits sharp during these stages so as to spot possible loans, calques and other kinds of transfer as well as general reflexes from reconstructed sources where these are to hand. The reason for doing this is that the ways in which loans appear or in which earlier forms may have been transmitted, can give valuable hints about patterns in the present-day state of the language under examination. The Albanian word mbɾɛt ('king'), for example, to take an isolated case, is reminiscent of IMPERATOR. Whether it is a reflex of the same early form, or a loan from Latin/Italian, it has lost the vowel between **p** and **r**, as well as other syllables. This may be a common feature of Albanian; if it is, we might, by recognising it elsewhere, be able to spot other loans, or identify a lot of other reflexes which might have escaped us if we had not noticed the MBRET / IMPERATOR case. This insight might also help us to recognise internal relationships in the language.

Hungarian provides a similar example of an even more general kind. The recognition of such Hungarian words as

baɾat   *friend*

astal   *table*

olaˑs   *Italian*

sɛɾda   *Wednesday*

tʃɤtœɾœk   *Thursday*

laˑslo·   *Wladyslaw*

as being loans from Slavonic provides an immediate clue to the basic Hungarian syllable structure **CV(C)** that will be found to recur throughout the language. All of these forms have initial consonant clusters in the source languages, as exemplified by Polish:

br -	*friend*
st -	*table*
vw -	*Italian*
ɕr -	*Wednesday*
tʃf -	*Thursday*
v w -	*Wladyslaw*

We are given here a pointer to Hungarian structural rules *before* working through our Hungarian material: and, of course, we are provided with a diagnostic for recognising loan words even from sources unknown. So, for instance, Magyar PREM 'fur' is a loan, we can hypothesize, even though its origin may not be immediately recognisable.

A more far-reaching case, in which a knowledge of the patterns of loan material helps us to work out relationships within a language, is provided by Welsh. The forms ɬaːeθ *milk* and saeθ *arrow* show the regular correspondence of Latin -kt- LACT and -tt- with Welsh θ . This has its implications for such Welsh material as mamaθaꞏd

mother and father

kaθaxiꞏ

cat and dog

and

taꞏdamam

father and mother

kiaxaꞏθ

dog and cat

in which 'aspirate mutation' of voiceless plosives after *and* is in evidence. If we take further into account such forms as TATWS AC ABLAU ('potatoes and apples') or MAIR AC EYNON ('Mary and Eynon') where the conjunction is ak we might wish to see 'aspirate mutation' as the result of a general development in Welsh in which (kt) > tt > θ and kk > x . The end of *cat* is also relevant. In doing this we posit the 'vowel junction' form of the conjunction as being **VC** in *all* cases in our abstract treatment so

kaꞏttakkiꞏ > kaꞏθaxiꞏ

This approach also provides an account of why the consonant of the vowel juncture form is what it is, and not some other consonant: and of why 'aspirate' mutation is restricted to initial voiceless plosives. The initial impetus for such a set of solutions can be provided quite easily in recording-work by noticing the shape taken by Latin loans such as SAETH and LLAETH.

In order to see these kinds of links and relationships, it is necessary to have a reasonably unprejudiced attitude about what languages are like, about what 'can happen' and about what can be related to what. It is not immediately apparent, for instance, that Kikuyu ðɷvu is the 'same word' as Swahili supu : both mean 'soup' and are borrowed from English. The correspondences involved are quite regular, as shown by

Swahili	Kikuyu	
kisima	ɣeðima	*well*
siagi	ðiage	*butter*
pilipili	viɛiviɛi	*pepper*
kikapu	ɣekavɷ	*basket*
mpira	mɷviɛa	*rubber*
siafu	ðiɛaku	*ants*

This suggests but does not demonstrate that the word may have been transmitted into Kikuyu *via* Swahili. In the *ants* example we find a f ~ k relationship; this is one that we are not immediately conscious of in Indo-European languages, though we do feel more at home with both k ~ h and f ~ h and we may want to hypothesize a Swahili historical succession k > h > f before u. This will suggest that the sequence **hu** does not occur in Swahili, and that if it does occur it will be in loan material, or, in indigenous material, be attributed to a source other than earlier **ku**. This will provide clues as to the status and structure of such words as huzuni 'grief' and kuhusu 'to concern' which are in fact Arabic loans, or huu 'this'

(Class 3) which has a constituent break between h and u . These thoughts about possibilities of Swahili structure and history have arisen from our examination of a small amount of related Kikuyu material.

It is also desirable that students learn how to conduct the research as a sequence of work. One crucial requirement is that the material collected should be collated and studied regularly with a view to its orderly and manageable organisation and manipulation later. Also by going through the gathered material questions for future sessions can be formulated, gaps can be identified and the groundwork laid for the formation of hunches and intuitions that will need to be explored further. There is nothing worse than carrying on collecting more and more material without scrutinising it regularly with a view to setting up hypotheses about language forms and their relationships. Later chapters in this book will attempt to demonstrate how such hypotheses are to be set up, and how eventual interpretations of the primary material are to be approached. For the moment we close this chapter by pointing out the necessity for written records to be kept carefully. They should be checked regularly to ensure that glosses are present to match all entries, that all entries are legible, that any *ad hoc* symbols are explained. It is useful to number entries, so that they can be unambiguously and easily referred to in notes and cross-references. Records are best kept in pencil in the first instance or in erasable ball-point; for it is better to erase and replace than to cross out when using a complex notational system.

Part 2

Observing

In order to pursue any coherent work on the sound-structure of language linguists needs detailed written records of speech material. In order to produce such records they require techniques for analytic impressionistic observing and recording. Analytic observing and recording are two separate but inter-related activities: in this section we focus on the practice and some of the central principles of phonetic observation. The notational resources employed to reflect the details of observation are discussed in Part 3.

2.1 Problems in observation

Observation and description do not take place in a vacuum. They are always selective and ultimately theory-dependent. All descriptive work is underpinned and focussed by the observer's aims and assumptions. These form the basis of the observer's theoretical position delimiting and determining the relevance of observations. They determine, for instance, what will be foregrounded or backgrounded in observation. So one observer, having particular predispositions, may deem some readily observable features trivial, and not make a record of them, while another analyst with a different theory may view the recording of those same features as central or crucial to satisfactory observation.

All linguists have hunches, intuitions and hypotheses about what languages are like. These also inevitably influence the way in which observing is done because these hunches help the linguist to make decisions about what is considered relevant, or about what categories of event are to be considered the same, what different. Even the business of what events are discriminable in phonetic observation is in large measure the result of predisposition, training, experience and attention.

The scope of phonological statement that the linguist envisages making will also inevitably determine to some extent what aspects of any given utterance gets attended to and this, in turn, will contribute to the kinds of phonological units which will be postulated. If linguists are primarily interested in establishing and making statements about interactional relevance then they are likely to be interested in observing such things as the fine details of pause, audible in- and out-breathing and other details, which though ever-present would probably not be attended to by a linguist whose primary interest was in the phonology of lexical items.

2.2 Degrees of detail in observation

We have suggested that all descriptions are constrained or focussed in various ways and can never be said to be complete in any objective sense. As the observer's aims and assumptions change so will aspects of the observational description. Even given a stable set of aims and assumptions it is possible to observe in varying degrees of detail. In addition we hold that it is part of the linguist's job to develop techniques and resources which will allow for the refinement and extension of the ways in which observing is done. (We will have more to say about phonetic detail and its importance for phonological analysis in Part 4, *Interpreting*.)

Because of our predispositions and theoretical assumptions about the organisation of sound structure in languages, we take it as axiomatic that the linguist engaged in phonetic observation should have the ability to respond to as much of the observable material as possible, since, no matter what phonological theory one may adopt, success in subsequent analysis is limited by the quality of the description on which it is based. Our view is that it is not possible to have too much phonetic detail. Part of the reason for this claim is our belief that at the beginning of work on language material we can't, in any interesting sense, know beforehand what is going to be important. Consequently we must attend to and reflect everything that we can discriminate. We do not claim though that any set (or sets) of observations and the resulting impressionistic records are complete or exhaustive of what has been observed. Categories of observation and description are indefinitely extensible. There is a limitless number of parameters that could be specified in the description and categorisation of an event or events. The particular theory that has been chosen will in a particular case only delimit a general space within which sub-sets of relevant parameters can be located. One of the issues in observing is to establish reasonably well-motivated criteria which can be invoked to decide which parameters to include and which to exclude (see Part 5 *Intonation and Interaction* for the way in which one approach to the analysis of conversation delimits relevant parameters). Depending on the way in which we as observers chop up the ecology of speaking so various parameters will or will not be admitted to the description.

2.3 Focus of phonetic observation

The aim in making phonetic observations is to produce detailed analytic records of spoken language which will be subsequently used as the basis for phonological analysis. Utterances are clusters of phased (cotemporal) dynamic events. If one looks at a cine-radiographic film of someone talking, the general effect of the movements of the speech organs is of a number of pistons and valves working together but independently in a very complex way. So we need to think rather carefully about observing and analysing these dynamic events and to consider what the implications are of particular kinds of observation and analysis. The events we are concerned to observe and analyse are complex. Consequently the methodology adopted in observation and used to arrive at the phonetic record is also complex, as is, inevitably, the record itself. The events are complex in that they are movements made audible. Thus our observing might be directed towards ultimately producing a record of the movements or of the resulting noises or some combination of the two.

2.3.1 Partitioning off speech

Before we make a choice as to which course we will take, we need to consider in more detail what our purpose is. Since the people engaged in this phonetic observing and record-making are linguists they will reasonably focus on and give primacy to those aspects of the spoken material which are most linguistic. That is, they focus on those aspects which they hypothesise are most central or contribute most to the linguistic events taking place. We make the assumption here that it is analytically valid to focus on the speech aspect of language events separately from other observable components. In doing this we automatically set aside from analytic consideration body-gestural components of doing talk. We will not explore the implications of doing this. But it is possible that quite different hypotheses would have to be entertained and quite different analytic statements made if we partitioned off speech in different ways, eg. by including gestural components. It would then, for example, be useful to know in some precise detail the extent to which percepts of linguistic events are driven by visual stimuli. We know that such things as telephone communication are possible and routinely unproblematic, however, and we take it that auditory stimuli are thus minimally sufficient. In addition we know from other everyday evidence that visual stimuli alone are not - not for ordinary speakers and hearers at least.

From this we can decide to focus our observing on auditory aspects and couch the resulting records in terms that are primarily auditory (how far we extend this working partition depends again ultimately on what the analysis is directed towards). What we do not know though is what elements of a complex auditory signal are attended to overall by listeners. So to do phonetic observation we need an expertise in observing, appreciating and eventually recording that will respond to and reflect as much as possible of all that is audible. However, as we have indicated the audible material we are dealing with has an organic origin. It results from organic movements. And if we assume that all listeners, and not just linguists, perceive speech at least some of the time by kinaesthetic means then we will need to attend closely to (and have a record of) organic movements as well. Ideally then our observational techniques will be organised around getting as much information as we can about

❑　　a complex and coordinated set of movements

❑　　a set of auditory experiences that relate, perhaps in a
　　　complex way, to these

2.4　Principal techniques of observation

2.4.1　*Analytic impressionistic observation*

We use the term 'analytic' here for two main reasons. Firstly, as we have indicated earlier observation is not a raw data gathering activity. All observation has analytic aspects. Even instrument traces are the products of equipment which is designed to 'selectively attend'. Secondly, we require our observation to proceed by a conscious attempt to identify systematic parametric parts of the events under scrutiny.

We use the term 'impressionistic' to indicate that the observations and the eventual records concern the linguist's detailed subjective impressions of the spoken language material they are working on. We are not concerned at this stage with whether the linguistic-observational categories relate in any simple way to those employed by participants in any speaking situation. We will however address this issue in Part 5 in the study *Intonation and Interaction* when we consider ways in which the linguist can attempt to achieve a certain degree of congruity between analytic linguistic statements derived from observation and those categories employed by co-participants in conversation.

'Movements made audible' may be observed and appreciated relatively directly through hearing, vision, or even touch. They may also be appreciated in a way which is possibly less direct in that it may involve a collaboration of other senses and is not, in our everyday language, associated with a simple sensory name. We refer here to empathetic awareness of what is going on in the speaker's vocal tract: kinaesthetic awareness. Not all these modes of perception have the same role to play in linguistic-phonetic observation. Touching is not a central technique. However, the linguist may often use it as an ancillary means of discovering what their own vocal tract is doing when they imitate and replicate sounds made by other speakers (by feeling throat, cheek walls, lips, the effects of activities of facial muscles etc). But kinaesthetic, empathetic awareness and listening are central and complementary techniques in phonetic observation.

(i) Kinaesthetic awareness

This is perhaps the most important technique available for phonetic observation. Since, as we have suggested, phonetic observation should concern itself not only with sounds but also with the movements which give rise to those sounds, we need to have some way of making observations of movements. Some movements are visible and can be easily observed; we will discuss the use and contribution of visual observation of movement below. The great majority of the organic movements of speech production, however, will not be readily visible and must somehow be reconstructed on the basis of the heard material. In employing kinaesthetic awareness in observation, we are consciously attempting to construe the heard material as audible vocal gestures. Kinaesthetic or empathetic awareness is a common part of our daily lives. Nearly everybody will, at some time, have experienced something like hearing a person talking who is experiencing embarrassment for some reason and has felt that embarrassment with them; or has listened to someone talking with a frog in their throat and has felt a desire to cough for them; or has encountered someone with laryngeal pathology and has experienced a kind of bodily emmpathy in their own larynx. In phonetic observation the linguist attempts to consciously make use of this bodily empathy to replicate the organic movements (and also the sounds), of the speaker(s) under observation. The linguist will then introspect on those productions and attempt to conclude analytically what their component parts are, how and where they are taking place in the vocal tract. In order to engage in impressionistic observation we believe that linguists must be actively engaged in attempting to replicate aspects of the speech they are describing. Ideally the results learned from empathetic introspection should be offered for assessment by the speaker they derive from listening to. Does that speaker accept them? Are they as close to the original as the analyst can get them? What kind of fine tuning, what small adjustments of the speech producing mechanism, must be done to get them closer? This procedure too must, of course, be subjected to introspective analysis which must feed into the emerging description. Introspection on replicated productions is best if done silently - experience teaches that it is considerably easier to gain conscious awareness of kinaesthetic sensation when the accompanying auditory sensations are absent.

(ii) Analytic parametric listening

In phonetic observation, listening needs to be primarily and consciously analytic-parametric. Phonetic observation begins by listening to speech in terms of independently varying auditory and movement parameters and not in terms of unanalysed, static postures and transitional glides. So, for instance, linguists need to listen to features of laryngeal and glottal behaviour independently of co-occurring oral articulatory concomitants of particular auditory sensations. They need to be able to untease the various strands of the auditory sensation into component factors. It is necessary to have such techniques, in part, to help to free themselves from prejudices (eg in describing events) which they might have by virtue of knowing and speaking their own language. If linguists have no recourse to analytic listening they have no real way of observing with what speakers actually do. Any listening in observation would be constrained by contingent factors, for example by whatever set of symbols were available for record-making. Nor would a linguist be able to make any coherent analytic description of complexes of events not previously encountered. They could well be unable to transcend their own language prejudices. It is essential to employ listening techniques which are responsive to the fine detail of observable features of utterance and which avoid insofar as it is possible any reliance, conscious or not, on preordained phonetic categories.

(iii) Reference, Relativistic and Holistic Listening

We need to distinguish three main kinds of analytic listening all of which are parametric but in rather different ways. These three kinds are reference listening, relativistic listening and holistic listening.

Reference listening. This is the least important kind of parametric listening but one which provides a starting point for more sophisticated observation. In reference listening we employ reference categories of various kinds provided by an institutionalised general phonetic (and phonological) theory. Typically these are categories which allow us to mentally and overtly identify auditory stretches or various extents of speech gesture and movement. Reference categories represent established (but not necessarily well-motivated) ways of temporally segmenting continuously varying phonetic parameters. This initial segmentation thus yields time-slices of utterance of extents which may or may not be linguistically arbitrary.

In reference listening we employ general phonetic categories of, for instance, initiation types, phonation types, articulatory topology and categories of cavity resonance. The alphabet of the International Phonetic Association (see Part 3) provides one such set of reference categories couched principally in terms of places and manners of articulation for a canonical vocal tract topology. Thus for instance, a voiceless, palatalized bilabial fricative, a creaky voiced dental nasal, and so on. In reference listening the analyst will attempt to refer what is heard to such categories and will employ various devices in record-making to indicate where the perceived event(s) exhibits what are deemed to be noticeable differences from the reference categories. Category terms have as part of their make up a range of within-category similarities and between-category differences. Different classificatory schemas may or may not make explicit the criteria for admitting similarity and difference. The most commonly used phonetic reference categories, those of the IPA, are sets of co-incident, cross-parametric articulatory-acoustic configurations and the kind of descriptive terms which are employed to label these configurations often reflect their canonical status: fricative (reference category) as opposed to friction (analytic observational parameter), plosive (reference category) as opposed to plosion (analytic observational parameter). Because of the arbitrariness of the way parameters are bundled together in reference categories (see further in Part 3) it is often the case that reference categorisation lies rather uneasily beside analytic parametric observations. Consider, for instance the reference categories such as 'nasal' and 'nasalised', as opposed to 'nasality' which is a label for an auditory percept which is taken to relate to a complex setting(s) of the vocal tract which may or may not be temporally co-extensive with one or more of the given reference category segments.

The justification for employing such reference categories, however, has already been discussed, that is, the practical need for general categories which allow the linguist to deal as far as is possible in a detailed way with the full repertoire of sounds that the human vocal tract can produce in language. Another, related, reason for employing reference categories is that we constantly assume that we are not dealing with an infinitely large number of different events when we engage in observation of spoken material. We assume that some classes of events recur that these classes are linguistically, and possibly perceptually, salient and that they can be related to our reference categories in a coherent and systematic way.

Relativistic listening. As well as employing reference listening in our observation we also need to listen in a more directed fashion in relativistic terms. When, for instance, we first listen to auditory complexes which we identify as vocoid portions of a spoken utterance, we will typically try to refer these in as precise way as possible to a set of reference categories - usually those of the Cardinal Vowels. But very quickly, as we listen to more material and work our way into the language, we will want to relate these vocoid portions, some of the time, to each other. There are two principle reasons for this. First 'internal' relating of auditory complexes assists us in making more precise observations and helps us to identify small differences which might have escaped us if we had solely been relying on our auditory memory of reference qualities. It thus refines the results of reference listening and helps us to adjust our listening to take into account the individual voice-quality characteristics of the speaker(s) eg to normalise for vocal tract (length) differences. Second, as linguists we are interested in working towards an explication and statement of the systems and structures of languages. So what is important is not only the precise qualities of any given sound complex, but also its relationship to other similar complexes in the same language. The linguist as phonologist wants to know for a given vocoid portion, whether it is for instance closer, more open, further back, or shorter in duration than the vocoid portion(s) in other stretches of utterance?; if its quality varies, does it vary in the same kinds of ways as variation in other similar vocoid portions of utterance? Or we might focus in relativistic listening on overall relative resonance differences (see further below on holistic listening), and want to observe say how much 'clearer' one part of an articulatory movement is than another, or how prominence covaries with articulatory events. Provided that the linguist understands the motivation for and is explicit about such observational practices, relativistic listening is both necessary and legitimate if we genuinely want to respond to as much of what is observable as is possible. It is necessary when beginning work on any language material to have some external points of reference. However, such reference categories are best treated as stepping-off points, not end points, in observation. They provide suggestions of things which might be useful to attend to further in detail, not an *exhaustive* set of features to attend to.

When we start listening analytically to language material, we will usually begin by relating and allocating parts of the complex of what we hear to these starting reference categories. This means that our initial analytic impressionistic listening must, by default, concentrate on observing those things which are proposed as relevant reference categories by phonetic theory. Because of this the linguist must be constantly on guard, constantly willing to critically scrutinise such categories and entertain new possibilities and relevancies. What observers need is a willingness to countenance and describe new auditory categories, for instance, which may serve in the future as relevant cardinal categories. This goes hand-in-hand with a willingness to refine or abandon old, unsatisfactory categories. For instance, once linguists have decided to listen systematically and analytically to resonance features of consonants they may decide to elaborate a more detailed set of categories than they began with. (By resonance here we refer to the auditory correlates of particular overall oral cavity configurations.) Resonance is, of course routinely encoded in the vowel symbol stock in the IPA but is not treated in a similar integral way in the consonant symbol stock. However if we listen parametrically rather than in terms of pre-selected feature bundles then there is no motivation to ignore the observable changing resonances which characterise all points of utterance, consonants included. Just how many categories the linguist decides to attend to in observation is, of course, affected not only by the limits of their auditory capabilities (eg how consistently they can recognise different resonances) but also by the hypotheses they entertain or construct as to how many do some kind of functional work in the language under examination.

It is rather difficult to say what motivates a refining or rejection of old categories of analytic listening. The example of the elaboration of resonance categories is a case in point. The linguist may decide to refine existing categories for instance because they have found it irritating to keep allocating noticeably different auditory complexes to just one category (rather than a number of categories) - having operated previously with say a binary resonance distinction of 'clear' (palatalized) versus 'dark' (velarized); or, related to this, they may have observed regularly resonance differences which simply do not fit with the existing categories: for example an articulatory movement or gesture during which the resonance changes in some manner (as against the current orthodoxy which treats resonance categories such as 'velarized' as if they are non-dynamic); or perhaps they may, through analytic experience, have found that it is phonologically useful to distinguish more than two categories.

Holistic listening. In order that the impressionistic records, which are a product of analytic listening, should be as rich as possible, it is useful to employ another kind of auditory analysis in phonetic observation. This we refer to as holistic listening.

In holistic listening we try to attend to auditory features which characterise whole stretches of utterance. That is, rather than

- ❑ attending to short auditory stretches as being composed of small cross-parametric time-slices which we relate to reference categories

or

- ❑ listening in analytic parametric terms where we attend to changing values of a single, consciously isolated (auditory or movement) parameter,

we

- ❑ attempt to listen in terms which attend closely to the details of the overall characteristics of longer stretches of the material.

This kind of auditory analysis is motivated directly by assumptions we make about the nature of phonological systems and structures, in particular the frequent importance for phonological statement of establishing such 'stretches' for morphological, lexical, syntactic and interactional delimitation and subsequent analysis.

The kind of listening we are discussing here is necessarily indeterminate in a number of ways. Firstly the range of phenomena which may be candidates as holons is not fixed *a priori* (primarily because we are not operating here with reference categories). The overall characteristics of stretches may be relatively simple in parametric terms - say 'markedly lip spread throughout' or may involve a number of parameters - 'laxly articulated, relatively central in resonance throughout'. Secondly, the extents of these overall characteristics are not fixed.

2.5 Contribution of visual information

We know remarkably little about the relationship of vision and sound in the perception of speech. We suggested above that visually available gestural information would not be of central concern to us as linguists. This does not mean, though, that visual observation has no role to play in impressionistic phonetic work. Quite the opposite. In doing phonetic observation it is important to pay attention to at least part of what a speaker can be seen to be doing.

Such attention can yield valuable, perhaps essential, clues and cues about how they are producing what they are producing. It is possible to gather a considerable amount of detailed information concerning articulatory and other vocal tract movement during speech by watching carefully. We can observe such things as movements of the chest, throat wall, larynx, jaw, lips and cheeks, and sometimes the tongue, and we need to take the fullest possible account of such things. We take as an example one particular speaker of English who was systematically observed producing the utterances *more ice* and *more rice*. The two utterances showed differences that were available to both the ear and the eye:

❑ differences could be **heard** in the vocoid portions of the two versions of the word *more* and in the resonance and durational aspects of the period(s) of tongue tip approximation (at the end of *more* and beginning of *rice*)

❑   differences could be **seen** in kinds of jaw movement
the speaker made in producing the two utterances.
In the *more ice* utterance at the juncture of the two
words one major jaw lowering movement could be
observed to happen. It began towards the end of the
vocoid portion and reached its most open phase during the beginning of the vocoid portion in the word
rice. At the same place in the *more rice* utterance
two jaw lowering movements were consistently observed. The first, and smaller opening movement
reached its maximum at the end of the word *more*
and the second movement (slight jaw raising, coincident with a noticeable resurgence of lip rounding,
followed by a noticeable lowering) began around the
beginning of *more* and achieved its most open state
during the early part of the vocoid portion in *rice*.

Many of the categories which we use in phonetic observation
are mixed auditory-visual ones. Categories of lip activity are a prime
example. It is not an uncommon experience to listen (rather than
watch and listen) to a particular auditory complex and judge it to be
'rounded' only to discover on looking that whatever the lip-posture
is it is certainly not 'rounded'.

Categories of lip activity and their timing relationships with other
phonetic parameters provide a striking example of possibly important
differences which can be observed visually but which may pass un-
remarked if observation is exclusively auditory.

An appropriate example can be found in some observations made
of a North Welsh speaker. The following impressionistic records are
taken unedited from records made at face-to-face informant sessions:

1

maximal rounding

he saw a dog

2

maximal rounding

not as close rounded as expected

I saw a wheel

3

no observable rounding

it's Wynn's stone

4

no rounding here cf 'wheel'

it's Wynn's cart

These examples illustrate different phasing relationships between lip-rounding with respect to other articulatory components. In 1 and 2 the maximum of lip-rounding co-occurs with the initial back-of-tongue velar closure rather than with the period of following (canonically rounded) labial velar open approximation; and, further, in 2 with a period of laterality and alveolarity. By contrast in 3 and 4 the maxima of lip-rounding, under similar conditions, were observed to co-occur with the open labial velar approximation rather than with the preceding articulatory complex. This is, in terms of conventional phonetic wisdom, rather unexpected.

There is an important difference between the morphological

structure of the utterances of 1 and 2 on the one hand and 3 and 4 on the other. In 1 and 2 the portions under consideration are word internal ; in 3 and 4 the portions of interest occur across word boundaries. It would seem then that detail of local maxima of lip-rounding for this speaker has a morphological function. Where the relevant complex involving open labial velar approximation does not occur across a boundary, ie is word-internal, the phasing of lip- rounding with other articulatory components is such that it is greatest before the period of labial-velar open approximation. However, where there is a word boundary there is no noticeable lip rounding co-incident with the articulatory complex preceding such open approximation.

A similar phenomenon can be observed for many speakers of English in utterances such as *this shop's a fish shop*. Here, though there may be similarity of juncture between the words *this* and *shop* on the one hand and *fish* and *shop* on the other in terms of tongue body disposition, it is frequently the case that the onset and timing of lip rounding in the two cases relative to other articulatory components is different. For many speakers who produce the period of final friction in *this shop* with palato-alveolarity the onset of lip rounding begins later (and gets progressively closer through to the beginning of *shop*) than that in *fish shop* where it is typically present throughout the period of final friction. Here this difference reflects the difference in phonological status between the ('assimilatory') palatality at the end of *this* and the lexically relevant palatality at the end of the word *fish*.

The following material further illustrates the importance of visual information in phonetic observation; the words represented are taken from impressionistic records of a child aged 5:9 years who is in speech therapy.

slap   slow

slip   glass

$$\theta \cdot \underset{\langle \rangle}{f} \; \mathfrak{X} \overset{..}{:} \overset{\sim}{} \;^{N} \overset{?}{}^{\circ}$$

$$\overset{\bar{\partial}}{b} \underset{>}{\mathfrak{v}} \; \underset{\underline{\;\;}}{a} \overset{\sim}{} \; ?^{h}$$

flags   *black*

$$\underset{\sim}{\rho} \underset{>}{f} \; \overset{..}{\varepsilon} \cdot \phi$$

$$q \underset{\underset{w w}{+\iota}}{f} \; \overset{..}{:} \overset{\sim}{} \;^{N} ? ?$$

playing   *clowns*

$$\overset{\sim}{\underset{\underset{+}{w}}{\theta}} \; \overset{\sim}{\underset{+}{b}} \; \overset{\sim}{\underset{w}{?}}^{h}$$

$$\overset{t}{\iota} \theta \; \overset{\bullet}{\underset{+}{\mathfrak{X}}} \; \overset{\sim}{\underset{+}{\lambda}} \; ?^{h}$$

drop   *top*

$$\varsigma \; \overset{\bullet}{\underset{<}{\underline{\varepsilon}}} \; \overset{\bullet}{Y} \; \overset{\bullet}{\underset{+}{\omega}} \; \overset{?}{\underset{w}{}}^{h}$$

$$p^{-} e \underset{..}{\phi} \; \overset{?}{\underset{w}{}}^{\circ}$$

lip   *bib*

There are two chief points of interest to us here:

- ❑ the lip activity which is coincident with the glottal closure at the ends of the tokens of *slap, slip, drop, top, lip* and *bib*.

- ❑ the (lip) air-channel information here indicated by the subscript < or > at the beginnings of the tokens of *slap, slow, slip, glass, flags, black, playing* and *clowns*.

Both these visually observable aspects of the production of these tokens are crucial for an analysis of this child's speech.

In this child's speech there are large numbers of lexical items
which end in glottal closure. These items predominantly correspond
to adult tokens with plosive-type endings. So we find:

hat   hot

lick   back

bad   lid

dog   bag

Notice that the child makes a consistent distinction between tokens
corresponding to adult words with final voicelessness or voice by, in
the first case audibly exploding the glottal closure and in the second
not audibly exploding the closure. The co-incidence of lip rounding
with final glottal closure is restricted to those items corresponding to
adult forms with final bilabiality. It is not the case therefore that all

this child distinguishes with respect to word final plosivity is 'voice' versus 'voiceless'. She also consistently distinguishes final plosivity with bilabiality from plosivity with other places of articulation by means of the visually observable lip-rounding which however makes little contribution to the **auditory** effect

Visually observable lip-gesture also plays a role in the second aspect of this child's speech. Again we have a phenomenon which is easy to observe visually but rather difficult to detect purely by auditory observation. At the beginning of tokens of words such as *slap*, *glass* and *playing* the child produces articulatory complexes one component of which is the lateral passage of oral airflow. In the case of *slip*, *slap* and *slow* the laterality is coincident with tongue closure in the region of the alveolar ridge. In most tokens of these words the lip-channel is obvervably uni-lateral. The child holds the right side of her lips closed together; the left side of her lips is slightly apart and drawn up and back (as in smiling). The subscript > is intended to symbolise this unilateral channel. Where < appears it indicates (if on its own) that the channel is right side. If both < and > appear this symbolises a lip-disposition wherein both lips are firmly held together in the middle with both sides slightly apart and drawn up and back as described earlier. This laterality corresponds to laterality with alveolarity in adult speech. Where the adult forms have initial friction with alveolarity preceding the laterality (as in *slip* and *slow*) the child produces a noticeably long period of voiceless alveolar laterality. Where adult forms have initial articulatory complexes in which the place of articulation for the initial closure in different from that for the laterality (as in *playing* and *glass*) the child produces lateral labiodental friction on the release of the initial closure. (This is related to a pervasive feature of her speech having to do with quite general 'assimilatory' effects.) Thus, though the child is not producing exactly the same kinds of initial events as occur in adult tokens of these words, she is modelling many of the salient features, for instance: appropriate phonatory state, articulatory closure and laterality. Moreover, the presence of laterality here serves, in part, to distinguish these items from others such as:

crown   *crack*

frog   *brick*

In these instances we find word beginnings which closely resemble those of *clown*, *flag*, and *black*. However, though there is labiodentality after the initial occlusions there are none of the lateral channel features which were observed to co-occur with it in those other items. Indeed the lip-disposition of the labiodental approximation in *crown*, *crack*, *frog* and *brick* is observably different from that occurring in items such as *clown* and *flag*. In *clown* and *flag* the labiodental approximation was such that the top teeth closed against the middle (to front) top of the bottom lip. In the case of *crown*, *crack*, *frog* and *brick* the approximation could be seen to be between the top teeth and the inner surface of the bottom lip. (The labiodentality in last these cases is best viewed as corresponding to the open labiodental approximation produced by the child's parents and peers in words such as *crown* and *brick*.)

The intertwining of visual and auditory information in making observational judgements such as those discussed has its implication for phonetic observation (eg from tape recorded material) carried out in the *absence* of visual information. In such a case linguists are forced to rely very heavily on what they know about the speaker and the language under study. If they know nothing they have to go by experience or make assumptions. To say, for instance, that a vocoid is 'rounded' or 'spread' on the basis of a tape-recording rests on quite a different kind of observational practice/analysis than where a linguist can see the person speaking. The nature of the guess-work involved when linguists work on tape recorded material means that the impressionistic observations which emerge need to be treated with appropriate reservations.

2.6 Observing and record making

In the course of this part we have discussed ways in which impressionistic observation can profitably proceed. In doing so we have touched on a number of things which may influence the ways we do observation:

❑ the skill, training and general experience of the observer

❑ the mode of observation of the spoken material - whether or not it gives access to visual information

❑ the categories of the phonetic theory employed

❑ the categories of the phonological framework in which the observed material is ultimately to be situated.

In addition to these the precise nature and form of the notation which is employed in record-making can influence observation in a subtle and pervasive manner. We will discuss this issue in more detail in the next section. As a preface to that discussion we note here that there is a reflexivity between observing and record-making in that their categories are mutually reinforcing. This is particularly the case if the notation we employ to reflect our listening is a segmentalised cross-parametric one. Such a notation system (eg IPA) can tend to focus our auditory observation as if we were really dealing with punctual phenomena. It is very easy, even for experienced observers, to listen as if the only relevant categories were those enshrined in the symbols and symbol stock: and to fail to notice some feature or set(s) of features if the notation being employed does not provide a ready way of symbolising them. Even if such things are noticed it is often hard to resist the urge to squeeze them into some almost-appropriate category offered by the notation to hand.

Even if we do choose to attend to and represent a specific feature or event, the very form of representation we choose can channel our listening in certain, perhaps unexpected or undesired, direc-

tions. The observation and notation of pitch phenomena is a good example. We can decide to make an impressionistic pitch record, for
instance, either in terms of (a) a continuous 'pitch trace' or (b) in
terms of 'discrete levels' and 'movements' allocated to syllables.
Thus the same utterance may be transcribed as follows:

(a)

(b)

The choice of one or other of these ways will inevitably direct our
listening accordingly. In the case of (a), the continuous pitch trace, we
will need to listen to pitch variation at as many points as we can and
will pay attention to such things as pitch movement through nasals.
(We will want, after all, to relate the observed pitch material to accompanying articulatory material eventually.) If we record in the
second way the locus of our listening is prescribed for us as the syllable and we may be less disposed to attend to movements through
nasals at, say, syllable initial place. Again, we are likely to pay more

attention to on-syllable pitch characteristics and to treat between syllable movements or differences in a discrete fashion. So a decision taken about how to notate can restrict the kinds of variation we will attend to and affect the way in which we do that attending.

In Part 3 of the book we will examine in detail some of the resources available for impressionistic record making. We will also examine some of the ways in which resources may be extended and developed so that the delicacy and detail of our observing can be reflected in our impressionistic records.

Part 3
Recording

3.1 Graphical representations

We have already talked about the linguist making written records. These records are made up of marks on paper. The marks are taken from predetermined sets of symbols. Linguists have produced many such sets of characters for recording speech. They fall into two main classes: those that are devised expressly for the purpose, and those that are adapted from existing sets of characters, such as the Roman alphabet. A discussion of a number of character sets devised for the purpose of making records will enable us to comment on both general characteristics and particular idiosyncrasies. The six examples which follow are drawn from four centuries and two continents. They differ from each other in three main ways

- ❑ the appearance of the characters

- ❑ the degree to which they are systematic

- ❑ the kind of systematicities which they represent

3.1.1 Specially invented notations

The first three examples are of the kind that are purpose built: the final three are adaptations of the Roman alphabet.

The adapted sets vary in the extent to which properties of the original are preserved. Character sets are typically adapted

❑   by changing the referents of existing character shapes

❑   by expanding the number of characters

The second of these procedures can be effected by taking characters from other alphabets, so β ; by devising characters, so ☉ ; by modifying characters in a number of ways: developing new integral characters on the basis of existing ones (ꝳ), or by such devices as reversing (ꟼ) and turning (ᴣ). To the best of our knowledge all the systems for recording speech which are adaptations of other character sets are unprincipled in the way they implement these two forms of adaptation. The first example is Robert Robinson's *Vox Vivenda* as used to record a number of proverbs in Spanish.

Robinson presents the rationale for his system in his book *The Art of Pronunciation* of 1617. The date when the Spanish records were made is not known, and we are not entirely certain that they are records, in our sense, though this seems likely in the light of the variable renderings of orthographic **s**. At all events, Robinson almost certainly meant his characters to be used for this purpose amongst others. Robinson's characters are non-Romanic, though some are, on his admission, taken from contemporary cursive forms of the Roman alphabet. They are alphabetic, in that each represents a particular selection of values of different parameters. They are segmental in that no links are, or can be, overtly made over 'places' as identified: there is one exception to this which we shall come to later. They are, in the main, non-systematic in that the character shapes themselves display no systematic relationships with the phonetic categories they encode. There is, however, a resemblance between the characters for long and short vowels, the one being a turned or reversed version of the other in a number of cases.

The one way in which Robinson's characters are not fully segmental is in his treatment of voice and voicelessness. He indicates the voiceless members of pairs such as **p**, **b**, **s**, **z**, by a mark over the character used for the voiced one. Further he combines initial and final voicelessness in a syllable in a single complex mark which can be seen in the third proverb at the beginning of the word **Sus**. This is one way too in which Robinson's characters might be said to be systematic. In his examples of English he uses the voiceless diacritic over vowels to show initial ʰ , which extends the systematicity and shows Robinson's excellent grasp of the relationship between the 'aspirate' and the 'mutes'.

The next example is taken from shows Francis Lodwick's *Universal Alphabet* of 1686. This again is non-Romanic, and only partly alphabetic. It is segmental in the sense used above.

The Universall Alphabet.

The Table of Consonants

	1	2	3	4	5	6	7
1	b	d	J	g	=	=	P ʃ
2	P	t	ch	k	=	=	
3	m	n	gñ	ñg	=	=	
4	=	dh	J	g	v	z	B ʃh
5	=	th	sh	ch	f	s	
6		ñ					

8	9	10	11	12
ʃ	y	r	w	א

The Table of Vowels

The Lords Prayer in English.

Lodwick writes vowels above consonants, in the fashion of Arabic writing, and has to use a vowel carrier in words that begin with a vowel, as **our**, **art**, **in**, in the first line of the Lord's Prayer. He includes characters to correspond to the modern IPA symbols ʃ and ʎ , neither of which would normally be called for in making records of English, and it is clear that he intended it for use as a record making device. The set of characters is systematic in that particular columns and particular rows each have a distinguishing mark in common, added to a basic vertical stroke.

Our third sample comes from the year 1867 and is the *Visible Speech* of A.M. Bell. The sample shows a number of phrases in the

Upper Teviotdale speech of Alexander Murray, the first editor of the *Oxford English Dictionary*. The characters are non-Romanic. They are systematic in the same way as Lodwick's, and are also iconic in that they purport to have a resemblance to the postures and shapes that produce the sounds. It is only partly segmental, since many of the characters in the total set are for phonetic characteristics such as settings that extend over one or a number of syllables. None of these characters appear in the sample presented here.

Bell's character set differs from earlier ones in that the phonetic theory that underlies it is meant to be in itself systematic and exhaustive, and in that the correspondence between character shapes and elements of theory is an explicit one. Bell's system, being of this kind, provides a means of symbolising the whole range of human speech sound-types and ancillary sounds including even such things as snarls, yawns and snores. In practice it is often used with disappointing economy in Bell's illustrative material. But it was certainly intended to serve as a tool for making first-hand records.

3.1.2 Adaptations of the Romanic Alphabet

S.S. Haldeman's *Analytic Orthography* was first published in 1859, and is our first American example.

GREBO (§ 351a.)

649. *The Lord's Prayer* is given here from the dictation of a native, the translation being furnished by the Right Reverend John Payne, Episcopal Missionary at Cavalla. Nasal and stopt vowels (§ 350) are very common. Vowels unmarked, as to quantity, are *short*, and especially so when stopt. We have probable not marked all the stopt vowels.

ā bùa mɔ̆ˬ nɵˬ nɛ dɛ́ ɟū, naˬˈ nɟe'nɛˬˈ bɛ cɑˈ-ʃnɛ, nɟ ĕˬˈbo'
our Father thou he art there heaven, thy name let it have holiness, men

bŏ núˈ moˬˈ vaˈcɩˬ, moˬˈ naˬˈ *ŵrŏˈ bɛ nùˬ ɛ-dɛ́ˈ cŭnʊˈˈ mɔˬˈ
they must make thee their king, for thy mind (will) let it be-done-here world in

tɛnɛ́ˬ oˈ nĭ-dɛ́ˈ nɛˬ ɟù, h ɟ ˬ ˬ āmó, nɟ ɛ na ɟĕdŏˈ nɛ́'noˬˈ ɛ'nɛˬdìbaˈdɛ́, nɛˬ
as they do-there it heaven, give us day this food, and

beˈ pɔ́ˬˈ āmó, h ˬ v ˬ ˬ 'soˈ† co ā bonɛˬ cúcviˈ a ta tɛnɛˬ a nĭˬˈ
do thou put us forgiveness for our conduct wicked its account as we do

ā pĕ nɟ o nó, oˈ nĭˬ amó, bonɛˬ cùcviˈ moˬˈ h ˬ v ˬ soˈ† ɟɩ; nɛ naˬ
wo put who-they they do us conduct wicked unto forgiveness also; and not

naˬɛˬ amóˬˈ túdoˈtúˈ ā tĭdɛ́ ɟĭdíˈ, caˈ bɛ hā amó, cū ɟɛˈ
lead us temptation its way in, but (you) must take us devil from,

ɛmó, mɔˬ tɛɟɛ́ˈ cɩˬˈ nɛˬ mɔ vɛˈ-tĕ-ɟɛ́ˈ,‡ nɛ̆ˈ mɔ minɔˬˈˈ dɛˈ bìɛˈ
for thou art king and thou art-able-things, and thou shalt things all

ā nɟ è nɛ cŏˈmoˬ tĭ bìɛˈ, *amɛn.*
their glory have time all.

650. *In the following examples,* when the languages are not noted by parentheses, as in (*Armenian,*) we have taken them directly from the dictation of natives.

* This ɯ is perhaps nearer to *ooze* than to *awe*, §418. † The penult vowel is more open than *it*, or between this and *eight*. § 391a. ‡ te, things; je for.

It was produced in response to the offer of a prize for an essay on 'An analysis of the system of articulate sounds ... and an alphabetic notation'. One of the requirements of the competition was that, for the notation, 'as few new types as possible should be admitted'. This naturally constrains the design of the character set which is is alphabetic and Romanic. It uses such devices as turning to produce new characters, as well as diacritics and a range of modifications of existing roman letters. The referents of existing letters are changed, too - so, for instance, v denotes w . None of these changes appear to be principled; for example, turned upper-case Q, a consonant letter in the Roman system, denotes a vowel here, as does turned upper-case U .

Haldeman, like Bell, employs a number of additional symbols which are not alphabetic or segmental. So, for instance, he suggests the use of _____ for 'jaw open', though, again, it is not used in his examples. He also uses additional informal notes quite copiously: some of these appear in the sample. It is clear from its use in this way that it was expressly intended for application in the making of first-hand records.

Haldeman's character set has a lot in common with the next example which is that of the *International Phonetic Association*. Designed and first brought out in the final twenty years of the nineteenth century, it is, with a number of modifications, still in use today: and is indeed probably the most widely-known set of characters for the presentation of phonetic and phonological records and analyses. Its characteristics remind us of Haldeman's set. Turned **m** and **c**, consonant letters, are used for vowels, there is little systematicity in the set, and it has no explicit phonetic theory attached to it. It will form the basis of the symbol stock used in this book and, as we shall have occasion to talk about its properties later, we shall say no more about it here. The sample is taken from records made by one of the authors of Migaama, a language of southern Chad.

1. A dog's leg

2. A cat's ear

3. Cats' ears

dɘ: tɕo ßes̰ɹ̰ɳgeˑjˑo̰ˑ

╲ _ ‒ ‒ ╲ _

4. He is driving his oxen

t̓a̰ßak·â̰ᵊ ko̰ˑdigëteˑ

‒ ‒ ╲ _ ╲ _

5. He drank his water

ʒ a̰ˑ ʂeˑj ʔ̃ʌ̰↗ʔ (m̥) t̓ eˑ
                      (p)   taʔ?

╲ ‒ ╲ _

The last of our examples is the second to originate in the USA, and is
rather different from the rest. It is intended as a tool for making
records of spoken language. These records serve, though, as the basis
of studies of how conversation is organised and of the phonetic,
grammatical, lexical, paralinguistic and other devices, that relate to
the interactive shaping of conversation by speakers. The character
set is alphabetic and Romanic because it is, at base, the standard
orthography of (American) English, and it includes the conventions
of that orthography, such as having 'silent' letters in **night**.

```
Lottie:                                  [h h]Jeeziz Chrise shu sh'd see that

           house E(h)mma yih'av ↓no idea.h┌hmhh
                                          [
Emma:                                      [I bet it's a drea:m.<Wih the

           swimming POO:L ENCLO:SED┌HU:H?
                                   [
Lottie:                            [u-
                                    .

Lottie:    Oh::::::::: Kho:d we ˙hhihhh uh hu ↑We swam in the n:ude ˙hh

           Sundee night u(h)ntil aba┌ht ┐two u┐h'clo┐:ck. ┐
                                    [ehh]h e h]h e h]huh h]a:h ha┌:<
Emma:                                                             [
Lottie:                                                            [HUH


           ┌↑HA: HA:┐↓:.
           [       ]
Emma:      [˙he:hhhh]↓OH::: well I bed thghe moonli:ght'n the

           beauduhful stars the ↑WIND BLEW TERRIBLY ↓THOU:GH
```

This extended orthography is intended to capture unambiguously all
those events within the stream of conversation that might be suspected
of having importance for speakers and listeners as they carry out
their conversational talk. This list of things is open-ended, so the
recording system has to be open-ended and flexible. There is no
phonetic theory underlying the records, so no systematicity is called for
and the elements of the character stock are *ad hoc*. Unlike other character sets, this one is polysystemic, in that identical characters (here

letters) have different values at different places. This is because the orthography of English is itself polysystemic. So, the **gh** of **night** has not the same value as the **gh** of **thghe:** and the three **h**'s of **thghe** and **kho:d** have each a different value. This produces the possibility of manifold ambiguities. Is **light** the word $lait$ or the word lt plus 'gutturality'? In practice, though, context, abundantly present in these records of connected speech, serves to make ambiguity unlikely.

In its registration of such things as overlap notation, silences (of various kinds), in- and out-breaths and certain aspects of rhythm, this character set is a subtle and responsive instrument for making records of conversation. It has been used to excellent effect in this area by Gail Jefferson, who devised the greater part of it.

The things that all of these systems highlight are, of course, those which are deemed most relevant by the workers who produced them. They encode, though not always transparently, the theoretical and pragmatic assumptions of those workers.

3.2 Representation of postures and parameters

The characters in each of the samples discussed above all denote discrete segmental categories which are themselves combinations of more primitive parametric categories. This follows, in part, from adapting or imitating established alphabets. For those character sets specifically designed for phonetic work this is also the result of the position which implicitly or explicitly follows the long-established tradition of describing speech in terms of sequences of postures (also called speech sounds) and transitions. By posture is meant a (category of) articulatory state, typically presented in the phonetics literature in diagramatic forms such as this:

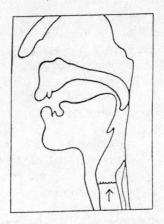

Transitions or glides are conventionally said to be the incidental transitory sound produced when the organs of speech are passing from the position for one speech-sound to that of another by the most direct route. The IPAA, too, embodies these assumptions.

We are not obliged, of course, to make our records using character sets which embody such properties. We might choose to concentrate on a mode of recording which selects and emphasises the continuous variation present in speech. For instance, we might highlight the movement aspect of utterance (movement of articulatory organs, laryngeal and pulmonic activities and so on) or the corresponding auditory aspect (such as sensations that we label 'falling pitch' or 'rising pitch' or 'friction'). If in our written records we concentrate on this continuous, dynamic aspect and try to deal independently but simultaneously with, for instance, the movements of tongue parts, lips, or nasal sphincter, we will have a parametric record.

A number of linguists have experimented with parametric representation of movement - though none of these are specifically designed for making first-hand records of speech. Here are two examples.

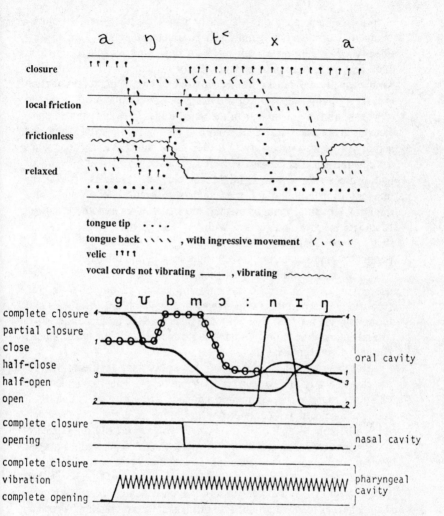

At first sight these parametric representations might seem to have a number of advantages over the segmental types of representation we discussed earlier. They emphasise activity and continuity of movement. They disentangle composite categories and reflect in a reasonably explicit fashion the timing of movements relative to one another. However, it would be wrong to assume that this kind of representation is more 'real' or accurate than a segmental-type record or serves as a better basis for phonological work. It is still an analysis in terms

of (pre-)selected categories. It is necessary to decide just what movements to record and to examine the parameters carefully - and to consider whether they are at all different in kind or whether indeed
they are genuinely independent. If, for instance, we represent pitch
parametrically we must consider what the nature of the representation
is. It certainly does not reflect a direct appreciation and
representation of movements of the vocal folds. Clearly such a parameter is qualitatively different from one having to do with visible lip
activity. It is also necessary to decide how much activity constitutes
a 'movement'; it is necessary to make guesses as to what movements
and degrees of movement might be relevant. What is meant by
relevant is determined by the linguists' theoretical beliefs and by the
kinds of structural categories they are developing hypotheses about.
Linguists observe and record with an ear to the kinds of entities
their theory contains. The principal function of the sorts of
parametric representations we consider is in fact to raise the awareness
of the linguist to the sorts of phenomena they are dealing with. Their
use, though, is subject to the same limitations as any other impressionistic work; and their effectiveness depends on the observer's skill
in making the records. They do not, then, provide an ideal alternative
to and improvement on non-parametric techniques, but have rather a
particular, and limited, use.

In contrast to this method of representation, segmental records
are cast in a way that we dub 'cross-parametric'. This means that each
character represents a compound phonetic category that is defined in
terms of a selection of parameter values. In selecting a set of segmental symbols the decisions to be made involve primarily the choice of
cross-parametric categories to be represented. Such record-making
systems offer a finite selection of parameter-values defining a
classificatory space in which 'speech sounds' may be allocated to
unique regions. The dimensions of the classificatory matrix are given
such labels as place of articulation or manner of articulation. The standard system of this kind is the alphabet of the IPA. The term 'alphabet' in the name 'Alphabet of the IPA' acknowledges that the system
is cross-parametric and segmental and that the segmental categories
are integrally (ie non-componentially) represented, in the form of
discrete symbols. In the case of the alphabet of the IPA the symbols
are letters of the Roman alphabet, in the main, eked out with selected
Greek letters and various makeshifts.

THE INTERNATIONAL PHONETIC ALPHABET

(Revised to 1979)

		Bilabial	Labiodental	Dental, Alveolar, or Post-alveolar	Retroflex	Palato-alveolar	Palatal	Velar	Uvular	Labial-Palatal	Labial-Velar	Pharyngeal	Glottal
C O N S O N A N T S (pulmonic air-stream mechanism)	Nasal	m	ɱ	n	ɳ		ɲ	ŋ	ɴ				
	Plosive	p b		t d	ʈ ɖ		c ɟ	k g	q ɢ		k͡p g͡b		ʔ
	(Median) Fricative	ɸ β	f v	θ ð s z	ʂ ʐ	ʃ ʒ	ç ʝ	x ɣ	χ ʁ		ʍ w	ħ ʕ	h ɦ
	(Median) Approximant		ʋ	ɹ	ɻ		j	ɰ		ɥ	w		
	Lateral Fricative			ɬ ɮ									
	Lateral (Approximant)			l	ɭ		ʎ						
	Trill			r					ʀ				
	Tap or Flap			ɾ	ɽ				ʀ				
C O N S O N A N T S (non-pulmonic air-stream)	Ejective	p'		t'				k'					
	Implosive	ɓ		ɗ			ʄ	ɠ					
	(Median) Click	ʘ		ʇ	ʇ								
	Lateral Click			ʆ									

DIACRITICS

- ̥ Voiceless ŋ̥ d̥
- ̬ Voiced s̬ t̬
- ʰ Aspirated tʰ
- ̤ Breathy-voiced b̤ a̤
- ̪ Dental t̪
- ̣ Labialized t̫
- ̡ Palatalized t̡
- ̴ Velarized or Pharyngealized t̴, l̴
- ̩ Syllabic n̩ l̩
- ̮ or ̯ Simultaneous sʃ (but see also under the heading Affricates)
- ˙ or ˴ Raised e˙, e̝, e̝w
- ˏ or ˎ Lowered eˌ, e̞, e̞ʷ
- ˖ or ̟ Advanced u̟, ̟y
- ˗ or ̠ Retracted i̠, i̠, ̠t
- ̈ Centralized ̈e
- ̃ Nasalized ã
- ̗, ʶ r-coloured a̗
- ː Long aː
- ˑ Half-long aˑ
- ̆ Non-syllabic ŭ
- ˒ More rounded ɔ˒
- ˓ Less rounded yˬ

OTHER SYMBOLS

- ɕ, ʑ Alveolo-palatal fricatives
- ʃˌ, ʒˌ Palatalized ʃ, ʒ
- ɹ̝ Alveolar fricative trill
- ɺ Alveolar lateral flap
- ɧ Simultaneous ʃ and x
- ɟ̫ Variety of ʃ resembling s, etc.
- ɪ = i̞
- ʊ = u̞
- ɘ = ə
- ɚ = r-coloured ə

VOWELS

	Front		Back
Close	i y	ɨ ʉ	ɯ u
Half-close	e ø	ɘ ɵ	ɤ o
Half-open	ɛ œ	ɜ ɞ	ʌ ɔ
Open	æ	a ɶ	ɑ ɒ

Unrounded   Rounded

STRESS, TONE (PITCH)

ˈ stress, placed at beginning of stressed syllable: ˌ secondary stress: ˉ high level pitch, high tone: ˍ low level, low tone: ˊ high rising: ˋ low rising: ˆ high falling: ˇ low falling: ˆ rise-fall: ˇ fall-rise.

AFFRICATES can be written as digraphs, as ligatures, or with slur marks; thus ts, t͡ʃ, d͡ʒ: ʦ t͡ʃ d͡ʒ: ʦ ʧ ʤ. c, ɟ may occasionally be used for t͡ʃ, d͡ʒ.

3.3 Characteristics of the IPAA

There are a number of important properties of the IPAA which we do
well to be aware of when employing it for the making of records.

3.3.1 Letter-shape to·parameter mappings

Relationships between letter shapes and parameters are random (contrast Bell's Visible Speech discussed earlier) and unsystematic in that
the same parameter-value is not consistently represented in every letter
shape. So, for instance, there is nothing in the IPA symbols ʂ f
which shows that the sound types they represent all exhibit the property of close approximation or friction. Similarly nothing consistently shows that k ɡ ŋ x ɣ   refer to dorsal-type articulatory events. They are arbitrary in that the selection of parameters involved in the definition of the symbols is not theoretically motivated.
So we find symbols which 'include' lip-rounding eg u o w , some
which 'include' lip-spreading eg i ɯ and some which 'include' neither, eg ʃ ʎ m   . Various problems arise from this. For instance,
because of the unsystematic nature of the IPAA, there is no principled
way of extending the stock of symbols and new, previously unencoun-
tered parametric configurations are difficult to integrate into the overall
scheme. This is because the dimensions and regions of the
classificatory space are pre-empted established and in advance.

3.3.2 Selection of parameters

In this pre-selected cross-parametric classificatory system those
parameter-values which are not selected for consistent representation
are often unspecified. This is clearly problematical: any such system
must necessarily ignore some parts of the observable phonic material
and afford it no theoretical status. In employing such a record-making
system we run the risk of producing records and analyses which do
not do justice to our observations. This means that IPA-type records
must be interpreted with very great care: some of the relegated material could well have primary linguistic status for all the linguist can tell.
A good example of this is provided by the following material taken
from the speech of a five-year old with impaired speech.

θ̆ɜ̌tˀtˢɪ̰̃j̃   fɔ̰̃tˀtˢɪ̰̃ʰ

fɪptˢɪ̰̃j̃   sik̟ˀtˢɪ̰̃nː

In *thirteen*, *fourteen*, *sixteen* we see syllable-final voiceless plosion with simultaneous glottal closure and tight, creaky phonation in the preceding vocoid. The adult forms in this Yorkshire variety show the same set of phonetic events. However, the child typically does not produce syllable-final fricative types, and in her version of *fifteen* we have, not f but p . However in this case there is no glottalisation and no preceding tight phonation. The phonetic sequence ɪp is not on a par with ɔ̰ˀt ~ ɪ̰ˀk and should not be taken as simply a substitution or replacement of f by p .

Now the representation of phonation types is not a primary category in the IPAA framework, and we are not encouraged, by using this framework, to take much notice of it. Over and above this, the reductionist approach which informs the phonological theory associated with the development and practice of IPA notation would actually encourage the analyst to see vocalic tight phonation as conditioned by the presence of the voiceless plosives, and in the present case to regard all occurrences of voicelessness with bilabiality and plosion as tokens of a canonical phonological-unit "p". This is clearly inappropriate here. We will argue below that such an alphabet-focussed approach has no place in phonology.

3.3.3 Gaps in IPA chart

There is no rationale for the gaps contained in the IPAA classificatory scheme. Consider the IPAA chart above. Some of the gaps are present because of physiological constraints on productive mechanisms. For this reason there are no symbols for glottal nasals, for example although there is apparently a category box for them in the IPAA chart. Other gaps are present simply because symbols have not been devised for the relevant sound-categories. So, for example, we do not yet have institutionalised symbols for bilabial trill, labiodental flap or velar lateral.

3.3.4 Arbitrariness of place of articulation

The kinds of place categories embodied in the IPAA are not those which a general phonetic theory would give. There is, for instance, a category post-alveolar, but there is no analagous category post-palatal. This means that actually occurring items that are descriptively post-palatal have to be assigned to either a kind of palatal or a kind of velar, ie c or k. Thus when we begin interpreting and start to collate, for instance, tokens of dorsal articulations so as to make preliminary analytic classifications, we have the problem of where to put, say, $\underset{+}{k}$. Should it be placed with items symbolised by k or by c? The IPAA's alphabetic basis makes it most tempting to group $\underset{+}{k}$ with k in the first instance - with a predisposition to relegate $\underset{+}{k}$ to secondary status, despite the fact that such a classification may be quite erroneous.

3.3.5 Implications of symbols

Character sets adapted principally from conventional writing systems can carry along with them certain undesirable presuppositions. Such presuppositions about symbols and their interrelationships can and do regularly constitute a major stumbling block on the road towards phonological interpretation. A ready instance can be found in the following material taken from Igbo.

$$ ɕ \cdot e\overset{.}{\underset{\equiv}{i}} j \tilde{ę}^{h} \quad \sim \quad ɕ e\overset{.}{\underset{\equiv}{i}} j \tilde{ɛ} $$

cook it

$$ ŋ \cdot g\tilde{ɔ} \; \overset{\sim}{\ddot{e}} j \overset{\sim}{\dot{ɛ}} \; \sim \; ŋ \cdot {}^{g} \tilde{ɔ} \; \overset{\sim}{\ddot{e}} j \tilde{ę} $$

$$ ŋ \cdot g\tilde{ɔ} \; \overset{\sim}{\ddot{e}} j \tilde{ə} $$

drink it

$$\text{ʌe̞ⁱ j̃æ̃} \sim \text{ʌe̞ⁱ j̃ẽ}$$

eat it

$$\text{ʌa̤ⁱ j̃ɛ̃} \sim \text{ʌa̤ⁱ j̃ɛ̞̃}$$

climb it

When we begin to examine such material with a view to talking about the vowel systems we find we have to deal with half open/open front vocoids symbolised by shapes such as ɛ̞ ɛ̈ ɛ̞ æ ɐ̞ ɐ . The shapes themselves may push us to lump together ɑ -type items as against ɛ -type items. It is very difficult to suspend the prejudices which these letter shapes carry with them. In the present case of Igbo, where there is a word-domain harmony system which distinguishes relatively opener from relatively closer vocoids, the grouping suggested above is entirely misleading and could lead to confusion and error at a later point in the analysis.

3.3.6 Phonological bias of IPAA

The IPAA is under-pinned by a particular kind of phonological theory. This is the cause of some of the problems we have identified. Other problems arise from the fact that it is underpinned by a *phonological* theory at all. So, for instance, the absence of special symbols for palatal and uvular frictionless approximants is a direct result of the fact that such items are not acknowledged as being, in any language, contrastive segmental units in word-phonology - the type of units that the IPAA is made up of. In fact these units are the kind that some conventional alphabetic writing systems reflect. The fact that the IPAA is constructed on similar principles to conventional orthographies emphasises again that it and cannot fairly represent general phonetic categories.

The problems that arise from the properties we have enumerated and illustrated can be seen as a kind of hierarchy. Some of them are less important than others. The problem of gaps is obvious and is openly recognised by the International Phonetic Association which allows for its remediation. In this case the IPAA can be extended by the user without theoretical complication. On the other hand problems arising from the theoretical underpinning are unstated and can constitute a more serious danger to the making of adequate records and analytic statement.

We have given extended consideration to this system because it is a widely used system for making records and because it is the system that we ourselves take as the foundation of our recording techniques. It should be clear that the problems we have identified in the IPAA are present to varying degrees with all of the other systems we have discussed. No set of descriptive categories is going to be exhaustive or satisfactory from all theoretical points of view. This means that we can in principle employ any system for phonetic recordmaking provided that we are aware of its properties, idiosyncrasies and deficiencies. We cannot begin interpreting and moving towards descriptive statements until we know, or have deduced, what kinds of (especially tacit) assumption are encoded in the record-making system. So, for instance, q and c tacitly share the property of denoting tongue-tip down, or convex tongue disposition as against apical $t̪$ $ɻ$ which are concave. This is apparent in either the form of the symbols, or the phonetic theory embodied by the IPAA, though it may be important in interpretation or phonological statement. The Visible Speech system of Bell, although radically different from the IPAA in certain respects, shares a number of its unspoken assumptions. For instance in $tʃ$ there is a tacit assumption that $t = t$. Bell's system, which is a direct forebear of the IPAA, also makes this assumption.

In the case of a parametric representation, like the one above in which vocal fold activity is represented in terms of an auditory parameter, there are problematic issues. The scale may include whisper (an intermediate state) or it may not. If it does not, we may record whisper on another parameter but which? The implications of our decisions are very complex and, as in all the other cases mentioned, are by no means transparent. Since the purpose of making records is to move from them into phonological interpretation we want a system that is not too committed to physiological events but which has the apparatus for close specification where necessary. And, despite our criticisms above, the IPAA is quite a good system from this point of view since it is relatively underspecified in its categories, and hence amenable to appropriate elaboration and development as desired.

A device like Bell's Visible Speech, on the other hand, stands or falls by the adequacy of the articulatory theory that it is based on. The categories of the IPAA are a blend of the the physiological and the auditory. Because there are various sides to the system, we are provided with a range of starting points in our route towards phonological statement. These strengths of the IPAA system make it a suitable basis for the working-out of a recording-system that allows for detailed, accurate and appropriate records.

3.4 Notation for Impressionistic Recording

We want our phonology to relate in as rich a way as possible to everything from, say, word-size entities to, say, interactive turn-size entities. So we require our impressionistic record-making system to take systematic account of at least the following, in addition to a basic articulatory skeleton:

❑ Long domain properties or sets of properties including pitch, tempo, syllable rhythm features, loudness features and articulatory and/or phonatory settings

❑ resonance features

❑ variability and co-occurrences

❑ relativisms

❑ phasing relationships

The ways in which the availability of such details in impressionistic records (IR's) allows the linguist to do phonological analysis will be discussed and illustrated in Part 4, *Interpreting*.

We give now illustrative examples of these aspects of our impressionistic records. These examples are intended to serve as a key for understanding the records which appear elsewhere in the book. They should also facilitate an understanding of the interpretive comments which accompany such records. What we present is not intended to be a complete system for impressionistic recording. It is, rather, a set of notational devices elaborated as the need has arisen over several years of impressionistic recording. While these notational devices are not intended to be fully systematic, the way that they have been elaborated reflects our theoretical position. This is apparent in the way that we resist the temptation to hypostatize symbols : we make no effort to engage in the invention of new phonetic symbols. This reflects our desire to background as much as possible the traditional implications of symbols, and to emphasise the parametric, the dynamic and the relative.

3.4.1 Notation of long-domain characteristics

(a) **Pitch** features are notated in a traditional (impressionistic) way on a relative syllable-by-syllable basis. Vertical displacement of pitch-marks is taken to indicate a higher or lower starting point for the syllable so marked while on-syllable pitch movement is indicated by the direction of the pitch-marks. We make some attempt to reflect the pitch-movement with respect to time characteristics in the particular way in which each pitch-mark is drawn. So ⌐ indicates a pitch fall where the bulk of the fall is accomplished early as opposed to say ⟍ where the pitch fall occurs late, the earlier part of the syllable having been perceived to be on a (relatively) level pitch.

Any notable excursions from what is taken to be the usual pitch range of the speaker are notated by writing "high" or "low" or suchlike where relevant and indicating the extent. For instance:

1

this is my father's sister (Ewe)

2

he hated the mushrooms (Ewe)

3 wɛ^rφ̣ị ̊g̈ȧ̈ö fəβɪh·ï· jɒṇɒ̃

when he go very he run and he walk(ing?) like that

(English - child in speech therapy)

So, for instance, in 1 the impressionistic pitch record reflects, on the third syllabic portion, a rather rapid rise which begins below the pitch of the second syllable and ends just above the pitch level of the first. This is followed by a low level pitch with a very small fall at the end.

(b) **Tempo** features are notated by using the musical terms for tempo change *accelerando* and *rallantando* underneath the relevant portions of utterance. We are principally interested in recording local, within utterance, changes in tempo, although we also note overall speed features of whole utterances.

4 jænạ̄s'ạ̈ jẹts'o:ɠo:ɠö:^ɦ

fastish _____ ⌐___ rall to end

he is standing tall, thin, like a wet chicken

(Hausa ideophone)

5   t' ɯ ɣ e̯ ṣ a̯ ŋ ʔ . ꞷ d̜ i d̜ a̯

        rall   *accel* to end

that's grass   (Korean)

(c) **Loudness** features of utterances or parts of utterances are notated separately. As there is no well established way of reflecting such features we have adapted, as others have before, musical notation and terminology. What we are interested in reflecting in our IR's is, as with pitch and tempo phenomena, the relative loudness characteristics of utterances. We employ notation such as f, ff and p, pp at relevant points in the IR to indicate louder (forte, fortissimo) and quieter (piano, pianissimo) portions as well as writing "diminuendo" and "crescendo", < and > to indicate loudness changes.

6   ʔ o̅ d̜ ˀ i̯ ꞏ j̇

          (variably quiet at end)

he ate it   (Twi)

7   ꭐ u ö d̜ ˀ i̯ ꞗ

    <   >

they ate it   (Twi)

8   ɣ β l ö e̤ ɲ ẽ̯ m e̤

          always quiet at end

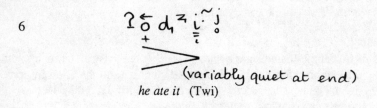

   < f   >   p

that's a mushroom   (Ewe)

9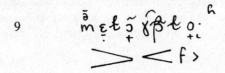

he hated the mushrooms (Ewe)

In 6 and 7 though the two utterances are grammatically related there is a difference in the kinds of loudness patterns associated with them (this is also true of other similarly related utterances in our Twi material). In the first the loudest part of the utterance is coincident with the first vocalic portion; the loudness then diminishes towards the end of the word. In 7 there is an increasing loudness during the first vocalic portion, and the loudness diminution at the very end of the utterance is rather abrupt. In 8 the overall loudness of the utterance is such that it reaches its perceived peak around the period of laterality and decreases from there to a rather quiet level (*p*) at the end of the word. By comparison, 9 has a decrescendo from the first syllable and then a noticeable burst of loudness coincident with the final vocalic portion. In both cases the increasing loudness relates to the syntactic structure of the utterances.

(d) **Syllable rhythm** features are notated separately too, in addition to durational features noted for parts of the articulatory skeleton. As with loudness features there is no widely agreed notation for syllable rhythm features. Consequently we use *ad hoc* notation writing — for (relatively) long, ◡ for (relatively) short and use the musical convention of 'dotting' to indicate half as much again'. We are not especially concerned about overrepresenting tempo and durational features (eg by writing say *i: n:* in the articulatory skeleton and also notating that particular syllable as rhythmically long, as we have found it useful to have in our records notation of such phenomena in different aspects. For it is not always the case that a short vocoid will be equivalent to a (rhythmically short) syllable.

The aim in notating all these features is not simply one of trying to achieve accuracy; rather, it is to have as many impressions as possible recorded together in some fashion, however *ad hoc*. The principle is that it is better to have things over-represented than not represented at all. This turns out to be especially helpful when later, as we move towards a phonological interpretation of these records, one of our primary aims will be to examine in detail interactions between parameters which serve to integrate and delimit stretches of talk.

10

how much is this   (Fula)

11

the leaf folded   (Malayalam)

12

he folded the leaf   (Malayalam)

In 11 and 12 the IR's show different rhythmic patterns coincident with the verbal portion. In 11 where the verb is intransitive the last two syllables have relative rhythmic quantities wherein the last syllable is somewhat longer than the penult (ie short-long). In 12, where the verb is transitive, the final two syllables are reflected as being of equal duration. (This rhythmic patterning is regular for such verb stem pairs in Malayalam.)

(e) **Articulatory** and **phonatory settings** are notated in our records simply by drawing a square brace above or below the relevant portion and labelling these braces. Again while we attempt to note as much as we can about overall phonatory and supralaryngeal tract settings, we make special efforts to reflect local changes in such settings. The status of the long-domain settings here varies. Although many of the kinds of features that we recognise are well-established traditional ones, some are not. We have made no attempt to fit everything into a taxonomic classification. This is largely because we are not yet sure what count as relevant classificatory categories (see below on the notation of resonance characteristics).

13

my brother kicked it (Igbo)

14

it's yellow (Sinhalese)

15 m̰ḛm̰ʌ̃k̚ʼo·d̰ḭʲeɡ̠ʌ̹ṣ̰sḛnə̣ʋ̣ẹ̃

central   back

lax

labiodental

I wave the flag (Sinhalese)

raised larynx

16 ɓˀt̰ɺ̥ʲɒë
    +·   +

tight cheeks

he copied it (Twi)

17 ɺ̰ǔɪ̰ḛJ̇ḛ̃ɤ̃

lax tense lax

eat it (Igbo)

tongue tip down

18 m̰ʷŋn̰uk:a̰ḛɲḭmḛ̃ɔ̰

suddenly spread

what's that? (Ewe)

3.4.2 Notation of resonance characteristics

The term **resonance** is used throughout this book to refer primarily to those features of consonants which are the auditory concomi-

tants of configurations of the oral cavity and/or movements of the tongue other than those which relate to the principal articulation. The kinds of resonance that we are concerned to reflect in our records are of the type labelled palatalisation and velarisation and usually treated under the heading of secondary articulation in the phonetics literature. The possible number of such oral cavity configurations and corresponding auditory categories is large. We have chosen to attend to a limited number determined principally by the (present) limits of our auditory capabilities. As we can routinely and reliably discriminate and identify a number of resonance categories we find it necessary to elaborate a more detailed notation for these secondary articulations than is provided by the current symbol stock of the IPAA. We refer to these resonance categories as palatalised, clear, half-clear, central, half-dark, dark and velarised. Using C as a symbol for any consonantal symbol we notate them using diacritics thus:

$$\varsigma \quad \c{\varsigma} \quad \overset{\overset{+}{\ni}}{C} \quad \overset{\ni}{C} \quad \overset{\bar{\ni}}{C} \quad \epsilon \quad \texteuro$$

In addition to notating the resonance characteristics of local portions of utterance we also attempt to reflect in our records the overall resonance characteristics of larger stretches. We have already given some indication of this in the examples above of articulatory and phonatory settings. The following IR's give further examples of resonance notation, both local, and long-domain:

19

he hid in the vestibule (Fante)

20

he inserted it (Malayalam)

21 (phonetic transcription)

the coconut fell (Tongan)

22 (phonetic transcription)

it's a pirate

(phonetic transcription)

it's a pilot

(Northern British English)

So, in 20 we can see that the consonantal portions towards the end of the utterance (eg ...) are characterised either by palatalised or by clear resonance. The consonantal portions at the beginning of the utterance are characterised by central or half-clear resonance. These resonance features are, in part, related to the grammatical category transitive.

In example 22 the records exemplify the notation of both local and long domain resonance. Here the first utterance is (relative to the second) characterised by overall backer resonance. In terms of local resonance the consonantal portions are central or dark in the first, as opposed to half-clear and clear in the second.

The resonance categories we recognise for consonants are not simply static ones. As secondary articulations they may, and often do, change while a primary articulation is maintained. Thus, for example, we may find a period of laterality which starts clear and ends dark or begins central and goes off half-clear. These effects and their notation will be treated in the section on phasing effects below.

3.4.3 Notation of variability and co-occurrences

We employ a variety of devices to reflect observed **variability** of utterances or parts of utterances.

- ❑ by writing vertically arranged arrays of symbols for observed different events or clusters of events at or around a given place in utterance

- ❑ by writing brackets around portions of the IR's we indicate that the portion may not always occur

- ❑ by writing arrows pointing in various directions to indicate range of vocalic variability Arrows are of two kinds: vertical and horizontal on the one hand, and diagonal on the other. Their uses are rather different. Horizontal and vertical arrows are employed to suggest closer/opener and fronter/backer ranges of variability.

The following examples illustrate these three devices:

Vertical arrays of symbols

23

it swayed   (Malayalam)

24

he climbed it (Igbo)

In the first case, 23, the IR reflects a considerable range of variability around the beginning of the utterance particularly with respect to the kinds of articulatory complexes at the first consonantal portion. At this place the speaker, in saying the utterance on more than one occasion, produced variations in dentality and velarity as well as in degree of occlusion. (As with the resonance characteristics of 20 this variability is related to the grammatical status of the utterance - here to the fact that it intransitive rather than transitive.)

In 24 a considerable amount of variability was observed throughout the utterance, particularly in the consonantal portions, where different kinds of articulatory events may occur. Notice, however, that although the speaker has on occasion produced this utterance with two portions having apical taps, the array of observed variability at these two places is different. Though there is overlap in what may occur, the second of these places sometimes admits of a lateral articulation while the first does not. As we will argue in *Interpreting* this kind of asymmetrical variability is frequently of phonological importance.

Two points require comment. First, the 'on the line' symbols have no primary status. They usually represent simply the first impressionistic response. If a particular parametric complex is not as common at a particular place in utterance, or if it is the 'predominant' one, then this is typically indicated by writing "rare" or "main" (or the like) as illustrated above. If a lack of variability is noticeable then this is typically noted by writing "stable", or something similar, and indicating the relevant portion thus:

25

not so variable (cf 'monkey' ?/ë;
'pineapple' ё/ə/ę)

cf ħ in 'best bundle' where 9 not variable

it's a shark (Tongan)

26

vowel very stable

cf 'flood'

bird (Danish)

The notes attendant on example 25 indicate that the lack of variability was striking, and thus of interest. In other cases where the same grammatical item occurs various vocalic qualities and ranges of variability are found. It seems likely that the non-oral nature of the glottal closure which begins the noun (*shark*) may be involved.

Bracketted symbols

27 [phonetic transcription]

when at fast tempo

his big stone   (Berber)

28 [phonetic transcription]

it's a breast   (Malayalam)

29 [phonetic transcription]

it was a long day   (Kiluba)

Example 27 illustrates two uses of brackets: those around subscript
ᴡ   indicate that there is variability of lip rounding; those around
ə and n   and the attendant comment indicate that these portions
are not present when the utterance is produced at a fast rate. The
symbolisation ɐ(·/n) indicates that when alveolar contact is not
present the preceding vocalic portion is longer. In the Malayalam example the brackets around the subscript . indicate that this portion
of utterance varies between more open ʌ and more close ʌ ; the
brackets around ɣ and ᶚ indicate that although this portion may be

present and may vary the speaker can produce the utterance without this portion.

Arrow symbols

30 (ʔ)↑oʦ̬ʉ̌ɤt̬ᵢ· æ e̱

he cut it up (Twi)

31 k̄ᵢ ɔᵘə̌ᵞ p̬ē̬ k̄ʷ æ·↓

it's a bat (Tongan)

32 ↑ɛ̱ɣə̱t̬a̱he↑ʲa̱ö↑

he hid the knives (Ewe)

We are not systematic in where these arrows are placed. They may appear before, after, above or below the symbol they apply to. Any ambiguity is resolved by *ad hoc* means. Diagonal arrows are employed to indicate that the variation in vocalic quality may variably be diphthongal, thus:

33 (ʔ)ᵢ·ɕə̌ɤ̌æ̱·ö̤ we↗

he combed it (Fante)

34 [phonetic transcription]

the long train (Cantonese)

In the Fante example the first vocalic portion is observed to vary in a more open range while the final portion varies in that it may have a closing, diphthongal quality. In the Cantonese example → indicates that the vocoid may vary over a range which is generally backer than that indicated by ɛ and may also vary in having a (frontish) closing quality towards its end.

As well as notating variabililty we endeavour in our IR's to indicate **co-occurrences**. By this we mean drawing attention to dependencies of the kind 'if variable feature(s) x, then also variable feature(s) y '. For contiguous co-occurrences we employ the convention of horizontally aligning the vertical arrays of symbols:

35   [phonetic transcription]

this man (Berber)

36   [phonetic transcription]

plantain (Fante)

Non-contiguous co-occurrences and complex variable co-occurrences are indicated by a tie bar to the appropriate portions sometimes with written comments. Where the variability involves pitch phenomena we notate this by writing the pitch patterns separated by backslashes as in 37 below

37

$$kʲe\tilde{ə̃}n_1d_1o̞↑$$

$$- \_ / \frown \_ / \rangle -$$

stove   (Luo)

$$kʲe\tilde{ə̃}ndö$$

$$- - / \overline{} \rangle / \overline{} \rangle$$

to marry   (Luo)

38

(phonetic transcription)

$$ʌ ʃ \text{ with } i ∼ e̞$$
$$\text{if } ʌ \text{ then } j$$

$V_2 i$ always
closer than
$V_1 i$

he ate it   (Igbo)

In 37 we have what may at first sight appear to be homophonous
forms. However, the pitch possibilities for the two utterances vary in
different ways. There is also articulatory variability in the second of
the utterances of a kind not observed in the first. In 38 there is
observed variability and co-occurrences of various kinds throughout
the utterance:

❏   the initial glottal closure is not always present

❏   the initial vocalic portion (a) varies in terms of
     closer qualities

- ❑ the portion (b) symbolised with ꞁ can vary in having post-alveolarity with friction - though it always has front resonance

- ❑ the following vocalic portion (c) can vary in terms of closer qualities - there appear to be two predominant kinds of quality here and either of these can co-occur with preceding friction or tap

- ❑ the following portion (d) varies, too, but not in terms of its primary articulation. The variation is in terms of resonance (secondary articulation) which varies in being more or less front - though not apparently in any obvious way with the qualities of the preceding vocalic portion (c)

- ❑ the next vocoid portion (e) also varies in terms of closer or opener qualities but here this variation has been observed to co-occur with variations in the resonance characteristics of the preceding portion

- ❑ the following portion (f) also varies - here we observe either open or close mid tongue approximation to the hard palate. Close approximation may occur here independently as it were, but the record reveals that it always occurs at this place if portion (b) also has friction

- ❑ the final vocalic portion (g) varies in terms of relatively fronter or backer qualities and may be followed by a period of labial closure variably with or without nasality.

Parts of the variability observed here (in both the vocalic and consonantal portions) turn out to be related to the system of vowel harmony operating in Igbo (compare also example 23, and see Part 4, *Interpreting* for a discussion of the status of variability in interpretation).

3.4.4 Notation of relativisms

Relativisms are noted within and across utterances principally in written notes. In addition we employ 'is equal to' and 'is not equal to' ties (⌢ , ⌐) to indicate specific places which contrary to expectations are notably similar or different. Horizontal square brackets are used to indicate larger portions where relativistic statements are appropriate.

The notation of relativisms has a rather different status in record making than other aspects discussed up to this point. It is fairly described as opportunistic as it frequently reflects some spur-of-the-moment observation or (analytic) hunch about the material being recorded. Some of the features which are focussed on as relativisms may be simply recoverable from other details of the impressionistic records but we often notate relativisms where we sense the possibility that alphabetic symbols may render opaque some of the relativistic details of observation. Relativistic observations may be language or utterance internal (eg differences of loudness, resonance or phonation, say, observed across two otherwise similar utterances), or language external (eg "not like English rounding") or what might be termed general linguistic (eg "k very front after back vowel").

34

$$ \overset{w}{\underset{\iota}{\ddot{\jmath}}} \cdot \overset{\sim}{\underset{}{\tilde{\jmath}}} \; h \; \overset{\sim}{\underset{}{\tilde{\omega}}} \; \overset{\tilde{r}}{n_{\iota}} \; \underset{\iota}{i} $$

Final V very close **not** nasalised
closer than 'sold it'

he saw it (Fante)

40

$$ \overset{}{\underset{+\iota}{\jmath}} \; \overset{\partial}{\underset{}{f}} \cdot \overset{\overset{\sim}{}}{\underset{}{\ddot{\omega}}} \; \overset{w}{\underset{}{e}}{}^{\iota} $$

initial V = that of 'shadowed'

it climbed it (Fante)

$\neq$ resonance

41    $\bar{g} \wedge\!\!{}_{+} \ell \cdot d\underset{\ldots}{\underset{\scriptscriptstyle\vdots}{\bar{e}}} k^{-} \overset{(\sim)}{\underset{+}{\bar{a}}} k^{-}$

backer than other utterances?

that's two stones   (Sinhalese)

42    $\ddot{o} s^{w} o d^{\vartheta} \underset{(\upsilon)}{\underset{\ldots}{\iota}} \underset{=}{s} \overset{\vartheta}{\tilde{\bar{a}}}{}^{n} ti\varrho \underset{\cdot}{\iota} \hat{l} g \underset{=}{\bar{a}} \acute{t}{}^{2h}$

always $\neq$ always
more open   backer

she bought a comb   (Fula)

43    $e \overset{\nearrow}{\cdot} \underset{(+)}{\bar{K}^{-}} \vartheta l_{4} \underset{=}{a} n_{\iota} \mathit{l}_{4} \phi \underset{=}{\bar{a}}$

$\ell \rightarrow \underline{a}$ transition odd
ℓ too clear for $\underline{a}$

it's light blue   (Sinhalese)

backer than 'he decreased it'

44    ${}^{\varsigma} \underset{+}{\wedge} \not\!\not{\tau} \overset{\omega}{\underset{\cdot}{\wedge}} \underset{\omega}{\underline{k}} \overset{\ddot{o}}{\omega} \underset{\cdot}{\iota} a \eta \ddot{u} \mathit{t}$

laxer rounding than 'he decreased it'

it decreased   (Malayalam)

45

≠ resonance

odd combination of resonances?

not m

my hand is hurting (Welsh)

46

backer
opener

it's a cockerel (Sinhalese)

tap cf 'cockerel'

tenser start
than 'cockerel'
V_1 closer

all closures firmer
than in cockerel

it's a hen (Sinhalese)

47   *[phonetic transcription: the parrot flew away]*

the parrot flew away   (Tongan)

48   *[phonetic transcription]*

*lip rounding more
like front than back*

to be tall   (Fante)

3.4.5 Notation of phasing relationships

By **phasing relationships** we mean the synchronisation of the separate parametric components of utterances. Almost any kind of written record gives some indication of such relationships, but writing alphabetic symbols in sequence carries with it the implication that all changes in parameters take place at the same time. However, we have found that there are phonological-analytic benefits to be gained from trying to be as responsive as possible to fine details of phasing and showing them explicitly in impressionistic records.

We have already, tacitly, illustrated the notation of some phasing relationships when we dealt with the notation of pitch, and loudness for instance. There the relative synchronisation was shown by the alignment of the pitch or loudness record with each other and with the articulatory skeleton. A good deal of the notation of phasing relationships is achieved by the careful placing of the various parts of the impressionistic record (eg symbols and diacritics) relative to each other. So, for instance, placing the diacritic relative to an on-the line alphabetic symbol implies different relationships between phonatory and articulatory activity:

49

$$\widehat{xм}$$
$$h\ u\ \overset{\text{x}}{\underset{\text{w' lo}}{d}}$$

*marked loss of voicing
at end*

human skin   (Danish)

50

$$\underset{\text{=}}{ş}\ \underset{\text{_}}{y}\ :\ \overset{?}{\underset{+}{к}}\ ə\ {}_{\circ}\ddot{b}\ddot{o}\ n,\underset{\text{ww}}{ə}$$

a sick farmer   (Danish)

51

$$\overset{ə}{f}\ \underset{\circ}{ɟ}\ \overset{?}{\underset{\iota}{ɛ}}$$

to call   (Fante)

52

$$\overset{ə}{t}\ \underset{\circ}{ɟ}\ \underset{\overset{\iota\iota}{}}{e}$$

to be broad   (Fante)

By placing the diacritic to the right of the final alphabetic symbol in
49 we mean to show that phonation is moving from voice into whisper
during and towards the end of the consonantal portion. In 50 by placing the same diacritic to the left of the symbol we indicate that at the
onset of bilabial closure phonation was noticeably not voiced but that
voiced phonation began during the closure phase.

Similarly in 51 and 52 the relative placing of the diacritic indicates the phasing of phonation with respect to the apical articulations.
(This relationship was systematically produced by this speaker and

appears to have to do with the status (plosive or non-plosive) of the initial consonantal portion.)

The following examples serve to indicate the notation of resonance phasing with respect to other articulatory components:

53

now she's reading it

(English - child in speech therapy)

54

this frog (Chaga)

55

wash it (Igbo)

56

resurgence of loudness during *l*
cf plural fuɬɓɛ̈ʔ

he saw a Fula (Fula)

In 53 the resonance co-incident with labio-dental approximation is shown to change from central to clear (notice that this is not simply due to the qualities of the neighbouring vocalic portions). (Some linguistic implications of resonances changes in this child's speech are discussed in Part 5 *Aberrant speech*.)

In 54 the record indicates that during the period of laterality the resonance changed noticeably from palatalised to velarised, though the dental place of articulation was maintained throughout.

Similarly in 55 the notation reflects the kind and phasing of resonance at the utterance beginning. The initial consonantal portion begins clear and during the period of apical friction becomes central. (This kind of resonance change was typically produced by this informant at the beginnings of imperative expressions where 'long' consonantal portions occurred.)

In 56 the IR indicates that loudness and resonance are phased in a particular way with laterality. (The phasing relationships here are relevant for the analysis of the morphological constituency of the utterance as the accompanying note suggests.)

In addition to the notational features we have explicitly discussed a number of other notational elements appear from time to time in the impressionistic records. These we regularly use as an informal but valuable adjunct to the principal strands of the records. These additional elements include notes (in words), and drawings (typically of lip disposition).

Notes may be descriptive and entirely subjective and have to do with such things as auditory effects ("dull"), articulatory effects ("lips together at sides only"); they may be relativistic ("backer than in 39"), or comparative ("not like English", "not English w rounding"). The following provide exemplification:

57
$$\underset{\iota}{\text{o}} \; \bar{\text{k}} \; \text{ω} \; \tilde{\underset{\pi}{\text{ş}}} \; \underset{\iota}{\text{ɣ}} \; \tilde{\text{m}} \; \land \; \grave{\text{v}} \; \text{f} \; \underset{\iota}{\text{i}} \; \text{j}^{\text{ə}} \text{'}(\text{ɦ})^{(\sim)}_{+}$$

ɔ = top lip further out than bottom – almost ɔ$_f$

he hid in the house (Fante)

58   ɒ ꞁṣ ̃ι (ɪ̃)

φ = bottom lip in
lips tensed laterally

he caned him   (Fante)

59   m æ ə ꞁ tˢ ι̃ ə n ʌ æ· u ꞁ̥

↘ not ŋ !

this house is big   (Welsh)

Though these notes and drawings are ancilliary devices we try not to relegate them to decorative status when we begin to interpret the records. Given the nature and restrictions of IPA type symbols, no matter how elaborated they may be with diacritics, there are bound to be aspects of the spoken material that can be easily observed but not so easily reflected in terms of symbols or even words. In doing interpreting towards phonological analysis we take seriously all the detailed observations reflected in IR's no matter how they are represented.

The provisional nature of large parts of the record is shown by the sometimes liberal use of "?" as a problem marker. This is usually a reminder to listen again carefully to (that part of) the utterance.

We have devoted considerable attention to detail in impressionistic record making. This does not derive from a gratuitous interest in detail for detail's sake. Such detail is not an additional extra, or something which whilst 'nice to have' is only of trivial interest. As we will demonstrate in the following Part, this detail can provide the minimum basis for phonological analysis.

Provided with a full set of records of the elaborated kind we regard as necessary, we can go on to the first stages of interpreting, where, away from the utterance of the material, we begin the search for patterns and relationships. These patterns and relationships have to be interpreted as being the external aspects of other, more abstract, systems that will accordingly need to be presented in more abstract theoretical terms.

Part 4

Interpreting

4.1 Introduction

In the previous parts we have explored some of the requirements that thorough-going observational methods place on the making of impressionistic records: and we have discussed the nature and properties of such records. We now know that whilst records of spoken language events may be quite detailed, they are not a facsimile of those events. For one thing they are in a different medium, the written medium. For another they are set out in terms of an analytical recording system. In making our records we refer the spoken matter to the recording system, and map it on to it. So the records present a particular kind of analysis of the material.

Impressionistic records, then, are a combination of an aide-memoire, needed because we do not have prodigious auditory memories, and a preliminary and imperfect analysis of a particular kind. As we move towards our eventual goal of making linguistic statements, there is a stage at which the records are looked at with a view to seeing how they can be interpreted. In working on such records in this way we are reanalysing parts of them and trying to recognise recurrences, regularities and categories of either an overt, an apparent or a covert kind. At this early stage of this set of activities that we call *interpreting*, there is no set of established procedures. The process is neither mechanical nor straightforward, in either the simple or the linear sense, though a number of principles underlie it and will be outlined shortly.

Interpretative work often entails seeing something as something else. If regularities are covert they have to be seen into, as it were. If a category is apparent it can be discarded at the next stage of interpretation. This means that the shapes, patterns and categories that we have before us in IR's made for a particular language can be quite different from those we may present in a phonological analysis made for that material. Here, straight away, is an example. The material comes from Migaama, a Chadic language spoken in Southern Chad. The following array of verbal forms were taken down from an informant. Chadic languages have a rich verbal system usually set out in the literature in terms of a number of what are called grades. These have to do with kinds of tense and aspect, generally speaking. The forms 1 - 10 given here are the grade forms for the first person singular: the records show no more detail than is required for the purposes of the demonstration:

	I *beat*	**II** *leave*	**III** *cry*
1	tamme	oome	erce
2	tamanna	okomma	erecca
3	tammiɗe	oomiɗe	erciɗe
4	tamanɗo	okomɗo	erejɗo
5	tamanɗe	okomɗe	erejɗe
6	tamanne	okomme	erecce
7	tammu	oomu	ercu
8	tammo	oomo	erco
9	tammeero	oomeero	erceero
10	tamma	ooma	erca

	IV	**V**	**VI**
	run	*jump*	*cut*
1	gaɗɗe	sadce	reppe
2	gaɗakka	sadacca	repekka
3	gaɗɗiɗe	sadciɗe	reppiɗe
4	gaɗaɗɗo	sadajɗo	repeɗɗo
5	gaɗaɗɗe	sadajɗe	repeɗɗe
6	gaɗakke	sadacce	repekke
7	gaɗɗu	sadcu	reppu
8	gaɗɗo	sadco	reppo
9	gaɗeero	sadceero	reppeero
10	gaɗɗa	sadca	reppa

These forms show little in common. The final vowels ring the same changes in 1-10 for all verbs, but, apart from that, most other regularities are common to only a sub-set of the six verbs. So, grades 7 and 8 have consonantal gemination in some verbs; but not *leave*, *cry* and *jump*. Grade 5 has gemination before the ending in only some verbs. Grade 5 matches grade 1 with regard to gemination in *run* but in no other verb; and whilst grade 7 always matches grade 1 in regard to what happens at the intervocalic place, for different verbs the things that happen are different.

Our first task is to make some decisions about stems and endings, to get some idea, that is, of morphological shapes and identities. In the cases of all these verbs we might want to hypothesise that the morphology is complex, such that verb **I** sometimes has a possible infix **-an-** which appears nowhere else in the six. If this is so, verb **I** is in a class by itself. Verb **II** might have an infix **-k-** appearing in the corresponding grades to -**an**- in verb **I** (2, 4, 5 and 6) but this is an infix into a possible stem, **o-om**, not into the stem-ending junction, which is where -**an**- goes in verb **I**. So **II** is in a class by itself, too, and a different class. If we interpret in this way the phonology is being elaborated in a very simple way as a set of elements identical in constituency and arrangement with segmental phonetic elements suggested by a naive view of the record. But the morphology is being made very complex, as we now have three morphological classes at least.

Another method of analysis is to try to keep the morphology constant, and to assign all complexity to the phonology. In such an approach a worthwhile move would be to assign the irregularity we have just noted to the lexicon, that is, to the stem in morphological terms. This immediately removes the morphological problems we have just considered, since we are now positing at an abstract level the stems **taman**-, **okom**-, and, by analogy, **erec**-, **gaďak**-, **sadac**- and **repek**-. These we might now go on to regard as being mediated through a set of matrices or templates. If we allow **taman**- and the like as basic abstract stems, we shall have to also allow structural places in our provisional templates to be filled by zero ($\emptyset$) to embrace forms such as 1, 3, 7, 8 and 10. Given this we can establish templates as follows:

1   (C)VC∅C - e

2   (C)VCVC - C a

3   (C)VC∅C - i d e

4   (C)VCVC - d o

5   (C)VCVC - d e

6   (C)VCVC - C e

7   (C)VC∅C - u

8   (C)VC∅C - o

9   (C)VC∅C - e e r o

10   (C)VC∅C - a

These can be seen as mediating the abstract material so as to preserve the first syllable of what we have called the stem in a constant (C)VC shape throughout all these forms. If zero did *not* occur in our templates then, for instance, in 3 above we would have (C)V|CV|CV|CV. In 4 and 5 the alternative analysis leads to CV|CV|C|CV: this gives an isolated C, which cannot form a syllable, and the analysis is disallowed. It will be seen that in grades 2 and 6, in which gemination appears, our templates show C-C at the relevant places. But in, for example, grade 7 they show C∅C. That is the -nn- of **tamanne** may be gemination, whereas the -mm- of **tammu** (< tam∅n-u) is not. This second case falls together with others such as **reppu, repeddo, gadde** (< **repek-u, repek-do, gadak-e**). These are all instances of a phenomenon whereby, at certain places where consonants abut, some phonetic feature or features exhibit a stretching over the whole abutting complex. The outcome of this is that gemination in Migaama can be seen to be of two kinds, one of which is, as it were, spurious. In some cases then, gemination is an apparent category, and shown to be so by our interpretation of patterns.

The interpretation has shown up, too, a number of covert categories such as syllabic zero. This is a phenomenon that serves to preserve certain structures; alongside it we have identified the stretch phenomenon mentioned above which serves to consolidate structures. Neither of these two structure-regulating phenomena will show up in an interpretation that simply elevates the phonetic categories of the records to phonological status, an interpretation which would fail to introduce regularity into this apparently irregular situation. In addition to what we have discussed there are a number of phenomena in our newly interpreted forms that suggests that we might want to interpret further. One is that in all of our proposed verb stems the second vowel is the same as the first: and the other is that the consonants at C_3 are a limited set of **n**, **c** and **k**. Now this latter may be simply the result of looking at a small number of verbs, and it would be foolish to place a lot of emphasis on it at this stage . But this is precisely the kind of observation that phonologists should enter into their mental bank for later checking and reinterpretation, for the set is made up of one palatal, one velar and one nasal, that is, precisely those categories that frequently operate as oppositions in phonological systems. So we may be looking here at complex, rather than simple, forms. For instance the structure might be $(C)VC\text{-}\partial^R$ rather than $CVCVC$, where we are dealing with an extension to verbal stems, having the generalised phonological structure ∂^R. In this tentative formula ∂ stands for a syllabic associated with the same set of phonological oppositions as the syllabic of the stem; and ^{R} stands for a three-term system of nasal, front or back consonantal syllable closure. All of these speculations would have to be subject to more extensive and deeper interpretative work on the language; and all are at this stage subject to revision or even abandonment.

4.1.1 *Purposes and Expectations in Interpreting*

Two factors affect, to at least some degree, the way in which we do interpretation. One is the purpose or purposes for which we are doing the work. The other is our expectations, which arise either from linguist's intuition or from various points of theory.

If the purpose of doing phonology is, say, to prepare a writing system for a literacy programme we might be predisposed towards a segmental analysis and would want for problem areas solutions that are both practical (eg to printers) and acceptable (eg to learners). This purpose would also be best served by an approach which sought to capture the phonology of the language in a single all-embracing system.

Similar, though not identical, considerations would apply if we were preparing a teaching or reference grammar. In this case we might be aiming to provide a systematic notation or transcription couched in IPA terms or something very like them, rather than a Romanic writing-system, and certain principles of language-study would prevail over more practical or pragmatic factors. It is awkward and expensive in printing, for example, to include tone-marks in the writing system in, say, a West African language. In addition, native users of such languages routinely say they do not need them, and tend to neglect their use even when they are available. So both practical and pragmatic considerations go against their use. But in a reference or teaching grammar of one of these languages tone-marking would almost certainly be indispensable, and a tonal analysis would be the prerequisite to such a marking-system. The approach to this analysis would itself be influenced to some degree by its intended application: and, when completed, it would almost certainly look different from an analysis that aimed at providing the abstract basis for relating the tonal patterns of a number of related languages. Yet both of these would be analyses based on interpretations of the same material.

Interpretation may, in addition, be partial or overall: and this in different ways and for varying reasons. If attempting the preparation of a reference grammar one would presumably want overall coverage. But a linguist working on the nature of vowel-harmony phenomena might look at only this aspect of a language and present an analysis of this alone. In a similar case a linguist might do a partial analysis of, let us say, the vowel system of a language as an illustration of the cogency or otherwise of a particular phonological approach or simply to show how it worked. There is a necessary interplay between what light languages throw on linguistic theories and what light linguistic theories throw upon languages: and, in performing interpretation, linguists may be focussing now more on the language, now more on the theory, or taking up a relatively neutral position.

The purposes, then, of our interpretations should and will influence the way in which we carry them out. It is wise to have a clear grasp of one's motivations at the outset. This is not to say that simply rooting around in language material is illicit: it is after all our most fundamental research tool and serendipity is at its most effective in this situation.

Partial analysis may be not so much a matter of purposes, though, as of expectations. Expectations arise, of course, from a number of sources: from what one has been taught, from a particular theoretical orientation, from the kinds of hunches one has learned to play and from the range and kinds of languages one has dealt with. In short, expectations arise from the totality of one's past experiences. And theories themselves arise in part from observations and intuitions within linguistic work in general. It is common, though not standard practice, to treat loan vocabulary as at least potentially different phonologically from indigenous vocabulary. In some theories this can take the form of a requirement, in others be simply recommended. The reason for this is that many linguists have found such treatment more satisfactory in the sense that the ensuing description is more elegant or more explanatory. And in their turn these characteristics may be regarded by particular linguistic theories as either more or less desirable requirements of linguistic description. To the extent that theories require one or another of these properties to be found in analysis, to that extent the linguist will be predisposed to interpret in a particular way. Similarly, the extent to which a particular theory insists on the universalist nature of its categories or of their combinations, will encourage a linguist working within that theory to interpret perhaps recalcitrant material in a certain way. Experience, expectations and theory come together to provide the matrix in which we work.

4.2 General approach to Interpreting

In interpreting impressionistic records we operate with a number of principles which provide guide-lines for the making of phonological analyses.

> **strict demarcation**: we draw a strict distinction between phonology and phonetics. Phonology is formal and to be treated in the algebraic domain; phonetics is physical and in the temporal domain. This distinction leads us to talk of phonetic *exponents* of categories in the phonology, and to countenance the setting up of arbitrary (in the Saussurean sense) but systematic relations between phonological categories and their parametric phonetic exponents.

> **non-derivation**: we view phonology as best treated in declarative, rather than process, terms. This principle encourages us to seek non-process accounts of phonological phenomena.

parametric interpretation: it is essential not to be restricted to the domains and categories superficially imposed by the shapes of the impressionistic record on the language material. This principle leads us to interpret impressionistic records with reference to component parameters and their synchronisation in time.

variable-domain interpretation: we should give equal priority to the recognition of features or sets of features over whatever domain. That is, interpretation should not restrict its interest to 'segment-sized' units. This leads us to explore language material for putative long-domain phenomena and to establish stretches.

variable-relevance interpretation: we should be prepared to accept any parameter or group of parameters as of phonological interest at particular points in structure. For example ɯ is nasal, voiced, bilabial, half-dark, pulmonic, non-lingual, non-lateral, lax, non-pharyngealised, continuant, non-creaky, extended, approximant, spread. Any one of these, or any group of them, may be what is relevant. So, a non-lateral, non-lingual nasal is what this phonetic bundle is phonologically at a certain point; whilst elsewhere it is a voiced non-lingual lax continuant. It is not necessarily always a voiced bilabial nasal, phonologically.

congruent level interpretation: we should systematically and differentially relate the phonetic detail of utterance to the various levels of linguistic analysis (eg interactive, grammatical, lexical).

polysystemic interpretation: we must be sensitive to the fact that different phonological systems operate at different places in linguistic structure and reflect this in our phonology.

parsimony: we endeavour to minimise the number of phonological primitives we employ

system-symmetry: we endeavour to look for and elicit symmetry in the systems we identify

The last two of these principles are widely held and characterise many otherwise very different approaches to phonological analysis. The others reflect our particular view of the nature of phonological analysis and phonological representation. Because some of the principles we have sketched are, if not controversial, at least not generally accepted it is necessary to consider some of the implications and consequences of working with them.

4.3 Preliminary interpretation

4.3.1 Congruence of levels and allocation of complexity

One of the first tasks that arises during the process of interpretation has to do with deciding on the relationship between various elements or phenomena in the record and other descriptive levels such as morphology and syntax.

The problem can be artificially illustrated by English. Many English nominal and adjectival 'learned' compounds contain the element -o-, unaccented. For example:

Graeco-Roman

Balto-Slavic

Franco-Prussian

Sino-Tibetan

cardiovascular

A linguist who knew no English would have the problem of deciding whether this was best treated as a morphological entity, or as a morphologically empty phonological entity serving to link two accented lexical phonological forms; or, a third possibility, as a phonetic filler only with no status in phonology. Having made a decision on this the linguist then has the problem of a word like PIANOFORTE. Since PIANO exists (whereas BALTO, CARDIO do not) is PIANOFORTE comparable in its structure with GRAECO-ROMAN. Is it two morphological elements or three? On decisions like this some of the ensuing phonology might depend. If we take -o- to be some kind of 'filler', why is it o ɔ , as against ə , say, an otherwise common unaccented vowel in English? We might want, then, to attempt to account for rounding here, which

we should be less tempted to do if we took -o- to be a morphological
element in its own right. We might also want to think about this issue
by treating different word-classes separately. It is essential when doing
phonology to move as quickly as possible towards an understanding
of syntactic, morphological and other structures in the material. This
is principally because the phonetic material itself has to be assigned to
categories at these other levels, as manifesting them in the spoken
medium. It is not always a simple task, though, to gain an insight
into these underlying structures and categories on first acquaintance.
There are a number of reasons for this. One common one is that
languages often have 'non-matching' categories in them, so that various particles, say, in a language under study, might correspond to
nothing in the English gloss and be at the outset impenetrable. Secondly, categories, though common to two languages, may be used differently in each, as when a quantifier 'some', say, is used generally
to pluralise. It is possible to take such a portion as a plural marker
situated within the area of morphology; only certain syntactic structures will show it up as a (lexical) quantifier. So in Ndogo:

kɔ̀

leg

kɔ̀jɛ́

his leg

ǹdákɔ̀jɛ́

his legs

kɛ́dʑɪ

road

kɛ̀dʑímɛ̃́

my road

ǹdákɛ̀dʑímɛ̃́

my roads

The last form looks in each case like **plural + noun + possessive**. But

ǹdákazaygɔ tazɔ́

crocodiles   three

and

ǹdá lambó kazaygozó tazɔ́

?   small   crocs   those   three

make it apparent that ǹdá is not a simple pluralising prefix, and
that its status may need more working out.

In other cases we may have a firm idea of what certain portions of a structure are, yet be left with indeterminate portions
which

- might be part(s) of the identified portions

- might be a separate as yet unidentified morphological or syntactic entity not paralleled in English structure as suggested by the English gloss: Japanese **wa**
  would be a case of this

- might be not really separate portions in structure but
  elements of the phonology of the portions already
  identified; so-called epenthetic vowels are a case in
  point here

and there are other possibilties. A situation of this kind is exemplified
now from Bakosi.

sàbɛ̣́dɛ̰

it's an orange

it's a dog/dogs

it's a person

it's a book/books

it's a stone

it's firewood

it's oranges

it's people

it's stones

Here we can observe that only one portion is regularly present, and is of approximately the same shape, namely - *de* etc at the end. But its tone is different from case to case. This *could* be a copula. If it is, then either it has a number of different forms - *de* , - *nde* , - *bede* ,- *mede* or some nominals have

singular	plural
sàbɛ́ɛ́	bìsàbɛ́ɛbɛ́
àlʼáà	mìlʼáàmé
mùdɛ́ɛ	bàdɛ̀ɛ̀bɛ́

(but m̂bwɛ́ɛ, plural m̂bwɛ́ɛ . If the second of these possibilities is the case we have two kinds of plural, since *she is selling oranges* is

àsúmè bìsàbé

she is throwing stones is

àpìmèʔ mìlʼáá

In fact we may have three kinds of plural, since *two oranges* is

bìsàbɛ́bibɛ̀

giving bìsàbɛ́ɛ̀bɛ́

bìsàbɛ́

and a possible bìsàbɛ́bi

as plurals for *orange*, singular sàbɛ́ɛ . The last of these could be bìsàbɛ́bi , of course, if, for the time being, we allow a falling pitch to be the phonetic correspondence of a high plus a low tone in a junctional configuration.

This is already providing a complex morphology for the nominals. If we put this analysis on one side and take up the idea of the copula having various forms, such as those listed above, we would remove some, but not all, of the complexity from the nominal forms. If we accept that the copula is a two-part form and that one part, the first, replicates the first part of the nominal with which the copula forms a syntactic whole, we would get a case of agreement between elements in syntactic bonding, a phenomenon well attested in the world's languages.

To demonstrate this kind of phenomenon we want ideally, though, to get away from forms where there are ambiguities about boundaries between an assumed 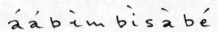 (from *she is selling*) and what follows it. A look at the material produces

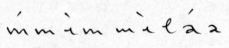

my oranges

alongside

my stones

where - **b** - and - **m** - reinforce our idea about an agreement of satellite elements which involves phonological replication.

A number of areas remain to be gone into

- ❑   the endings of the nominals in the *it's* . . . utterances

- ❑   tonal patterns

- ❑   the identification of all the agreement particles

- ❑   minor oddities, such as the appearance of **g** in *it's a book* as against **ɜ** in *my books*.

We also have to suppose a system in which singular and plural forms fall into various ones of the agreement classes: and this would need to be fully explored.

The phonology and morphology of the junction portion between nominal and copula is still not clear, though we have established that the copula is at least a two-part form: and that, in principle, it exhibits agreement with the nominal it refers to, just as qualifiers ('my') and linkers ('of') do. We say 'in principle' because, in some cases, it is difficult to see in the material what the agreement is. And, even when we can see it, we shall have to relax our earlier statement about such agreement replicating the phonology of the nominal, since in some cases it does not do this. But, though the phonology and morphology are complex, the 'bonding' or 'agreement' system works regularly; and this seems to be the neatest answer to the various forms and patterns we have encountered.

In handling all the material of the nominal + copula boundary we are faced with a difficulty when we look at *it's an orange* or *it's a book* where there is no apparent agreement particle: similarly in *it's a person*, *it's a dog*. We are assuming now that the agreement controller in the nominal is at the beginning, so b i̱ -, m i -, b a -, m e - and n -. For this reason we would regard the first d of m u d ɛ·d e as being in the 'stem' of the nominal, if we set up a provisional pair of categories 'initial particle' and 'stem', IP and S.

In the problem cases we have two ways of looking at the structure. We can say either that these have no initial particles, or that they have particles which are manifested here as zero. We are pushed in the direction of one or other of these interpretations by other evidence.

The problem we have here is that there are effects taking place at the nominal + copula boundary that are not immediately easy to grasp. This results from our not yet knowing what the *total* syntactic structure of this piece is.

A possible clue to one solution of this is provided by the possessives:

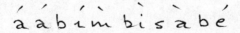

my oranges

éétʃìǹkálà?

my books

ḿmímmìlá

my stones

éétʃímm̀bwé

my dogs

áádímlàń

my firewood

In these forms the agreement particles b-, tʃ-, d- etc are preceded by syllabic elements aa-, ee-, m-. It is not clear what status these have, but if we introduce them into the structure of the copula we get

```
bisabe   aabede
kalak    eede
mɪlaa    mede
mbwe     eede
lʌn      aade
```

The phonetic realisation of these will include ɛɛ at the juncture -e-a-, a half-open front vocoid relating at the same time to the phonological elements half-close front and open front. Other cases are straightforward: κ + ee has $ke:$, e + ee has $e:$, aa + m has $a:m$. The *firewood* case is more complex. *Firewood*, $\ell\,tt\,n$, is disyllabic. Our phonetic records shows $\ell\,tt\cdot n$ with a clear (= palatalised) final syllabic. If we postulate this as a front syllabic in the same class as - e then n + aa is acceptably seen as manifested in $\varepsilon\varepsilon$. These effects are seen elsewhere in the language. So

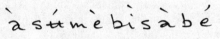

she is selling oranges

$$\grave{b}\grave{\imath}s\grave{a}b\acute{\varepsilon}\grave{\varepsilon}s\acute{u}m\,e$$

the oranges she is selling

where $\varepsilon\varepsilon$ relates to the juncture - e - a -. So we are dealing with a phenomenon of phonetic realisation which is quite general in Bakosi.

Certain morphological assymetries remain in this material. For instance the 'reconstituted' morphology of *they're oranges* is a five-part structure but in *they're books* we have

$$\kappa a l a g \qquad e - de$$

and for *it's firewood* we have

$$\ell\,tt\,n \qquad a - de$$

Two phonological matters remain to be accounted for: one is the duration of the vocalic nuclei at the nominal + copula boundary: the other is the overall tone patterning. One possible solution of the first problem is to posit that at the abstract level that we are considering here all utterances are of the same structure, ie nominal + 3 part identifier, the 3 parts being in the case of *book*

$$e + e + de$$

in the case of *firewood*

$$a + a + de$$

All items are now structurally equivalent and the phonetic length is accounted for as a realisation that relates to *two* syllables.

In the matter of the tone patterns we have interpreted the
‾ ‾ ∨ ‾ ‾ notation for *it's some oranges* as low-low-high,
which accords with *oranges* in all other manifestations, followed
by low-high-high. This latter interpretation is less certain, but is bolstered by high-high on the corresponding portion of *it's some stones*
which can be taken as having overall the same tonal configuration as
the *oranges* sentence. In the *book* sentence the notation
‾ ‾ ‾ ‾ looks like high-low-high-mid or, now, high-low-
high-high-mid. And in *it's firewood* we have ‾ ‾ ‾ , or high-
high-mid-mid-mid. Writing in abstract terms, we might present this as

$$kálag \qquad é + é + de$$

and

$$lűn \qquad a + a + de$$

to stand alongside

$$bìsàbé \qquad à + bé + dé$$

and

$$mìlá \qquad à + mé + dé$$

There is a lot of complexity still here in the tonal arrays. But this can be largely resolved if we hypothesize that in this language sequences of more than two highs (in this syntactic structure at least) do not occur, any third item that would count as phonologically high being rendered as mid in pitch. We could now envisage as the tonal structure of the above items the following:

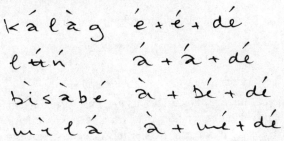

if we add a convention that takes mid pitch as the usual manifestation of highs following a 'lowered' high.

These proposed interpretations introduce a great deal of regularity into what looks, at first sight, much more confused. It may not be the right interpretation but, given the regularity that ensues from its adoption, it is worth testing, modifying and adapting. The possibility that the tonal suggestions are not totally correct is provided by

bisabebilan

three oranges

though this is a different syntactic structure and possibly not included within the scope of the 'three highs' rule. This is another area we should have to explore and test.

In making these interpretative steps with the Bakosi material we have used two insights that are of paramount importance in interpretation, and can be called basic. One has to do with interpretation beyond the symbols; the second with the provisional identification and characterisation of relevant 'stretches' of the impressionistic record. Though we will discuss these activities separately, in practice they are carried out alongside one another. As with so many aspects of linguistic analysis there is an interplay between them - each kind of interpretive activity informing and shaping the others. Interpreting beyond the symbols can entail

- ❑   seeing beyond the segmentality of the symbols

- ❑   seeing beyond the immediate reference of the symbols

4.3.2 *Seeing beyond the segmental representation*

An examination of impressionistic records in terms of parameters is the most basic kind of interpretation that we undertake. Apart from theoretical reasons for examining IR's in this fashion, it serves a very important consciousness-raising function. The symbols we employ in making our records impose a particular kind of discrete classification on the observed material. The categories so imposed are given by a theory of phonetic notation, not of phonological theory, and are therefore not necessarily (some would simply say not) appropriate ones to employ in making phonological statements. There is, for instance, no *a priori* evidence that the 'nine segments' of a transcription such as

$$s\,\tilde{æ}\,n\,ɹ\,ə\,k\,ɬ\,ɔ:\,z̥$$

have any kind of linguistic validity. They are simply one way of representing some rather generalised observations about an utterance. Indeed one might ask why count 'nine' here? What about the nasalisation tilde (=10), or the length mark (=11)? Is 'nine' some kind of theoretical claim or simply a response to the discreteness of the Romanic letter shapes?

Phonological analysis is essentially about functional relationships. The categories offered by phonetic theory are referential and not functional. We need to distinguish carefully between a theory of phonetic notation and a theory of phonetics. Phonetic categories are explicitly not functional ones although they are often used as if they were. For example, the voice/voiceless arrangement for consonants in the IPAA matrix often seems to have been taken to have straightforward phonological implications. In turn this appears to have led many linguists to assume contrastive phonological status for θ / ð in English. However the restriction of ð in word-initial position to items from the grammatical system and of θ in the same position to non-grammatical (lexical) items suggests that there is not a simple phonological contrast here.

Earlier we suggested that notation can often push type of analysis in particular directions and encourage particular 'solutions'. Because of the kind of phonological analysis *we* pursue, which does not recognise segments as primes, we seek and engage in an interpretation of the IR which emphasises dynamisms and continuities. One way of achieving this is to construe the IR as a reflection of the putative articulatory motions and manoeuvres which gave rise to the auditory impressions on which the record was based. It should be clear that the more detail of utterance the linguist has been able to respond to at the observational stage, the more accurate such a parametric interpretation can be.

In our treatment of Bakosi we have taken the item *l-ṏ-ṅ* as being disyllabic, and as having a clear final syllable: as being structurally on a par with such an item as *bìsàbé* . This involves taking ṅ as more than it appears to be. Specifically it involves taking the front resonance feature of this syllabic nasal as an important and phonologically relevant component.

We have suggested already that a fruitful approach to the interpretation of spoken language material is to emancipate oneself from a too strict adherence to a segment-by-segment model. We can do this best if we regard segments as the interweaving of a number of phonetic parameters as in this Bakosi case. These parameters will be more than just those named in traditional phonetic nomenclature of the kind that attaches to our daily symbols. Thus, there is a lot more to ɣ than voice, velarity and friction. It must have an attendant lip position; the front of the tongue must be doing something; the 'voice' will be of a particular kind, and so on. Any one or any combination of these may be relevant in any way, morphologically, lexically, grammatically or in interaction, and at any point in formal or interactional structure.

4.3.3 *Seeing beyond immediate reference*

We need to learn to view things in different interpretative ways. The non-systematic, cross parametric nature of a recording system like that of the IPA is likely to obscure the kinds of dynamisms, continuities and overall phonetic patternings we are interested in. This is well illustrated by the following material.

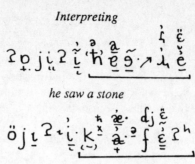

he saw a stone

he saw some stones

The bracketed portion of these Fula utterances can be taken to be singular and plural of the same lexical item, STONE. Here the impressionistic records present what are apparently considerable differences between the two forms. But in how far is this difference a result of the symbol shapes we have been using? If it were customary to show h by the symbol ꝁ̣ , for instance, these two items would at once look more alike. Or if, alternatively, we examine the record with a view to describing overall articulatory setting parametrically, then kʰæ·ᵃfɛ can be seen to be generally laminal, produced with the tongue tip down and the tongue body arched, as against haɾɛ̈ , which is generally non-laminal and apical. The differences that seem so striking in the IPA-type characters seem considerably less compelling under this interpretation. This looking beyond the symbols and beyond the limitations imposed by their shape and arrangement is a crucial insight in phonological interpretation. In the case of these examples such parametric interpretation may allow us to proceed more sensitively to a generalisation about one aspect of the phonetics and phonology of the number system in nominals.

In this Fula example we have looked at the phonetic elements h and ᴋ in relative, but only relative, isolation. It is important, too, to learn to interpret symbols with reference to the stretches they appear in. So, for example, ɣ , a 'voiced velar fricative' is produced by a gesture of the back of the toward towards the soft palate and pharynx wall; it has no explicit lip-position. w has an explicit lip-position, and could be rewritten ɣ̚ , or ɣ̟β . In utterance-pieces that are in general spread and close ɣ might stand as the congener of ɣ̚ elsewhere, the two to be grouped together as a phonological velar 'glide'. In fact we have such a representation in impressionistic records of a Bantu language, Chinsenga, where it almost certainly needs to be interpreted in this way.

ï t ɕ ə n̩ ị t ɕ ə k̚ ' ɯ̄ m̃ y̆ ĕ̃ ʰ

it's a finger

The whole of the final syllable in this utterance is open, spread and dark (retracted front vocalic quality and velarised nasal). Several interpretative approaches present themselves: ɣ might be the phonetics associated with a velar approximant in an open syllable where a corresponding approximant in a close syllable would be ɡ. So ɣ has a relationship with ɡ. If this were so, m preceding ɡ would be expected to be syllabic, since consonantal sequences of the type m ɡ do not occur, even in abutting conditions, in this language. Evidence of a *prima facie* kind for or against the syllabic nature of m is now to be sought in the pitch records. We have two possibilities for this utterance

Both of these show it as primarily six syllables, a finding which militates against a 'syllabic nasal' solution. We can investigate, instead, the possibility of ɣ being, in a spread syllable, as w in a rounded one. The C + velar glide configuration is a common one in Bantu languages, so this new interpretation is acceptable and is supported by the provisional syllable count.

4.3.4 Templates

This Chinsenga example shows the importance of having basic syllabic templates to operate with at a relatively early stage in interpretation. If, for instance, CCC- is ruled out, even in a provisional set of templates, things which look like CCC in the records are immediate candidates for reinterpretation. The Xhosa item

$$\iota \, \mathbf{\gamma} \, \chi \, \mathbf{\underset{\iota}{i}} \cdot \mathbf{z} \, \wedge$$

herbal remedies

cannot be **VCCVCV** since clusters are not permitted in Xhosa template configurations. All Xhosa templates are derived from **(V)CV(n)**. The symbols $\mathbf{\gamma \chi}$ in the Xhosa utterance are to be referred to the phonological item $\mathbf{\gamma}$ plus the syllable feature 'aspiration'. This is regularly heard as χ in Xhosa when accompanying clicks because of the back-of-tongue closure and release which is part of their productive mechanism. Before we can satisfactorily come to grips with all the ingredients in a complex phonetic event, and interpret them towards an analysis, we need these kinds of templates or skeletal frameworks to view them against. Such templates are particularly valuable when we are dealing with cases, frequent in comparative work, where identical ingredients are differently phased or otherwise differently combined in speech. In the Chinsenga example above, for instance, yet two more interpretations of $\breve{\mathbf{\gamma}}$ are open to us:

□   the final syllable could contain a diphthong, more appropriately written, as a first approximation as $\mathbf{ue}$, perhaps.

□   the salient property could be the velarisation of $\mathbf{m}$, as in a language like Polish or Russian, where consonants are associated distinctively with a pair of resonances. In this case, we would view $\breve{\mathbf{\gamma}}$ as part of the manifestation of the velarity associated with $\mathbf{m}$.

Our choice between all the possibilities is, as we have seen, conditioned by what we know about Bantu languages in general, *viz*, that they rarely have phonological diphthongs or independently and distinctively velarised consonants. So the solution adopted is by far the most likely one. If we know nothing at all about Bantu languages it will take longer and require more work to get to the 'correct' solution; we should have to look for further putative diphthongs, for instance.

What we are doing in making these choices is setting the material against skeletal frameworks, templates, of different kinds, namely CCV as against C ᵂ V as against CV (where V is an *ad hoc* symbol for 'diphthong'). They are identical in being each one syllable and in relating to the same phonetic make-up; but they differ in the make-up of the syllable in terms of empirical structure.

Templates of differing degrees of generality are often useful diagnostic devices for interpreting phonetic material against, and are useful pre-structural devices. Their provisional status can be shown by using lower case c and v, for them, say, or turned letter-shapes such as ɔ , ʌ .

4.4 Stretches

As we have shown, the activity of interpreting beyond the discrete symbols of the IR can have considerable implications for the kinds of phonological statements the linguist may make. In particular there are implications for the kinds of entities proposed as phonological primes in such statements. For instance, it is likely that abstract entities relating to notions of punctual contrast at a given place, such as phonemes, distinctive features will be disfavoured. That is, local articulatory complexes reflected in the symbols of the IR are unlikely to have any pretheoretical primacy (cf generative phonological and phonemic approaches, where such articulatory complexes *do* have primacy). Conversely the kind of interpretation we have been discussing is likely to highlight and encourage the recognition of phonological features having 'long-domain' relevance, as with 'dark' syllables in the Chinsenga case above.

Up to this point we have been concerned with showing some of the ways in which it is possible to 'interpret beyond the symbols' of the impressionistic record. In doing this we have been considering already established pieces of language, that is, word-size chunks. However, if the material we have for interpretation consists of connected text, whether interactive or not, where the identification, delimitation, description and analysis of the pieces themselves is part of the job of interpretation, then features of the 'long-domain' type may be of prime importance. This is so if the linguist is working towards explicitly non-lexical phonological statements having to do with the workings of, say, grammar or interaction. In the Bakosi material above attention was paid, in working on tonal matters, to features of long-domain relevance associated with particular identified syntactic pieces. Features that are suspected candidates for long-domain relevance we

call **stretches** in the interpretative phase of our work. Such stretches
frequently provide the background against which elements of lesser
domain must be interpreted: hence the establishing of stretches is the
logically prior activity. In reality the two operations of seeing beyond
the immediate reference and segmentality of the symbols proceed in
parallel.

4.4.1 Stretches and 'non-distinctive' features

We have talked about the attitude we take to the job of making
records and we used words like 'impressionistic' and 'parametric' to
describe one aspect of the approach we take to the recording of material. We take this approach because it can be shown that a lot of
phonetic clues to structures of all kinds (syntactic and morphological for example) are present in speech. These clues are often encoded as the fine detail of the production of sound or, more typically,
by whole sequences or chains of phonetic features that do not contribute to those complexes of features by which word-size items are
often said to be minimally identified and differentiated. For although
we have been talking of parametric interpretation this should not be
taken to imply here that the long-domain features recognised are uni-
form phonetic features in the sense of one phonetic feature = one
long-domain feature. It may be necessary to abstract in interpretation sets or sequences of features and call the set or sequence by one
label having minimal phonetic motivation (at least in conventional
terms). The kinds of features we are talking about here are as important as those more attended to in conventional (ie lexical) phonological accounts. Indeed, for certain purposes (eg in governing interaction, or in avoiding homophonic clash) they may be more important. By important here, we mean several things. Important for how
the language works as a system; important in their implications for
linguistic variety, linguistic relationships and linguistic change;
and, because of all these things, important in phonological description.

It is a common, but fallacious, belief that some features are distinctive and some 'non-distinctive', and that these 'non-distinctive'
features are redundant to analysis. The relevance and 'distinctiveness' of features depends, to a large extent, on the particular aspect of
analysis which is being pursued at any given time. For instance, some
features which might be claimed to be redundant in the analysis
of lexis may well prove to be distinctive when considered in the
context of grammatical or interactional analysis or more extensive
contexts in general.

When we come to carry out interpretation it follows that, having this set of beliefs and preoccupations we will carry them over into this stage of the overall analysis. So, as a first or early analytical exercise, we are predisposed to scan the material in our records, for phonetic properties that might be interpreted as important in marking stretches of utterance as integrated wholes such as syllables, morphemes, words, rhythmical feet, phonological or grammatical phrases, clauses, junctural structures etc. Such an exercise has two main parts and involves looking for (i) delimitative and (ii) integrative features and sets of features.

It is important to emphasise that interpretation is a cyclic process, and consists of a series of examinations of the material, setting up at each pass one or a number of hypotheses. At an early stage such hypotheses are about stretches. The stretches that we look at and isolate out at the interpreting stage may well be candidates for later recognition as integrated structures. Formal analytic statement will be couched in terms of structures of formal elements contracting formal relationships with one another.

4.4.2 *Establishing Stretches*

Some of the features that serve to mark stretches as such may be reflected transparently by the choice of symbols in the IR. Vowel harmony might be such a case. At other times integrative and/or delimitative stretch features may not be so transparently presented in the IR. In cases such as this we need to look beyond the selection of symbols in the IR.

The following Igbo material presents such a case. We can get an initial sense of utterance delimitation by attending to certain aspects of this Igbo material. In it a range of articulatory, phonatory and other effects occur over the end of utterances, either singly or in various bundles, and can be interpreted as markers of utterance cessation. They can occur individually in other, non-final, places, and have there no such implications. So, in themselves, there is not anything intrinsically 'final' or delimitative about them: this is *one* way in which they may function. These effects in Igbo are represented in the following examples, and include breathy phonation during and following the final syllable, nasality, laxness of articulation, and rallentando tempo.

he saw a wild dog

the dog ran into the bush

he chased it

Another kind of utterance delimitation can be found in Akyem Twi in sentences of the kind *it's a* . . . . If such utterances end in a vocalic portion then there is always also glottal closure. The following material is illustrative:

it's a snake

it's a monkey

it's a yam

it's a messenger

Compare the following utterances all of which also end in a vocalic portion:

he shot it

she sold it

it bit him

they bought it

it fell down

Here, where we have different grammatical structure(s) there are no occurrences of complete glottal closure after the final vocalic portion.

4.4.3 Identifying stretches

Once we have catalogued the patterns that are typical phonetic indices of an 'utterance' or class of utterance, we can go on to identify phonetic patterns that reflect possible utterance parts. Pitch patterning effects are common here. For instance, beginnings of many types of utterance are often characterised by an overall climb in pitch in both tonal and non-tonal languages.

Stretches of this kind, are not, of course, isolated through examination of phonetic patterns alone, though these may be suggestive. We also want to know whether the items 'utterance' and 'part of the

utterance' have any correspondence with putative elements of
analysis at other levels, say the morphological or syntactic. Stretches
have to be of assumed linguistic relevance in order that they can be
carried forward in analysis. If they were simply sequences of phonetic
material united by the sharing of one feature or group of features it
would be possible to find large numbers of such things in any body of
utterances, and they could be of virtually any length. The Kiluba sentence

it's the dog I lost

is voiced throughout. This might be a feature of Kiluba utterances
in general and assignable to some such syntactic unit as the sentence.
It might conversely have to do with the phonological presence of
voicing at some particular place in the sentence and the materialisa-
tion of this at all subsequent places; or it might be completely fortuitous and without linguistic function. Which of these it actually is
can only be approached by an inquiry into the regularity and relationships of this feature or combination of features. But in many cases it
will be fortuitous. Allocating 'significance' is one of the principal
tasks of interpretation, and one that is particularly important in the
study of stretches. To do it we need again to know something about
morphological and syntactic entities and relations. As we know, a certain number of intuitions will have been formed about these during the
recording and early interpreting stages. It is important to establish
such intuitions consciously as soon as possible during this early activity and to preserve them for subsequent testing. They might not all
be right, but some probably will be. We illustrate what is meant from
Sinhalese.

it's a dog

it's a bull

it's a snake

it's a stone

it's a fish

it's a bitch

In these Sinhalese utterances it seems unlikely that the 6 nominals selected (at random) should all end in dorsal closure. So we have to consider the possibility that the syntactic or morphological structure that relates to these utterances is not the equivalent of the English **pro + copula + article + nominal**, either in that the constituents are different, or that the order is different, or both. It may be **copula + nominal + article** or **demonstrative + nominal + case-ending**, or **nominal + numerator**. These three, and other, hypotheses will have to be put to the test. It is clear from this Sinhalese material that one phonetic pattern that is associated with utterance end (at least in these utterances) is phonetic variability. The final articulation shows a very wide range of possibilities, a range which is not equalled by the range of variability of phonetic dorsal item(s) at the beginning of the second syllable, for example. This variability might be associated with utterance endings or with this final morphological element, wherever it occurs, or with this total structure. This case demonstrates the circularity of the interpretative task, and shows also, as will later cases, that hypothesis-making and testing has to be conducted at a number of levels of linguistic organisation at once.

Certain problematic decisions arise when identifying patterns. One such choice is the extent of the stretches over which patterns are identified and established. It is possible for patterns to operate over almost any extent of stretch, even the material corresponding to a whole conversation. And it is legitimate to consider such a range of possibilities, since we are allowed to assume that any utterance or set of utterances given by informants have some kind of coherent linguistic status for speakers of their languages, and this might well be phonetically characterised in some way.

A second problem that comes up at this stage is that of the 'reality' of the patterns we have isolated. By this we mean that some linguistically important patterns may be obscured by the very nature of the notation system we have used for recording. Or, conversely, certain patterns may lie before us that are in fact only apparent.

We need a good knowledge of phonetic theory for the pattern-finding stage. What is also required is an awareness of the prejudices and presuppositions hidden in the notation system: and an intuitive sensitivity to language patterns and relationships in general terms. This is can only be acquired through exposure to work of the relevant kind.

4.4.4 Looking for integrated stretches

In working with stretches, we need to be liberal in what we take to be a stretch, taking our cues from putative syntactic or morphological portions as readily as from the phonetic. Since the establishment of phonologically significant units is our prime goal, though, we shall want to give priority to phonetic material, in the expectation that phonetic patterns will later be referrable to syntactic and other categories. In the Limburg Dutch material below a lot of stretches are marked by relative frontness or non-frontness of articulation occurring over a number of adjacent syllables. We say 'relative' frontness and non-frontness since a sound of the ə -type that is relatively 'front' in one stretch may be construed as relatively 'non-front' in another. It is patterns that are ultimately relatable to systems of contrast that we are interested in, moving away from phonetics pure and simple towards phonology. The term 'backness' is avoided above since all of the vocalic material under survey is of a generally 'front' type. Even at this preliminary stage in interpretation it is desirable to keep terminology as orderly as possible: this goal is less likely to be reached if we start using words like 'back' of vocalic items that are phonetically 'front', even allowing for the fact that the first label would be in the realm of phonological vocabulary, the second in that of phonetic vocabulary.

1

it's an apple

2

it's a cherry

3

little sentence

4

just read that short sentence

5

it's two cherries

Our first job is to get some provisional idea of the basic structure of these utterances. 1 and 2 suggest that the nominal is at the end. 1,

2 and 5 suggest that ↰z / ↰ʂ and ʂɛ̠ᵗn̦ are copula forms, concording with, respectively, singular and plural nominals: ʂɛ̠ᵗn̦ in 5 going with *two* and a plural form *cherries*, as against ↰z / ↰ʂ in 1, 2 .   3 is to be roughly matched by a portion in the middle of 4, and the equivalent of English *two* can be provisionally equated with a portion in the middle of 5. We can, again provisionally, locate an article, numeral, or quantifier preceding the nominal, and an 'introducer' at the beginning of 1, 2 and 5: so we can sketch some sort of rough-and-ready syntactic and morphological structure on to the phonetic details of our records, together with some, again rough, lexical identifications.

Stretches might now be investigated. Stretches, we recall, are provisionally significant, that is, candidate units of systemic or structural relevance. Some stretches in the Dutch material above have been marked with ⌞⌟ .

In attempting to designate stretches we have firstly to do a job of selection and focussing. If we focus, in this Dutch material, on the stretches that coincide with or relate to the junction of the portions provisionally designated 'article' and 'nominal', we see that in 1 as against 2, there is substantial relative backness (1) versus frontness (2). So we have

1   ən ʔ a

versus

2   ↰ y̟ k æ

The stretches here are some part at least of the phonetics that serves to fuse, perhaps systematically, the linked grammatical elements in these utterances. This is the phonetics of sentences, as it were, rather than of a list of words. These stretches are, then, at once of phonological interest.

Features other than frontness and backness are to be isolated in this material. The phrase *short sentence* has two shapes that show considerable differences with respect to openness and closeness. In the one, at 4, phonetic differences link the first and last syllables with, respectively, what precedes and follows. 4 has the vowel sequence I a̠ (ɛ I ə I ↰) ẽ I as against 3 with -(ɘ ə ɛ̈)- where

( ) shows the boundaries of the word and | | the stretches.

4.4.5 Purposes of stretch delimitation

The purpose of establishing stretches is, then, two-fold. Firstly stretches frequently correlate in various ways with meaningful isolates at other levels. Secondly, contrasts and systems of opposition are best looked for within such stretches and interpreted within this context. It is not given *a priori* that contrasting systems will be the same either in their abstract properties (eg the number of contrasting items) or in the physical attributes that manifest the contrast, as we move from one stretch to another. For these reasons the elaboration of stretches has to be an early task. This aspect of the relationship between phonetic matter as represented in the record, and categories at other, formal, levels, that we have not yet discussed, is that a phonetic feature, or set of features, may relate to these levels differently at various places. The Welsh utterance

it's a big house

is voiced all through, just as is the Kiluba utterance above. But in the Welsh case it is set off against an utterance

the house is big

which suggests that the voicing in

is of some phonological relevance. There is no place in the Kiluba utterance where a similar relation holds for any of the voiced portions. So the status of voicing in the two languages appears to be different. We might want to posit

and its complement

as stretches in Welsh. They are related in terms of (a) orality, relative darkness, relative openness, (b) nasality, relative clearness, relative closeness.

These would be provisional stretches, subject to revision. For we may find that *all* syllable-final nasals are clear, so that

is 'clear' not by virtue of being in this stretch, but of being in a stretch constituted by it alone, irrespective of the preceding material; or that it is clear by virtue of standing after

as well as by virtue of standing syllable finally, so is in two stretches at once. Or we may find a third possibility, that this resonance feature is random and has no systematic relevance for the delimitation of stretches.

The point should be made here that there is nothing at all mechanical or predictable about the way in which genuine stretches operate. In the Welsh material above we have

(a)

in MAE'R TY 'N FAWR (*the house is big*) as against

(b)

Y TY MAWR (*the big house*). In (a) nasality is distributed, drawing our attention immediately as a potential stretch, associated with this grammatical juncture. There is no similar phenomenon of nasality in (b), a different grammatical juncture. We note here how inappropriate, from the truly structural point of view is an 'allophonic' approach that would have it that 'vowels (*sc* all vowels) are nasalised in the environment of nasals'. The mapping from symbols to stretches is not simply one-to-one. There is no necessary relation between stretches as selected for examination and sequences of symbols in the IR. A stretch can coincide with just one articulatory or phonatory gesture. ʒ , for instance, is often worth considering for stretch candidacy, and there are indications that this is the case in our Limburg Dutch material. No more need boundaries coincide, and a given notational element may be mapped into two successive stretches. If, for instance, an alveolar nasal starts dark and ends clear, we might want to begin or end a stretch half-way through the nasal, or even regard the dark section (which will not be represented by any single integral symbol) as a 'stretch' in itself. The setting up of stretches is part of the analyst's task: they are neither artefacts of the recording system, nor products of a discovery procedure. Indeed, the recording system can easily mask what might be possible useful stretches. The fact that a consonantal sequence

$$\phi \ldots h \ldots r$$

is as a whole , and relatively 'more open' or 'laxer' than a sequence

$$m \ldots ʔ \ldots d$$

is not immediately apparent from what we see.

4.5 Parametric interpretation and phasing

One of our aims in seeing beyond the symbol-segmentation is to try to take account of the dynamics of utterance; and in particular to attempt to get a sense of the ways in which the concurrent articulatory components of utterances are synchronised. This synchronisation is called **phasing**. Interpretation that concentrates on parametric phasing differences is a profitable way of moving towards phonological analyses when making linguistic comparison of any kind, as in dialectology, child language study or historical investigation. A set of illustrative collections of material follows, the first of which deals with child language. Consider the consonantal representations in the following:

(A)

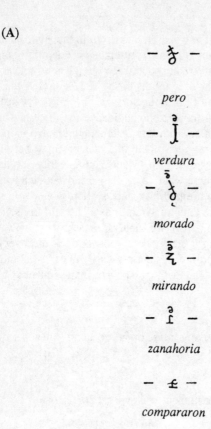

pero

verdura

morado

mirando

zanahoria

compararon

These selected portions of impressionistic records reflect parts of utterances produced by a young (4 year old) Mexican Spanish speaking child. The portions of immediate interest are those which correspond to adult (parental) forms, where there is concurrent realisation of voice and apical ballistic contact (represented in the orthographic glosses by 'r'.) All of the child's productions can be seen to be apical, and though not all involve ballistic approach and release all are 'short' and all, like the parental forms, have central or back resonance. Compare these with the forms below. The portions of immediate interest here are those which correspond to periods of voice and intermittent apical contact with clear resonance in productions of the same lexical items by the parents. (These portions are represented by 'rr' in the orthographic glosses).

(B)

Monterrey

perro

perro

perro

zorro

zorro

tierra

arriba

horribles

In none of the child's versions at (B) do we find the same punctual co-incidence of features as are present in the adult forms. We do find similar features but with a different arrangement in time. From a 'segmental' point of view the forms of the adult and child differ greatly. But from the parametric point of view the similarities are striking. We find that the child's versions all involve repeated apical contact and an overall raising of the tongue front towards the hard palate (palatalisation) all over a relatively longer period than in (A). The child is thus preserving the phonological contrast of the adult forms by means of the same phonetic components differently arranged.

A second example deals with the comparison of forms characteristic of different tempi, for a given speaker. In some Home Counties accents, notably that of Surrey, pieces consisting of velar plosives + lateral are produced with velarity throughout. So *clone* is $\text{k}\widetilde{\text{t}}$- , *cleanse* is likewise $\text{k}\widetilde{\text{t}}$ – as against *lens* with $^{\text{ə}}\text{ɭ}$-. *Cologne* is $\text{k} \text{ə}^{\text{ʔ}}\text{ɭ}$ - , the lateral here being syllable initial but not in a cluster. In rapid speech, as produced by one Surrey speaker, *cologne* can be $\text{k}^{\text{ʔ}}\text{ɭ}$-, with no ə present. A comparison of rapid speech *clone* and *cologne* shows $\text{k}\widetilde{\text{t}}$ - as against $\text{k}^{\text{ʔ}}\text{ɭ}$ - in initial position. A mechanical segmental and minimal-pair type of analysis of the rapid colloquial style for such a speaker pushes us into a position of setting up a syllable-initial contrast of 'clear' versus 'dark' l for this kind of English. This is completely out of line with the generality of English accents, and shows the danger of comparing incomparables; in this case fast and slow tempo.

In doing phonology we examine the overall scatter of forms, including their slow tempo and fast tempo versions, so as to produce maximally generalisable representations. In the speech of this speaker $\text{k}^{\text{ʔ}}\text{ɭ}$ - is a fast tempo phenomenon, $\text{k}\widetilde{\text{t}}$ – both a fast and a slow tempo phenomenon. $\text{k}^{\text{ʔ}}\text{ɭ}$-, as well as being tempo-related, is marked by resonance as disjunctive, once stretch-type features are taken into account. We will have more to say in Part 5, *Dialect and Accent* about resonances used by speakers of certain kinds of English in the production of 'liquids'.

This case illustrates the importance of stretch features and their phasing for formal pieces and for the identification of such pieces even when certain features referrable to the piece are no longer observable in their *temporally sequenced* form. There is no difference between the phonological ingredients of the tempo-specific tokens of *cologne*, the difference is to be found only in the temporal arrangement (phasing) of the phonetic ingredients. Templates are again of relevance here.

The phenomenon described here is not at all uncommon. A parallel example comes from Lutooro. The two forms *kɔhumɪʃʌ* *kʼumɪʃʌ*

mean 'to collide'. The first occurs in slow tempo speech, the second in
fast tempo speech. The second of the forms is distinct by virtue of the
breathy onset of the first syllable from

kʼumɪʃʌ

which is a slow tempo form and means 'to swallow'. Comparing one
slow tempo and one fast tempo form here would again produce a spurious contrast at one place in structure.

Our third example is of comparative work in the narrow sense of
language comparison. Languages often show identical phonetic material differently disposed with regard to C and V elements or to syllable elements in general. An example is provided by an array of material from a number of Bantu languages:

ɛmɓwa   (Lutooro)

mɓwa   (Swahili)

ndzɾa   (Xhosa)

mɣɾa   (Venda)

The forms all represent the word for 'dog'. All of them are disyllabic.
All of them have initial nasality and end in an open vocoid. The initial
nasality coincides with the first syllable in all cases, so our template begins to look like

$$\underset{\text{\tiny!}}{n} C \ldots V_\alpha$$

where . . . is unresolved as yet. All of them have lip-rounding or velarity or both at the beginning of the second syllable which is plosive so we expand our formula to

$$\underset{\text{\tiny!}}{n} C_{pl} w V_\alpha$$

All have palatality at some point between the beginning and the onset of the stem vowel; this can only be placed on a higher level in our formula giving

$$\overset{\displaystyle y}{\overbrace{\underset{\text{\tiny!}}{n} C_{pl} w V_\alpha}}$$

This formula is a useful interpretative device for helping us unravel bundles of phonetic material as we add to our Bantu comparative corpus. Our attempt will be to see Bantu 'dog' items in these terms, or in terms that relate to it in degree of generality. Fang ŋ v ə , for example, appears to be neither ʸ or **pl**, nor possibly, α (it is written **mvu** in the Fang orthography). But it is nCwV.

Once the linguist countenances parametric interpretation and the phasing relationship generally, it becomes possible to engage in a kind of phonological interpretation which *begins* by interpreting beyond the segmental basis of the phonetic notation. Two brief studies in such interpretation follow:

❑   the first, drawn from IR's of an urban Tyneside speaker from the North East of England, suggests ways in which apparent morphological differences in the forms of DO and DO NT might be treated phonologically

❑   the second focusses on some issues of lexical distinctiveness in the speech of a native of Hemsby in Norfolk. It concerns the pronunciation of words such as DO and DEW, FOOD and FEUD It illustrates how 'interpreting beyond the segment' with phasing relationships in mind can provide some novel solutions to old issues such as 'phonological deletion'

DO and DON'T and in Tyneside speech

The following material is taken from the speech of a localised Tyneside speaker from Gateshead. The forms are typical of localised speakers, male and female. Accented words are printed in bold in the glosses.

1   ẽ d̪ ɹ ɤ ḭ̃ n̩ ʔ

I **don't** *like that*

2   æ̃ ɛ̃ ə̃ ɤ̃ ə̃ n·

I **don't** *know*

3   ə d ə ɯ ḭ̃ n·

I don't **think** *so*

4   j ə d ə g̊ ə̃ n

what you don't **say** *because...*

5

I *do*

6

I *do*

7

I *do*

8

I do

9

I do

10

I do

11

$$ə\,\bar{d}^{z}\underset{+}{ı}\;\overset{ə}{d}\overset{?}{ı}\,\underset{ı}{t}·$$

I **do** *do it*

12

$$ʔ\,j\,ə\,\overset{?}{d}\,ıɨ$$

you **do** *make money*

13

$$w\,ə\,\overset{ə̄}{d̠}\overset{ö}{ʊ}\,θ^Y$$

we **do**

14

$$ʔæ:\overset{ə̄}{d}ə̰̃\,ñ\,ʔ^h$$

I *don't*

15

$$ə\,\overset{?}{d̠}\,ö̃:\;ñ·$$

I don't *hear...*

16

$$ʔ\,jı\,d̠ə̄\,ñ\,ʔ\,t'$$

you **don't**

Faced with forms such as these the analyst might well wonder whether this speaker had two morphologically different forms for DO and DON'T: one form being rather like that found in standard English (12 - 16) (though with localised vocalic qualities), the other (1 - 15) being oddly different in having labio-dental articulation as part of its makeup. The variant forms are apparently not the product of material in the linguistic context. There is no evidence, for instance, that one of the forms can be accounted for as a variant conditioned by, say, place in utterance (eg final), or by accentuation, or by co-occurrence with particular verbs.

However, the 'non-standard' forms are not entirely different from their 'standard' counterparts. The two forms of DON'T are markedly similar in terms of their beginnings and endings, those of DO perhaps less so. The main problem lies in deciding on the status of the consonantal intervocalic portion in 1 - 4, and on what looks like the same portion occurring finally in 7 - 10. Are we to postulate that the forms of DON'T in 1 - 4 have a **CVCVCC** configuration while those in 14, 15, 16 have a **CV(V)C(C)** configuration? Is **CVV** the relevant configuration for the forms of DO in 7 - 10, but **CVC** the appropriate one for the forms in 5, 6, 11, 12, and 13? A parametric consideration of the details observed in the production of these utterances suggests that there may be relationships obtaining between the utterances which are more satisfactorily stated if we do not treat forms such as 'div' and 'divn't' as having a phonological C-unit at the place where the letter 'v' appears.

The impressionistic records reveal that, although the symbol v has been employed to reflect co-incidence of certain parameters, parameters other than simply voice and lip-teeth approximation have also been observed in this portion. For instance, the subscript diacritic at this point in the records draws attention to the fact that on no occasion in these utterances was friction observed to co-occur with labiodental approximation. Moreover the record suggests that on every occasion dorsum-velar approximation was observed at this point in the utterances (whether the lip disposition involved labiodental or bilabial approximation). In addition the symbols employed for the adjacent vocalic portions indicate that they are of retracted or back of central quality. Taken together these details suggest that the primary difference between items such as 1, 2, 3, 4 and 14, 15, 16 is best seen as a difference in one of phasing of the exponents of voicing, labiality and velarity over the vocalic nucleus, rather than as a difference in syllable-type or as a case of morphological suppletion. We are not dealing here, then with a paradigmatic labio-dental consonant or 'the (phonological) vowel i ' or ι .

Further evidence for such an analysis is to be found in forms such as LIVE, LIVING, GIVE, GIVING, SEIVE, RIVER. For this speaker (and others on Tyneside) the labiodentality in such words may co-occur with friction, the coincident resonance is typically central to half-clear and the vocalic portions are routinely closer and fronter than in the 'divin't' forms. In addition we find patterns similar to those of DO in forms of TO.

DO, and DEW in Norfolk English

The next body of material records some of the speech habits of an individual who comes from an area in England which is conventionally described as one where 'j-dropping' or 'yod-deletion' can be found. These terms are generally taken to indicate the absence of a post-consonantal palatal glide at the beginning of words such as DEW, DUKE, PEW, TUNE, and MUSE. As a result of such 'j-dropping', speakers from this area are said to have identical pronunciations of items such as DO and DEW, FOOD and FEUD. That is, such words are claimed to be minimally distinct, in other accents, by virtue of the presence or absence of j . Consider the following assortment of items, taken from IR's of this speaker:

	1		2
do		dew	
food		feud	
boot		Bute	

First, note that if these records are taken at face value, the items in

Column 1 are not homophonous with those in Column 2. They differ in their rimes. Parametric interpretation suggests that there may be interesting things to be said about differences and similarities here. The relationship between items in the two columns may be more fruitfully stated in parametric terms than by employing notions such as 'j-dropping' or 'deletion'.

If we background the obvious differences between each word and the others in each set we can see that the differences between these two sets (1 and 2) of items can be appropriately summed up in terms of relative frontness or backness of consonantal and vocalic resonances. That is, the items in Set 2 all have clear resonance (here symbolised **C**) co-incident with the initial occlusion and rather close, frontish beginnings in their vocoids (overall relative frontness). In addition, if the words have consonantal endings these too are accompanied by clear resonance. By contrast, the items in Set 1 have dark or non-clear resonance initials and non-front non-close beginnings to their vocoids overall relative backness). So observed frontness and backness components reflected in our IR's are assigned by parametric interpretation to phonological units whose domain is at least the syllable. This leaves only punctual features such as apicality and plosion to be stated for the syllable initial in items such as DO and DEW.

An interpretation of these words which assigns primacy to a (non-occurring and punctual) **j** -item to the exclusion of all other fronting effects present is patently not the most felicitous way of accounting for the material. For this speaker, at least, 'deletion' is not involved: rather we have a particular phasing of the parameters in terms of their relationship to syllable organisation. The parameters are the same in other accents, but with their values differently phased.

4.6 Systems

Alongside structures we shall also want to set up provisional systems. As we do our interpretation we shall be making preliminary guesses and interpretative ventures about possible significant oppositions to be recognised at various points in structures.

Systems are, essentially, permutations: closed sets of elements operating at places in structure. They will almost certainly be different for different patterns and types of structure. **TP** (tense particle) is a structural element of the morphological type. **St-Ex** (stem plus extension) is a structural pattern of the morphological type. **VF-VI** (vowel final plus vowel initial) is a structural pattern of a phonological kind.

Other structural patterns are configurations such as, **CVCV**, for example or, more abstractly, **C(V)C(C)VC** which incorporates **CCCVC, CCCVC, CCVC, CCVC, CVCCVC, CVCCVC, CVCVC** and so on.

Because structural patterns and elements can relate closely to grammatical, interactive and other categories, we should expect systems at different places to be different. A three-term grammatical system will often have, at least at some places in its phonological correspondences, a system of three terms in phonology. Stretches may themselves be the phonetic correlates of these phonological systems. By isolating stretches, and interpreting them against the structural background they occur with, we are often on the way towards a set of phonological systems having multiple and/or extensive realisation. An example of the interpretation of stretches in terms of system can be found in Malayalam. The following Malayalam material is taken from the notes of a postgraduate student working alongside us. We include records from this source so as to enlarge the data base we draw on with work produced by researchers other than the two authors, but trained in the same tradition. The following six utterance records are of interest, and comprise a group of nominal phrases, the structure of which is at the outset uncertain:

1

it's a tree

2

it's a jack-fruit

3

it's cassava

4

it's a boat

5

it's a net

6

it's a pot

These are either two-part or three-part structures, consisting of, perhaps, an introducer, a nominal stem, and, possibly, a final element which may be a case or class marker of some kind. Or, the structure may be a demonstrative plus a nominal and a final identifier ('is'). There are, of course, other possibilities. An urgent first task is to gain some idea of the actual structure of these utterances. One way to do this is to compare them with the corresponding negatives, to pluralise them, to introduce conjoint nominals, and so on.

Let us assume that this is done and that we are satisfied that what we have before us in these six utterances are six tokens of **demonstrative + nominal Stem + copula** and that we have decided on working structural formulae for **dem** as **VCV**, **nom stem** as **CVC...** and **copula** as **...CV**, where the three dot elipsis means indeterminate. We are unsure here as to the boundary between stem and copula in nominal pieces. Several considerations might be taken into account in an attempt to decide this issue. It must be borne in mind, before we go into these, that 'boundary' is a morphological notion first and foremost. It would be naive to think in terms of putting a line in an impressionistic record, or in a working structural formula of the kind that we would be attempting to make, so as to show a 'boundary'. In looking at the Malayalam material, we are, rather, trying to decide what aspects of the phonetic material are to be assigned to what phonological elements in the formula that relate to the nominal and its satellites.

We have decided that the nominal stem is located at second place in a 3-place syntactic structure with stem **CVC...** . For the purposes of analysis at the outset we have imposed a restriction on the material by limiting the sample to stem vowels of the open class. Two sub-classes occur, grouped around ⅌ and ⋀ , denoting respectively front and back half-open central areas. After the putative stem **CVC** only two vowel types occur. This is not a methodological restriction of the kind introduced for stems, though it may follow from it. These two vowel types centre around ℮ and ⋀ and the complex in which they occur always includes ȷ̇ (front) with ℮ (front) and ᴍ with ⋀ : ᴍ and ȷ̇ stand to each other as minimal versus maximal tongue constraint (ᴍ has no integral tongue posture, ȷ̇ is in itself a tongue posture); and as nasal versus non-nasal. Both share voice and continuance. The vowels that accompany (precede) j and m fall into two discrete areas:

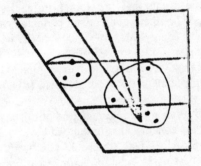

One of these zones is front and close, relatively speaking, the other back/central and open. An inspection of the articulatory resonances that imbue ᴍ show that they are either back or central: the resonance of ȷ̇ is of course front and close by definition.

The vowel at the end of the utterances is, too, of a number of phonetic types, fronter varieties occurring after ȷ̇ and the clearer cases of ᴍ , and backer varieties in 4 and 6 where ᴍ is of a darker resonance. And, transferring attention now to what we have in the matter of consonants in stems, we find that clear stem consonants assort with the whole array of clear final elements in 1, 2, 3 and 5, as against generalised darkness for the same portions in 4 and 6. Final

CV(C) of these putative **CVCV(C)** items shows a strong phonetic unity, along with the following copula syllable. Initial **CV**'s show a similar uniformity, so ⟨m⟩ ⟨ʔ⟩ ⟨ʊ̃⟩ ⟨ʔ⟩ in 1 and 5 as against ⟨ʊ⟩ ⟨ʌ⟩ ⟨ɋ⟩ ⟨◌⟩ in 4 and 3. We can also notice a frequent, but not, on the face of it, standard, matching in resonance and quality between the two syllables of these (putative) disyllabic nouns. So 1, 2, 5, are front throughout, and 4 and 6 are back throughout. 3 is, relatively speaking, back throughout, too, though ⟨ρ⟩ shows some front resonance when before the centralised **e** .

And, finally, the final syllable of the 'introducer' can be heard and, in these records, seen to share in the general qualities of the accompanying nominal, just as the final marker does. So ⟨ʒ⟩ in 2, before ⟨t⟩⟨ɕ⟩⟨ʔ̩⟩ , ⟨ʔ̲⟩ before ⟨ɋ⟩ and ⟨ʊ̃⟩ , rounded and closer before ⟨m⟩ , and so on.

This is a very small assemblage of material and we have made comparisons over it that may not be definitive, or may even be misleading in some ways. For example, we have included in the list items having long as against short consonants at C_2 in the nominals. The phonetic events that are found in the neighbourhood of long consonants, with their consequent phonological interpretation, may be different from what we find in the neighbourhood of non-long consonants. But the observations we have made are compelling enough to make it worthwhile carrying them forward in further analysis. The phenomena they embody seem to be basic and regular in this language.

How are we to begin our interpretation of this material? It seems difficult to avoid the conclusion here that we have to do with a difference in system, System 1 and System 2, as it were. One has to do with overall frontness of articulation throughout the piece: the other has to do with darkness distributed in the same way throughout the piece. Both types appear in the identifier clause and the conclusion is worth considering that they are associated with particular nominals, though their stretch manifestation exceeds the assumed boundaries of these.

It is noticeable that in the material we have looked at, liquids of various kinds appear, associated with both types of piece; so ⟨ɾ⟩ and ⟨ɭ⟩ with clear pieces, ⟨ʏ⟩ and ⟨ʔɭ⟩ with dark only. Apart from this we have ⟨tɕ⟩ in a clear piece and ⟨ρ⟩ in a dark one.

The remaining tasks include the setting up of total C and V systems for each system, 1 and 2; then at a more abstract level, drawing a common system out of these, if this is a profitable exercise.

We also need to check constantly against remaining, or new, material to decide on the validity of our conclusions and deal with exceptional cases or any bodies of material that might suggest revision.

it's a feather

suggests a revision of our set of what we can only call nominal-final junction markers to include a lateral. It also serves to reinforce our notion of overall phonetic features characterising pieces of this kind of piece in Malayalam, as also does

it's a broom

in the disyllabic set, against

it's a horn

The main question that might interest us here, though, is the detail of our interpretation. We are faced with a systematic difference between palatality and velarity as word or phrase phonological features. Presumably they are first and foremost word-features since the introducers and final particles partake of the phonetics involved. They do not have, that is, an independent specification of their own. In the interests of generalisation we shall want to establish a set of general elements of the C and V type, to operate in systems alongside the more fundamental dual phonological system of clear and dark. We shall need to investigate the extent of the phonetic manifestation of these fundamental phonological elements, and their role in linking phonetic material to other levels. We have seen the lexical role being implemented: but such characteristics often have grammatical implications. The Malayalam material illustrates the beginnings of an approach to system both of the kind that applies to pieces and that applies to punctual phonological elements. It also provides a case of variable relevance interpretation in the way it handles ᴍ and ʝ as systemically opposed.

The establishment of punctual systems is, in theory, one of our last tasks within the overall job of interpreting, though in practice we may be doing it alongside various earlier commitments. We leave it till last as these contrasts are those of minimal implication, either for other parts of the phonology or for other levels of analysis and statement. Contrasts of this kind are consequently made within stretches and in the knowledge of the other kinds of significant abstractions we have made. We will exemplify this punctual inventory-making from Polish.

Polish consonants in all positions enter into relationship with long-domain systems of palatality and non-palatality and these in turn with complex grammatical and lexical relationships. So, for instance, at syllable-initial position we find:

$$- w \ni \mathfrak{z} \dot{\imath} t \mathfrak{c}$$

to put

$$\ell \varepsilon \mathfrak{z} \varepsilon t \mathfrak{c}$$

to lie

related semantically, and phonologically as C(palatal) to C(non-palatal). In the same situation, but related grammatically in this case, we find:

$$n \ni \mathfrak{c} - \dot{\imath} t \mathfrak{c}$$

to carry

$$\jmath \varepsilon \mathfrak{c} - t \mathfrak{c}$$

to carry

The stem-syllable final congeners for these two pairs are to be seen in related nominals, for example NOCLEG (NOC - 'night' + LEG) 'a night's lodging' and WYNOS (WY + NOS) 'carrying away'.) We can regard these six words as showing at both syllable initial and final places various basic consonant types under palatal and non-palatal conditions. In these cases the consonants are ℓ , $\mathfrak{z}$, $\hbar$ and S . Patterns arise as follows

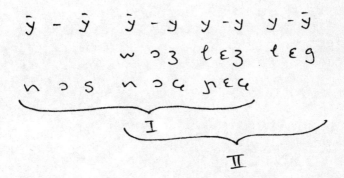

where $\mathbf{y}$ = palatal and $\mathbf{\bar{y}}$ = non-palatal, and upper case symbols are used to show phonological abstraction over a range of material. It will be noticed that the two basic roots **W-G** and **N-S** contract different relationships with the palatality system, **W-G** being **II** and **N-S** being **I**. A partial extension of this listing for single syllable-initial position would be as follows:

ʸ and ȳ have, by definition, implications for the phonetics of the syllables they characterise, as well as having   their schematic working in the grammar and lexicon. For the basic close front vowel, for example, here **I**, we have i in ʸ syllables and ɩ in ȳ syllables. The corresponding phonetic occurrences for the basic open vowel **A** are ɛ and a . This is illustrated below:

ȳ **TI**

ti

thou

ʸ **TI**

tɑi

to thee

ȳ **BIW**

ɓiw

he was

ʸ **BIW**

biw

he beat

ʸ **MIS**

miɢ

teddy-bear

ȳ **MIS** ʸ

miʃ

mouse

ʸ **MAR** ȳ

umjɛra

he is dying

ȳ **MAR** ȳ

umarw

he died

The phonological units represented by the upper-case symbols have (as far as we know) no relevance, nor does any component of them have any relevance, that we want to state as extending beyond the place in structure occupied by the unit. There is nothing to say about the **M** of *die* or the **Ɓ** of *beat* at least in synchronic phonological terms, other than that they stand at these places, occupying a slot in the structure of these lexical items.

It is worth adding here that the material above is illustrative of only one system, which is the central system in Polish phonology; loan words show different patterns, so

sine

which is impossible in the central system
and cannot be stated in the terms applied to that system.

4.7 On the relevance of detail for interpreting

In *Observing* and *Recording* and throughout this Part we have placed great emphasis on the need to attend to and reflect as much of the fine detail and variability of utterance as possible. The term 'detail' refers here to two aspects of the observed material:

- ❑ the detail in the records deriving from close impressionistic observation of a given utterance

- ❑ the detail of variability and co-variability deriving from our multiple observations of the same expression spoken a number of times.

In large part, our insistence on pursuing observation that is as detailed as possible is motivated by trying not to prejudge which of the phonetic aspects of a given utterance are going to be phonologically relevant.

When we come to the job of interpreting the impressionistic records, the detailed phonetic observations we have made serve a number of important purposes:

- ❑ they play a central role in allowing us to generate and warrant robust analytic hypotheses about the language material at hand;

- ❑ they can often help us to avoid postulating unnecessary theoretical constructs;

❑   they can direct our attention to things which are not part of received phonological wisdom, and suggest to us novel interpretations of the material.

We will illustrate each of these claims about the relevance of detail in turn in the sections which follow.

4.7.1 *Phonetic detail and the motivation of analyses*

This first example is taken from impressionistic records of Fang, a Bantu language spoken in parts of Gabon and Cameroun. Here the detail of interest is the resonances (secondary articulation) and coincident lip gestures of some of the consonantal portions. The IR's given below represent some of the noun forms elicited from a Fang speaker:

etƒǝɿ
shoulder

tɔm
branch

ŋgi̤bi
ŋgṿǝbi
hippopotamus

bikǝq
back-teeth

ndʋ̯(ǝ̱)
dam

elǝn
water-tortoise

kƒǝ̱l

tortoise

ɲfǝq
bag

ŋkƒǝ̱
salt

tʃǝŋ
neck

ŋkɔl   osən

rope   *squirrel*

In the complete corpus of nouns elicited from this speaker the following vocalic nuclei are found: ɪ e a ə ɔ o y   . One
rather odd feature of this list is the non-occurrence of a close back
rounded nucleus of an ʊ type. The sense that there is something
odd here arises from that fact that most Bantu languages display a
symmetry in the vowel sets which occur. This means that if say, ɪ
is present then ʊ will be present or if e is present then o will be
present. These nominal forms are also rather odd in that some appear to have the non-Bantu feature of sequences of consonantal
items at the beginning of the noun-stem. It would seem then that either the linguist must either countenance the possibility that Fang is a
rather unusual Bantu language in these respects or that these features
should be interpreted in such a way as to produce an analysis
which resolves these problematic aspects.

A consideration of the detail of the impressionistic record
suggests the latter possibility. We find

- the putative sequences of consonantal items as in
  shoulder, *night* and *dam* all involve labiodentality
  with friction and dark (velarized) resonance

- there are a number of occurrences of stem initial
  friction (including affrication) with simultaneous
  labio-dentality and dark resonance

- there is variability in the realisation of words with
  stem-beginning plosivity: alternative pronunciations
  are possible, one of which has a vocalic portion and
  one of which does not (eg *dam*, *hippopotamus*). If
  there is a vocalic portion present in such cases, it
  is always ə . There are no other possibilities.
  Careful attention to the quality of this schwa reveals
  that it is different from that central vowel occurring
  in words such as *branch*, *bag* and *squirrel*. The

schwa in words such as *shoulder* and *beard* has a
tongue position which is maximally neutral on all
dimensions except that of backness. It is somewhat
retracted in quality.

These details taken together suggest that the non-Bantu lack of ᴜ
and presence of consonantal sequences may be related. In the sequence ᴋ f   for instance, which occurs in the item ᴋ f ᴚ ℓ
(*tortoise*), the following phonetic categories, amongst others, are
found

- ❑   labiality (labiodentality)

- ❑   closeness (of articulation)

- ❑   velarity (dark secondary articulatory resonance)

followed by

- ❑   vocalicity

- ❑   backness

These categories are notably similar to those of the vocoid ᴜ. The
observed detail then, suggests that we can interpret these categories as
equivalent to those of ᴜ but differing from it in terms of their synchronisation in time. That is, in ᴜ all these categories are phased
simultaneously, whereas in f ᴚ they are phased sequentially.
    This interpretation of the phonetic sequence (consonant plus f
/ v plus ᴚ) as being phonologically C-unit plus V- unit is made
without prejudice to the interpretation of any other occurrences of
this phonetic complex elsewhere outside this configuration. So, for
example, the punctual co-incidence of labiodentality and friction
(f / v) in the nominals f ᴚ p , o v o n , are interpreted
as stem initial C-units at the phonological level as is the co-incidence
of voicelessness and alveolarity (t / s) in the nominals
t ᴚ m , o s ᴚ n . In a similar fashion f in n f ᴚ q is
not to be related to a phonological V-unit but as phonological C+V.
There are several reasons for this. Primarily the phonetic detail does
not support such an interpretation: the vocalic quality in these items
is ᴚ and not ᴚ , and the labiodentality and friction are not accom-

panied by velarization. Another reason is that if stem-beginning ʄ / ᴠ were to be analysed as close back-V, Fang would then display a large number of stems with an initial vowel. This would run counter not only to the rest of the language, but also to the generality of Bantu languages, in which stems are initiated by consonants.

The kind of interpretation arrived at here might well have been achieved *without* access to the impressionistic detail we have discussed. It is clear, however, that such an interpretation is greatly aided and made more plausible where such detail is available and employed. The question is now not why there is no ᴜ in this language, but rather what is to be said of the way in which this language realises the phonetics of the close back phonological V-unit. This is much easier to answer given all the other cases of (darkness), rounding and labiality being related to labiodentality (eg English: HARROW, HARRO-VIAN; NEWT > EFETE; Hungarian: FALU, FALVI; MŰ, MŰVET; TETŰ, TETVEK) whereas the first question cannot really be answered at all.

4.7.2 *Phonetic detail and theoretical perspicuity*

The following material gives some illustration of the ways in which close attention to phonetic detail can serve in interpretation to reveal features of some theoretical importance. At the same time availability of such detail may be useful in avoiding unnecessary theoretical constructs.

We give three illustrations here all of which centre on the issue of the so-called 'neutralisation' of a phonological opposition:

❑ the first is concerned with the word initial r/w opposition in a young English child's speech;

❑ the second looks briefly at 'neutralisation' in one assimilation environment in the speech of four English speaking adults;

❑ the third focusses on the putative neutralisation of intervocalic t/d opposition in the speech of two adult speakers of American English.

We have chosen to focus on these particular cases because neutralisation is a long entrenched construct in many approaches to phonological analysis; yet we have found that many of the classic cases of neutralisation are in fact only apparent. Attention to detail show that oppositions are maintained in many such cases.

Neutralisation of contrast in child speech

In the literature on children's language it is not uncommon to find discussion of the significance of a child's ability to perceive but not to produce certain phonological contrasts of the adult language. Such discussions usually include illustrative examples of putative homophonous forms. In this context consider the following (prepausal) forms extracted from IR's of spontaneous speech by a Yorkshire girl 5:4 years old:

rich   *witch*

ring   *wing*

(ᴡ = outer lip-rounding, ᴍ = inner lip-rounding.)

Of interest here are the word beginnings where the child appears not to have acquired the (adult) contrast between initial labial-velar approximation (for WITCH, WING) and a post-alveolar approximation (for RICH, RING). Moreover a cursory examination of the material suggests that the child simply produces voiced bilabiality with open approximation for all these items. On closer inspection of the IR's, however, it becomes clear that she is not simply producing undifferentiated beginnings but that she is systematically and consistently maintaining differences between the two sets of items in terms of

- ❑ lip-rounding

- ❑ variability in lip-approximation

- ❑ resonance features co-incident with the word-beginnings

❏ durational and loudness characteristics of the word-beginnings

The labial gestures in 1 and 3 vary between bilabiality and labio-dentality with open/close approximation and clear resonance. Those in 2 and 4 are noticeably longer than those in 1 and 3, have increasing loudness (represented by <), have outer lip-rounding, and are always accompanied by dark resonance. Moreover the bilabial or labiodental portions are *never* accompanied by friction. Clearly in this child's speech these items are not homophonous in any linguistically interesting sense. Instead, rather more interesting theoretical possibilities and questions present themselves. Why do the distinctions between the sets of items take this form in the child's speech? What is it about resonance which makes it such a stable component of the distinction between these items? - whereas primary place of articulation is grossly undifferentiated. (Notice that the IR's given above reveal that there are whole word resonance differences between the sets of items. For further discussion see Part 5 *Child Language*.) Given that this child has w and ℓ as the dark liquids in her system set off against the clear liquids j and ʎ , we might further investigate neutralisation and homophony in children's speech in those varieties of English that have w and ʎ as dark liquids. (We know that different resonance associations with members of the liquid system have interesting phonological implications for adult speech. See further Part 5 *Dialect and Accent*.) We might also investigate the implications of these parametric combinations for patternings in language acquisition. Finally we might ask a fundamental question concerning the whole issue of homophony in children's speech. To what extent is homophony in children's language an artefact of particular ways of recording and analysing the spoken material?

Neutralisation of oppositions through assimilation

Neutralisation of oppositions and consequent homophony is often claimed to arise as a result of so-called assimilatory processes in adult speech. Statements to this effect can be found in most introductory texts on the phonetics of English. A conventional formulation of this kind might be that word-final alveolar consonants are particularly apt to undergo neutralization of oppositions in connected speech and that, such oppositions having been neutralised, the sense of an utterance may be determined only by the context. Such a for-

mulation is predicated on a view of phonological distinctiveness
which assumes that phonological representations consist of a linear
sequence of contrastive segments. The following material, elicited
in the course of experimental work on the resonance characteristics
of liquids, comes from four adult speakers of English. It represents
tokens of the words RAN and RANG in the context *ran quickly, rang
quickly*. The observed detail reflected in the IR's again raises
questions about the theoretical validity of the construct of neutralisation, and about the adequacy of a linear segmental view of phonological organisation:

Speakers	A	B
	RAN	RANG

In these cases although we can observe that there is some kind of
stretch cohesion in which the verbs end with nasality and velarity
we do not simply have coarticulatory/assimilatory neutralisation of
opposition. Though the junctural features in A are similar to those in
B the detail in the IR's reveals that these productions are in no case

homophonous. Furthermore, the differences between the two sets suggested by the observed impressionistic detail are of theoretical interest. We can see that:

❑ though all the verbs end with nasality and velarity the tokens of *rang* have audibly fronter contact/resonance for the final consonantal portions than do the tokens of RAN

❑ the tokens of RAN all have nuclei which in whole or in part are more retracted and more open than those is the tokens of RANG

Comparable differences are also to be found in parallel assimilatory contexts eg *kin came, king came*. Moreover this kind of differentiation is not restricted to the four speakers represented here. It is typically the case that differences are to be heard where neutralisation is claimed to arise from word-junctural assimilation. Similar effects can be observed other assimilatory environments. A sentence such as *in that case I'll take the black case* illustrates this well. In fluent connected utterance we typically find stretch cohesion (marked by velarity at the junction of the words *that* and *case* and at the junction of *black* and *case*). Again however we find regular and noticeable differences in the quality of the vocalic nuclei in *that* as opposed to *black*. The following IR's are of the *ran ~ rang* speakers S and C above:

S:

C:

For both these speakers the vocalic portions of *black* are fronter and more peripheral than those in *that*. For some speakers we have observed there is also a noticeable difference in the place of occlusion at the juncture of *that case* on one hand and *black case* on the other, such that in *black case* the occlusion is audibly pre-velar as opposed to velar or post-velar. All these observations strongly suggest the inadequacy of the simple but pervasive notion that phonological distinctions are typically realised by a contrast at one place in structure. It would appear that the linear, punctual theory of oppositions is a theoretical artefact born primarily, perhaps, of a particularly unsophisticated attitude to observation.

Neutralisation of intervocalic t and d in American English

The third classic case of putative neutralisation is drawn from American English material, and usually focusses on word pairs such as WRITER ~ RIDER, and ATOM ~ ADAM. Interest in such pairs arises because both **t** and **d** in American English may be realised as apical taps when they occur between two vowels. Many accounts of this phenomenon do, however, point out that while the **t/d** contrast may be neutralised, the vowels preceding the tap may exhibit length differences typical of vowel allophones before voiced or voiceless consonants, hence:

ɾɑɪɾər   ɾɑːɪɾər

writer   *rider*

There is a theoretical problem here, however, for segmental phonological analyses. For here, the only way that the two words are distinguished and contrast is by virtue of their vowels - a difference which is not distinctive elsewhere, being conditioned by whether or not the following consonant is voiced. However, when we examine closely the detail of IR's of the relevant material it becomes clear that there are other kinds of difference between the words which serve to distinguish them even where the pairs both have taps and vocalic duration is not discernibly different.

The material we consider here was collected as part of a psychoacoustic experiment. Two speakers (**DR** and **RR** are represented. Both are male and both come from Queen's, New York. We give impressionistic records for the two speakers' productions of the pairs:

WRITER, RIDER; WAITED, WADED; ATOM, ADAM; PUDDING, PUTTING.
All the words were spoken in the sentence frame 'Say ... again'.

	DR	RR
writer		
rider		
waited		
waded		
atom		
adam		
putting		
pudding		

(ɤ = 'molar r')

A number of points merit comment.

❑   while some of the word pairs exhibit durational
     differences between the pre-tap vocalic portions,
     these differences are not consistent and do not all
     operate in the same direction. It is not straightfor-
     wardly the case the **d**-words have longer vowels
     than **t**-words in their first syllables

❑   the word pairs are not however rendered homo-
     phonous; indeed they are phonetically different at
     every point

❑   all the pairs exhibit different qualities in the vocal-
     ic portions of both syllables. The **t**-words have
     generally fronter, closer articulated vocalic por-
     tions than do the **d**-words

❑   there is a general, overall difference in perceived
     articulatory 'tenseness' between the word pairs
     such that **t**-words have a more tense articulatory
     setting than the **d**-words For example, those **t**-
     words having plosivity in their makeup exhibit au-
     dibly firmer, sharper, closure and release of those
     portions. This 'laxness of articulation' in the **d**-
     words results, in some cases, in the speakers pro-
     ducing friction rather than plosivity (eg *pudding*
     where the initial consonantal portion is realised as
     voiceless bilabiality with friction). Conversely, in
     portions where an 'open articulation' might have
     been expected (eg the initial consonantal portion
     of *writer*), the tense articulation of the **t**-words can
     result in the production of friction

❑   the overall phonatory setting of the word pairs is
     also different. The **t**-words consistently exhibit
     creaky voice while the **d**-words do not

❑   the overall front or back resonance displayed by the
     vocalic portions of the words is also to be found in
     the consonantal portions of those words. That is,

for **t**-words consonants have clear resonance while for **d**-words they have dark resonance. In some cases the consonantal portions in the **t**-words actually have advanced places of articulation as compared with their **d**-word congeners - eg the nasal portions at the ends of *putting* for both speakers are noticeably front of velar in contact as compared with these portions in *pudding*. This may be something of an artefact, however, because for many speakers of English grammatical -ING is overall closer and 'fronter' compared with the sequence ING in lexis

It is apparent, then, that if the detail of utterance is responsibly attended to, the construct of neutralisation is an inappropriate one. Rather we have to address ourselves to the issue of how to represent whole-word phonological distinctiveness.

The situation we have discussed is not merely limited to the **t**- and **d**-words. Many speakers of American English display similar constellations of features in other word-pairs with intervocalic voiceless and voiced plosives. Nor are these kinds of patternings restricted to American English. Many British English speakers produce the same kinds of whole-word differences considered here. Such differences can readily be noticed in productions of LATTER ~ LADDER (where not only are both the vocalic portions in the **d**-word backer in articulation but also the initial period of laterality is backer in terms of secondary articulation than in LATTER). They are readily observable, too, in word-pairs such as RAPID, RABID and BACKER, BAGGER.

4.7.3 *Phonetic detail and the domain of phonological phenomena*

It is frequently the case that close attention to phonetic detail suggests that received phonological analyses require revision or at least critical examination. This is particularly so if, in interpretation, phonetic detail is examined with stretch-phenomena highlighted. In the following examples we will discuss reasonably accessible instances where the detail of observed utterance allows us to entertain rather different views of the domain of certain phonological phenomena than conventional accounts do.

Domain of phonetic exponency of mutation in Welsh

We have suggested in the previous section that characterisations of homophony arising from assimilatory phenomena seem to be products of a particular kind of observation and a particular attitude (punctual-segmental) to the interpretation of that observation. The benefit of having responsibly detailed IR's resides largely in the fact that if linguists have detail they can choose not to account for it, but if the impressionistic records do not ever represent it in the first place then it is not possible to recover it.

As with the case of neutralisation we have discussed, many of the traditional constructs of phonological analysis seem to arise from the elevation of a rather impoverished impressionistic response to 'phonological' status. Consider, for instance, mutation in Welsh which is classically treated as a punctually situated phonological phenomenon. A conventional account of one 'stem initial mutation' will typically state that under certain morphosyntactic conditions (1) voiceless stops become voiced (2) voiced stops become fricatives (3) voiceless lateral fricatives (a) lose their friction, and (b) become voiced.

An account such as this presents the phenomena as highly restricted in domain (initial consonant) and suggests that the phonetic features involved are restricted to manner of articulation and voicing. Examination of reasonably closely observed material from one North Welsh speaker suggests that such stem-initial mutation

- ❑ is not simply a punctually situated phenomena but that it has *syllabic* extent

- ❑ typically and significantly involves secondary articulatory resonances in addition to the kinds of manner and phonatory features already mentioned.

Observations of other Welsh speakers suggest that these characteristics are not idiosyncratic. The following examples are representative:

1 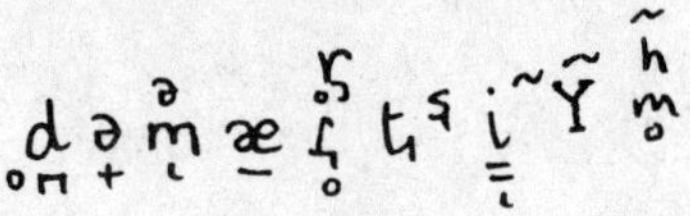

that's a house

2 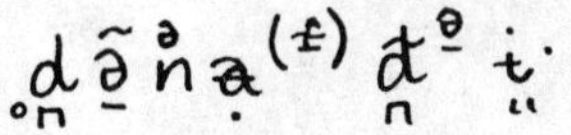

that's the house

3 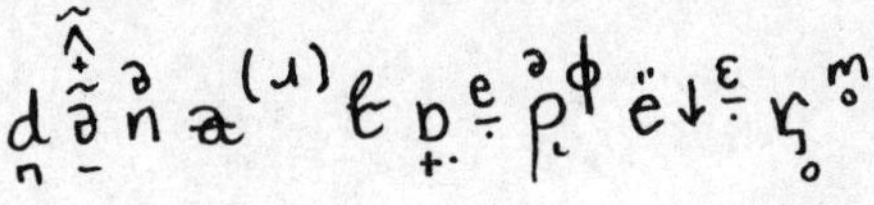

that's a path

4 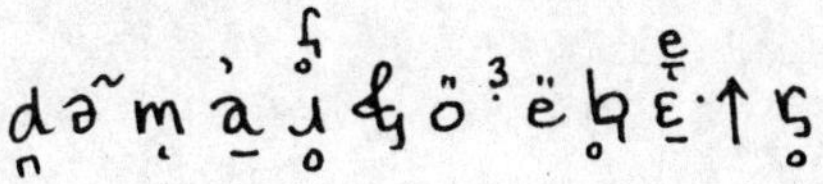

that's the path

5 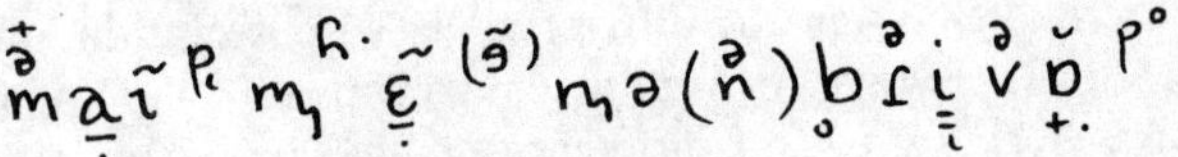

my head is hurting

6 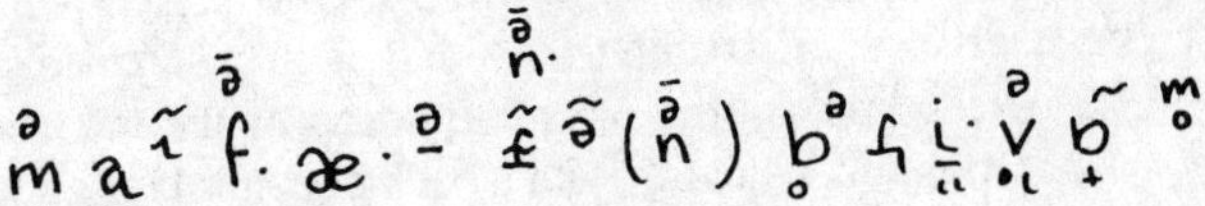

her head is hurting

7

his head is hurting

8

my father

9

her father

10

his father

There are systematic differences to be observed in the alignment of particular resonances with the initial consonantal portion of the nouns as well as systematic differences in the vocalic portions of the nouns.

In 2 we have the mutated form of the noun *house*. The initial consonantal portion of the noun differs from its non-mutated congener in terms not only of voicing but also of its co-incident resonance characteristics. It is noticeably darker in resonance. This effect is also perceptible in the vocalic portion of the noun where we find a backer more open quality with a back of central on-glide.

The mutated and non-mutated forms of *path* (4 and 3 respectively) exhibit the features expected from conventional accounts. The initial portion of 4 has alveolarity with laterality, voicelessness and friction while in 3 we find alveolarity with laterality and voice but no friction. But we also find that in 3 the initial portion is characterised by palatalised resonance throughout the period of laterality. The equivalent portion in 4, in contrast, is characterised by half-dark resonance. In 4, in contrast to 3 the vocalic portion following the initial laterality is relatively closer and more firmly rounded, though there is little difference between the final vocalic and consonantal portions in the two utterances. Having access to detailed records here allows us to see that we are not just dealing with 'changes' of manner and voicing in the initial C's. The features we have drawn attention to are recurrent in multiple productions of these utterances by this speaker, and the same patterns of features are found in other nouns with similar initial consonants and mutation patternings.

A brief consideration of some material from Scots Gaelic, another Celtic language, similarly shows that detailed IR's may reveal unexpected domains for phonological oppositions. The following IR's exemplify definite singular and plural forms of selected nouns:

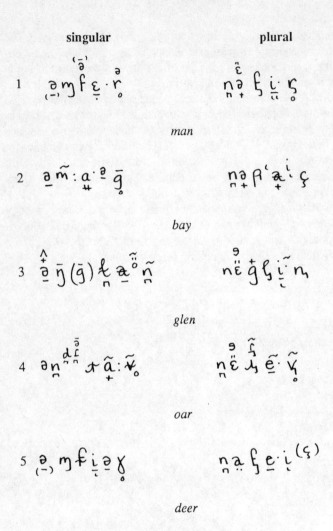

singular	plural

1   *man*

2   *bay*

3   *glen*

4   *oar*

5   *deer*

A conventional account of the plural formation of nouns such as these might refer to 'internal mutation of the root vowel', and in the case of nouns such as 5 and 6 'lenition' or 'replacement' of the final consonant. As in the case of Welsh mutation discussed above, such a formulation treats the phenomena as having a very restricted segmental domain. However, as the IR's show, although there are obvious quality differences between the 'root vowels' in the word pairs, there are also numerous other differences. These differences, like those discussed earlier, have a more extensive domain than simply the vocalic portions of the nouns. This is so even in 1, 3 and 4 where the primary place of articulation of the final consonantal portion does not exhibit the variation shown in 2 and 5.

The phonetic correlates of the singular/plural distinction in these nouns are distributed over the whole word. In all cases the consonantal portions in the plurals have a clearer resonance than do those in the singulars. Thus consonantal portions display central or dark resonance in the singular and clear or palatalised resonance in the plurals. This is not simply an automatic consequence of particular vocalic environments. For example, the initial consonantal portion of the singular of *deer* is dark (although before a front vocoid) while the initial portion of the plural of *bay* is clear, although it occurs before a vocalic portion which is open and noticeably retracted in quality.

Nor are these differences restricted in domain to the nouns themselves. They can be discerned in the forms of the definite article which precede them. The (non-accented) vocalic portions of these definite articles have notably different qualities; those preceding the singulars being open, central or back-of-central, while those preceding the plurals are noticeably front in quality. Thus rather than a singular/plural pattern involving simply differences in stem vowel of the noun, the IR's show that the phenomenon under consideration has a domain which extends beyond the word, of the kind which is treated elsewhere under the rubric of 'vowel harmony'.

A comparable case can be seen in the so-called anaptyctic vowels in lowland Scots (in words such as FILM and FARM) and in Scots Gaelic in words such as A'FALBH ('going') and GU DHEARB ('indeed'). The first two might be conventionally rendered as $f \iota \ell \ddot{A} m$ and $f \varepsilon r \ddot{e} m$, and an argument pursued that in the case of FILM the anaptyctic vowel parasitically adopts the velar quality of the preceding lateral. In fact, careful observations of these and similar words spoken by a number of lowland Scots speakers reveal that, just as the anaptyctic portion in FILM has a backish quality, the anaptyctic vocalic portion in FARM is regularly of a front quality - a quality which is also to be heard in the preceding apical portion, initial consonantal portion, the nuclear vocalic portion and the final consonantal portion. In the case of FILM, by contrast the initial and final consonantal portions, though sharing the same primary place of articulation with those in FARM are noticeably dark in resonance as is the nuclear vocalic portion. Exactly these same resonance patternings are to be found in the Gaelic items thus:

ˀfa̠tæ̠ˠ̥ ~ fˀə̄ˀḁ̠ꭤ̣ᵚₜₜ

dʲꭤɜˀꜱˀᵊḁ̣꞉ˠ̥ ~ dʲæˀꜱˀǣᵊḁ̥ˠ

In neither the lowland Scots nor the Scots Gaelic, then, are we dealing
with purely local quality differences attending on the 'liquid' + anaptyctic vocalic portion. Rather, we have once again a set of whole-
word differences. The presence of the anaptyctic portion can be
accounted for by a general syllable template restriction on the occurrence of two particular contiguous portions; and the quality of
the vocalic portion can be treated as an exponent of a (word-) long-
domain phonological unit.

Gemination in Malayalam verb stems

Gemination is a component of many phonological analyses. Many
languages exhibit autonomously long consonants, for instance, and
these are generally treated as 'geminates'. However, regardless of the
particular phonological theory underlying analyses which recognise
gemination, the phenomenon is conventionally viewed as having implications only for a particular consonantal place in the structure of
utterance. Malayalam is one language where geminate consonants are
said to occur. The language has a number of verb stems which can
function both transitively and intransitively. A conventional account
might say that the transitive forms have geminate consonants while
the intransitive forms do not. The following material suggests that such
a claim is not entirely appropriate:

1   ʌ̟ᴜ̠ᵡᶞəkˣö̈ᶜᴛᵃ̄̆ᴴᵗ̣

it increased

2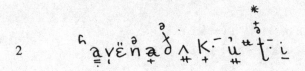

he increased it

3

it went inside

4

he inserted it

5

it folded

6

he folded it

7

$\Lambda \overset{+}{\underset{\iota}{\delta}} \cdot \overset{+}{\underset{\iota}{\Lambda}} \cdot \overset{+}{m} \cdot \underset{=}{\vartheta} \cdot \underset{=}{\gamma} \cdot \overset{G}{\eta} \cdot \overset{?}{\vartheta}$

it broke

8

$\underset{=}{\vartheta} \cdot \underset{\iota}{\vartheta} \cdot \overset{\vartheta}{\vartheta} \cdot \hat{n} \cdot \underset{\iota}{m} \cdot \underset{\iota}{u} \cdot \overset{*}{\overset{+}{\underset{=}{\vartheta}}} \cdot \underset{=}{\overset{·}{\varepsilon}} \cdot t_{\varphi} \cdot \underset{+}{u}$

he broke it

('Geminate consonants' are asterisked.) The first thing to notice is that the transitive forms do not all have consonantal portions which are longer than the equivalent portion in the intransitive forms. They may have, but this can vary across repeated versions of the same utterance. Notice too that the forms in 5 to 8 do not, at first glance, appear to exhibit the same kinds of relationship between the transitive and intransitive pairs in respect of the corresponding consonantal portions of the verb stem. However, the IR's show that whatever the patterns are, 'geminate' transitive forms are not simply different by virtue of a particular consonantal portion at one place in structure. The transitive and intransitive forms differ in terms of

- ❑ rhythm (and length)

- ❑ phonation

- ❑ consonantal and vocalic resonance

- ❑ variability

- ❑ tenseness/laxness of overall articulatory setting

The domain of these differences is considerably greater than a single consonantal place in structure. They encompass at least *the whole of the verb phrase*.

The rhythm and length differences between the pairs of utterances are primarily to be found in the syllable preceding and the syllable following the 'geminate consonants'. In the intransitive, 'non-geminate' forms the relative quantities of these syllables is short-long. In contrast, the same syllables in the transitive 'geminate' forms have quantities which are relatively equal-equal. There are regular 'length' differences too between the pairs of utterances in that initial consonantal portions of transitive verbs are noticeably longer in duration than those in the intransitive form.

(Rhythmic differences of the kind identified here are also to be found in many disyllabic noun-pairs where one form has a 'short' intervocalic consonant and the other a 'long' intervocalic consonant; for example

9

that's a head

10

that's a mother

11

that's a palm-tree

12

that's a pig

The vocalic resonance differences between the verb stems are such that transitive forms have syllabic-nuclei that are typically closer than intransitive forms (never more open), and typically fronter. Similarly the consonantal resonances are typically clearer (fronter) in transitives than in intransitives. These vocalic and consonantal resonances can be seen to encompass at least the 'it' morpheme - in the transitive utterances; for instance, the period of dental friction is always clearer in resonance than its counterpart in the intransitive utterances. The IR's show that there was greater observed variability across repeated productions of intransitive forms than across productions of transitive forms. In particular the 'non-geminate' consonantal portions displayed ranges of articulatory possibilities not observed for their 'geminate' counterparts.

The perceived articulatory tension settings are such that intransitive utterances are pervasively 'laxer' than transitive ones. So, for instance, where there is lip rounding it is always closer and firmer in transitive forms; plosives in intransitive forms tend to have lax closure and noticeably lax fricative release, and may even be realised as fricatives, which never occurs in transitive forms; and 'nasals' in intransitive forms freely alternate with nasalised vowels. These comments apply not only to the verb itself but to longer stretches of the whole transitive or intransitive utterance. This is can be further seen in the utterance pairs below.

13

the price increased

14

he increased the price

15

the pot broke

16

he broke the pot

The material considered here shows that however 'gemination' is to be treated with respect to verbal forms in Malayalam, it is clear that it cannot be legitimately construed as only having to do with a particular consonantal portion of utterance.

4.8 Variability

It is a commonplace, though rarely demonstrated, phonetic observation that the same expression spoken by the same person will sound slightly different each time it is said. Its phonetic detail will vary. Such variations are usually ascribed (i) to the labile, plastic properties of the vocal tract, and/or (ii) to the sociolinguistic or stylistic conditions impinging on the speaker and utterance. However our interest in variation in utterance production here is not centrally concerned with either of these. In discussing variation we are interested in delineating some of the ways in which variability can contribute to the formulation and elaboration of phonological statements. We will consider two principal types:

☐ where one portion of utterance varies and a phonetically similar portion elsewhere does not

☐ where one portion of utterance varies and a phonetically similar portion elsewhere also varies but with a different range of possibilities

We take it as axiomatic that if either of these kinds of variability occurs, then the relevant portions are potentially phonologically different. That is, we are dealing with candidate cues for phonological distinctiveness.

Both of these types of variability are extremely common. Like all objects of phonetic observation, however, they become more noticeable the more repetitions of the same utterance one has. In practice this means that access to this kind of variation is very easy in elicited face-to-face informant work and much less likely to arise in working with say recordings. It is, of course, completely unavailable in nearly all secondary-source analysis (eg of published language descriptions). The following illustrations should provide a flavour of these two types of variability.

4.8.1 Type (a) variability

In Albanian we find ə alternating with ə̥ in such items as

these doors

In other cases, ə̥ does not alternate with ə , as in

my house

Looking also at the stretches in which they occur we find that ə ~ ə̥ are in pieces that have voicelessness as an ingredient throughout. So both by virtue of the pieces they occur in and by virtue of the alternation they do or do not entertain, we might want to regard these as two phonologically quite different ə 's though phonetically they are very similar, if not identical. (Compare the different phonetic possibilities available for the first syllable the English word *potato*

$$p^{h\overset{\mathclap{\overset{\circ}{\partial}}}{\partial}}\ t^h\ e_{\partial}\ t^h\ {}_{\#}^{\wedge}\ \widehat{\omega}_+$$

$$_{(\circ)}b_{\partial}\ t^h\ \underline{e}_{\partial}\ t'\ \underline{\partial}\ \widehat{\mho}_+$$

This range of variability for ə , and preceding consonantal portions in quite different from the initial portion in *bodega*. In this word the initial consonantal portion does not vary between voice and voicelessness and the initial syllable does not admit of a voiceless nucleus.)

In many English accents (eg Tyneside) we find some disyllabic words which routinely end in a vocalic portion of slightly advanced, half-close back rounded quality. For example,

$$\underset{\#}{\widetilde{a}}\ g\ \underset{\underset{\smallsmile}{}}{\not\,o}\ \ddot{o}$$

aggro

$$p\underset{\underset{\smallsmile}{}}{\not\,o}\ \overset{\mathclap{\partial}}{\theta}\ \underset{\underset{\smallsmile}{}}{\check{v}}\ o_+$$

provo

$$b\overset{\partial}{\imath}\ \imath\ l\theta\underset{\smallsmile}{}$$

Brillo

$$w\ \underset{\cdot\cdot}{a}\ m\underset{\smallsmile}{z}\ \underline{\theta}$$

whammo

We find other items which may end in a vocalic portion of that same quality but which vary in that they allow for pronunciations with a range of frontish or central unrounded qualities, thus:

window $\quad w\underline{\imath}\,n_{\imath}d_{\imath}\imath \qquad w\imath\,n_{\imath}d\partial \qquad w\imath\,n\underset{\smallsmile}{d_{\imath}}\ddot{o}$

pillow $\quad p^h\imath\,l\underline{\imath} \qquad p^h\imath\,l\overset{\partial}{\underset{+}{}} \qquad p^h\imath\,l\underset{\smallsmile}{\underline{\theta}}$

piano pjãnɪ̥ pjæ̃nə pjãnɪ̥ θ̥

yellow jɛʎ̣ɪ̣ jɛʎ̣ə̟ jɛʎ̣ö̆

marrow mæɤ̯ə̇ mæɤ̯ə̣

The differences here are, in part, attributable to the different status of the words in the lexicon. The first set is comprised of 'shortened' forms of various kinds (AGGRO - AGGRAVATION, PROVO - PROVISION-AL), invented names (OMO) and forms where the -o- is a formative (WHAMMO from WHAM).

The material below, from Banda, presents a similar situation. Here, however, rather than relating to the status of the words in the lex-icon, the variability has to do with the ways in which a particular feature (labiality) may be instantiated in utterance. We find certain words, all nominals, varying as follows

skin akɔ akwa

spinach ŋgágɔ ŋgágwa

fish-scale kɷŋgɔ kɷŋgwá

Other words having a phonetically similar final vocalic portion do not vary in this way:

ɔtʃɔ

handle

fəʟɔ

camwood

kɷmɔ

nest

The first set of words all have plosion with velarity in the relevant syllable as part of their makeup, the second set do not. In this context labiality with vocalicity may be realised punctually (as a vocoid having back half open quality) or sequentially (as labiovelarity followed by an open vocalic portion).

The following material from Malayalam displays further examples of such variability. Here we find the initial consonant of verb stems varying in 1 and 2 but not in 3 and 4 where the initial consonantal portion always has firm, long closure with sharp explosive (unaspirated) release. The forms in 1 and 2 may have either short, rather lax, closure and lax release, or fricative-type beginnings.

1   ʌ ʤə kⁱ ω ɕa niu̯   *(lax rounding)*

it decreased

2   ʌ ʤʌ ×kᵍ ɛ̣ ʟ ʈ

it went inside

3   ʔv̆ə̃n̄ʌd̯ək̄·uɠɛ·t̯ɪϕ˝

he decreased it

4   ävə̃n̄ʌd̯ʌk̄ɟɛ̣·ᵊt̯ɪ̣ᶜɪ̣

he inserted it

The variability in 1 and 2 correlates with their status as intransitive
expressions while the lack of variability in 3 and 4 correlates with their
status as transitive expressions.

4.8.2 *Type (b) variability*

The material below, again from Malayalam, illustrates the type of
variability where two similar portions vary but over different ranges.
Here we present the variability observed for the intervocalic consonantal portion of the 'it' morpheme. This portion varies in both transitive
and intransitive utterances but it displays a much wider range of variability in intransitive utterances:

intransitive	transitive
-C-	-C-

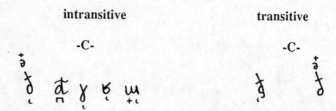

All the intervocalic consonantal portions of 'it' in intransitive
expressions have back-of-tongue-raising as part of their makeup. This
patterns with the resonance characteristics described earlier for the
intransitive verb stems. By contrast, this same portion in transitive
expressions has central or clear resonance co-incident with dental approximation. This patterns with the overall resonance of the transitive verb stems.

The following English material, from the speech of a young child illustrates again the importance of examining variability in the course of phonological interpretation. Here we see again that variability can provide vital information concerning phonological contrastivity. The consonantal portions exemplified correspond to adult word-initial and word-final f and θ .

f ~ f   f ~ φ

fat   *laugh*

f ~ θ   θ ~ f ~ φ

bath   *thank*

f ~ φφ   f ~ θ ~ θ

fry   *throw*

There are similarities here across the tokens of **f** and **th**. They have in common various kinds of labial approximation. But they also show differences. Thus initial **f** has labiodental or bilabial approximation while initial **th** may also have dental approximation. In addition the nature of the labiodental approximation exhibits a different range in the two cases. For **f** the lip-teeth approximation is either 'on top of' f or 'in front of' f the bottom lip (exo-labial). For **th** the bite position (when labiodentality occurs) is always behind the bottom lip f (endo-labial). Thus in the counting sequence *three, four, five* we observe

f -   f -   f -

Inspection of variability can reveal unsuspected regularities and patterning in language material. Consider the following pair of utterances from Igbo:

1   (phonetic transcription)

↓ ↗ with i~e
if ↓ then j V_2 i always
                                               closer than
                              he ate it V_1 i

2   (phonetic transcription)

if ↗ then ↗
j never j   ? no links between
                                               ↗/↓ and V qualities
                              he climbed it

The impressionistic records show that both of these utterances may
be produced with ↗ at the first two consonantal places. The ranges
of variability which these places show, however, is not identical. In 1
we see that these tap portions may vary in having fricative realisations. In 2 we see that the variation involves more open approximation, or other kinds of transient (flap) articulation. (In addition the
IRs show that in 1 we may have a fricative or non-fricative portion
near the end of the utterance j j ; but that in 2 this similar portion is always non-fricative.) This variability is associated with relatively more close or more open qualities in the vocalic portions of the
respective utterances. It may be that these consonantal portions pattern harmonically (in their variability) in a similar way to the vowels in
these utterances.

4.9 A beginning interpretation: material and notes

In collecting material for analysis in most situations the jobs of
recognising portions, establishing stretches and doing preliminary
collating all go on at once, often even while the material is being
gathered. In practice, after a couple of hours of gathering material the
investigator can write down a number of tentative observations of this

kind. It is in fact important that interpretation should begin to take place as early as possible. The feasibility of this can depend on, for instance, the complexity of the language. A language with a large consonant system, for example, will take some time to throw up all possible elements in syllable patterns. But a great deal can be got from a small corpus, particularly in the case of a language with a small number of C-elements. This is not because of the number of elements itself, which is no indicator of how complex or extensive such things as, say, junctural or noun-class systems might be. Rather that one can more quickly come to a grasp of the general architecture of the language. To show what we mean, here are a number of utterances from Tongan. They were taken down in three one-hour sessions with the informant in as detailed an impressionistic form as could be managed in the time. They are given here exactly as taken down. The notes that follow are based on those made by one of the authors over the period of the informant sessions.

1.
$$k^{(-)}_{(-)} \, o \, \pi^- \, \overset{\partial^?}{\underset{=}{e^+}} \, \eta \, g^{\downarrow}_{\gamma} \cdot \, \overset{\text{extent?}}{\underset{\downarrow}{\{}} \, 2^{(+)}_{=}} \longleftarrow \text{fast fade} \qquad \qquad - - \rangle$$

spread
variable
frontness

It's a monkey

2.
$$k^- \, o \, \pi^{\downarrow}_{\underset{+}{\overset{w+}{}}} \, \partial^{\partial}_{+} \, \overset{\partial}{f} \cdot 2^{\varphi} \, \overset{\partial}{n} \, 2^{+ \, (\cdot)} \qquad \qquad - - - \rangle$$

'_muffled_'

It's a pineapple

3.
$$\underset{(-)}{k} \, o \, \pi \, \overset{g^+}{\underset{\uparrow}{}} \, 2 \, \underset{+}{a^+} \, \overset{\circ N \, (\sim)}{\underset{\gamma}{}} \, \lambda^+ \qquad \qquad - - \rangle -$$

not so variable

It's a shark

4.
$$\overset{\text{lax, tongue tip up}}{} \qquad \text{firm}$$
$$k' \, \underset{-}{2^+} \, g^+ \, \overset{\downarrow}{\underset{-}{s}} \, \overset{z}{} \, i^+ \cdot \, \underset{+}{2}^I \, \overset{\vee}{n} \cdot \, \overset{\vee}{\underset{=}{e}}^+ \qquad \qquad - - - - -$$

no panting; ↑
rounding slight

null   _accel._
all spread + front

It's a banana

5.

tight

$k^- ɔ^{ʔ} ə^{ʔ}$ ... $p^- e^+ k^- æ^+ ↓$

(-) ↗

v. back   central and 'strangulated'

It's a bat

6.

$k ɔ ə^+ k^- ʌ^+ k^- ʌ̃ · ə$

(-)   +   (-) + =

— — — ⌐

vall.

It's a parrot

7.

bottom lip only?

$k^- ɔ ə · p^- θ · p^- ʌ õ ɣ$

— — — ⌐

p click-like, percussive?

It's a canoe

8.

$k^- ɔ^+ e \; m̃ \; ɒ^+ k^- õ π$

lax

— · — ·

un clear on, dark off.

It's a lizard

9.

$k^- o^+ e \; t^h \; ʌ \; k \; æ · w ·$

lots of tight central rounding

centralish   'strangulated'

It's a reef

10. $k^- \ddot{o} \ominus^\tau \ \tilde{n}^? \ n_i \ \underline{i}^\tau \cdot \overset{(\sim)}{\ddot{u}} \ w^{\cdot}_{\circ}$ fast fade   – – –
    (-)   _spread_   ⤸   tight protrusion

    It's a coconut

11. $\tilde{n} \ \underline{\varrho}^2 \ \overset{\varepsilon}{\ell} \ m_j \ \underline{a}^+ \ \overset{?}{\underline{t}} \ e^\tau \cdot \ \ell \ \approx N \wedge$ – – ⌐ – – –
   ½ dark   _backish_

    The shark died

12. $\overset{o}{n} \cdot \underline{a}^2 \ \vdots \ \ddot{e}^{\sim} \underline{t}_{\eta} \cdot \flat^+ \cdot \ ^{\sim} \ \underline{\gamma} \ \bar{F} \ddot{o} \, 2 \ \ddot{c}^{(+)} n^{(\cdot)} \underline{i}^+ \ddot{u}^{\sim}$
   moving back
       'throaty'   – – ⌐ – – – – –

    The coconut fell

         ≠
13. $\overset{(?)}{n \underline{\varrho}}^+ \ell \ e^{\pi} \overset{(\cdot)h}{\rho} \vdots \overset{w}{u} \cdot^w \overset{\ell}{n} \varrho^2 \ \bar{\underline{e}}^+ \ominus^\tau \ k^-_{(-)} \wedge^\tau \ k^- \tilde{\wedge}^{\frown}$

       – – ⌐ – – –

    The parrot flew away

                ← backer than n $\underline{e}^2$ above.
14. $\overset{\partial}{n} \underline{\varrho}^{(2)} \overset{\sim}{\varepsilon}^+ \ th_{\flat} \overset{\sim?\sim}{\ell} \underline{a}^+ \ \ddot{e}^{\,b?} \ \tilde{m} \cdot \flat^{\pi}_+ \ k^{\sim} \flat^\tau$
   all   _back_

        – – ⌐ – – –

    The lizard ran away

15. k̄ öᵇᵗ ʒ ǝɴ·ʌ⁺ ʒ e⊥ ᵍ⁴   _ _ _ _ _ (-) ┐

binar vowel sounds rounded, but looks spread.

← light central rounding

It's two sharks.

16. k̄ öᵍ ʒ u· p̃ö̈ p̃ʌ̃ ɣ̃   _ _ ¯ ¯ ┐

It's some canoes

17. kɔ⁺ʒ⁺ f̣ ǝ̃ɴʌ⁺ m̃·ɒ k̃ɔ̃ᴛ   _ _ ¯ ┐ _

It's some lizards

An examination of the records allows us to make a number of observations that can point the way for further work, and might even
serve already as the basis for formal statements about the forms of the
language. Not all these are about the sound-structure. One observation about 'portions' in syntax is that transitivity order appears to be
VSO, for example.

In terms of of sound-structure the following seem worth setting
out as parts of possible patterns in the language:

❑   there may be a case for vowel harmony system(s)
    involving both frontness and backness and openness
    and closeness

❑   vowels systems are possibly different at V_1 and V_2
    in nominals

❑   consonant systems: no fricatives at C_2; only stops,
    nasals and ʔ , so possibly different systems at C_1
    and C_2.

❑   accent: the phonetics suggests one accentual place
    for each word, manifested by an on-syllable fall (in
    declarative and deictic sentences)

❑   resonance: there is a considerable amount of reso-
    nance harmony; *shark* is back, *monkey* is front. This
    holds both in and between syllables. Some of it
    might be treated as consonantal dominance, with
    velars perhaps important as dominant elements

❑   glottal stop: appears in two statuses, one perhaps a
    member of a C-system, the other perhaps as an
    utterance delimiter. The first is always present, the
    second comes and goes

❑   utterance closers and delimiters regularly include
    nasality and centrality of vowels

❑ considerable variability of the phonetics of deictic particle in deictic sentences. This goes along with, and harmonises with, the phonetics of the head word. The possibility exists that all of this is to be treated as a 'stretch' in terms of sound structure, where the introducer displays phonetic features that link it to that nominal which is grammatical head and carries accent

❑ pitch movement of longer utterances shows stepping down movement preceding main accent and pitch pivot. The rhythmic pattern together with this downdrift suggest that the language falls roughly into that part of the rhythmic typology called stress-timed

❑ syllable structures are typically **CV**, plus perhaps **V**. A decision on this depends on how we go on to interpret the mark over the final vowels, and on whether we are impelled to consider seriously the admissibility of long vowels.

❑ generalities: few voiced plosives or fricatives

A large number of other things remain to be followed up: the status of creaky voice; the status of various kinds of lip-rounding (that observed for **o** is different from **w**); status of resonance of eg **m** in *lizard* ; the status of length in the same word; status of resonance of *bat* (dark consonant and retracted vowels); status of syllable final vocalic items.

In considering the Tongan material we have looked for patterns in the material with little attempt at interpretation. But it is necessary to accept the possibility that the material has to be interpreted in another sense. In this other sense we are sensitive to patterns that are not immediately apparent in the material; but which we might posit as worth establishing on some non-material level because they will, for instance, remove assymetries from the material or will deal with apparent complexities in what is a relatively simple way. We illustrate this by reference to two problems concerning syllable structure in this Tongan material. In the

words for *reef* and *canoe* we find complex vocalic glides in
the final syllables: we find a similar thing in *parrot* and
coconut. We need to interpret these glides, partly because
they turn up only in final syllables, partly because they are
restricted in what they are, and partly because they compli-
cate our explanation of syllable structures in this language,
otherwise quite straightforward. If we take them to be interpretable as syllable final consonants we shall have to re-
vise our notions of syllable structure here to include this special type. If we take them to be totally vocalic elements we
have either to introduce diphthongs into the vocalic repertoire or to explain them in some other way. And, if they are
diphthongs, we shall have an asymmetrical set of diphthongs,
as they all finish relatively back, though in different ways.
There are in this corpus no diphthongs that finish front.
Another possibility is to take these elements as separate vocalic items that constitute syllables in their own right. In this
case we shall have to look for corroboratory evidence in the
rhythmic and pitch records. Or, lastly, we might regard them
as part of patterns of our first kind, having to do, systematically, with endings: though then we are pushed into ex-
plaining why only utterances with these words in them end
in this way and others do not.

Part 5
Case Studies

The studies that follow are meant to illustrate the general approach to phonological description that we have set out in Parts 1 to 5. Each study arises from work carried out by one or both of the authors over a period of some three or four years. Consequently they are, and are meant to be, independent and self-contained. They are also to some degree experimental. Study 2, for example, experiments with the idea of a non-romanic notation for phonology, and Study 4 is an essay in polysystemicity, attempting to bring systematicity albeit of a complex kind into material that had seemed chaotic.

All of the studies are sketches in the sense that each could be taken much further: none says the final word on the topic. But the coverage is very wide. We have chosen the areas of work to show how an approach can be used fruitfully by speech therapists and conversation analysts as well as others working in difficult areas of our discipline well away from the idealised speaker-hearer or 'style familiere ralentie'.

Study 1

Aberrant Speech

Introduction

The study and analysis of non-orthodox speech is particularly difficult. There are a number of reasons for this. One is that techniques for description and analysis are not very well developed. Another is that, naturally, things that are non-orthodox are non-orthodox in different ways. Each case is *sui generis*. In addition there is always the theoretical problem of what status to confer on the material *vis a vis* the orthodox language material that makes up the majority of the linguistic matter of the surrounding culture; and, finally, speech of this kind is almost always in a state of flux. This may be because it is, in the case of many linguistically disabled children, for instance, changing in the process of adapting towards a norm. Or it may be, as in the case of stroke patients, that the lapses and errors are, to an extent, unpatterned in their occurrence.

For all these reasons, then, non-orthodox speech needs to be handled with some subtlety; it needs to be seen in its own terms in as far as possible before the attempt is made to map it on to other systems. The subtlety involved also calls for close and empathetic observation emancipated from traditional categories: and an equal care may have to be exercised in the matter of grammatical analysis. In this section we shall go through material from a child with what is sometimes called a 'phonological disorder'. The child was 5:2 years at the time the work was done: and the material derives from the child's talking about pictures in a child's storybook in response to questions about them.

System congruence

In this case-study which deals with connected speech we set up grammatical categories first. In the English BE + ING verbal aspect we might want to recognise three phonological items, corresponding to the person system namely a nasal, a sibilant and a vocalic. In orthodox speech these are manifested by

1   m   n   ŋ   ɳ   ŋ̩   ñ

as in *I'm opening, I'm bringing, I'm not bringing, I'm getting, I'm finding, I'm thinking, I'm wanting.*

2   z   ʒ

as in *he's bringing, he's shifting.*

3   ɹ   ə

as in *you're opening, you're bringing.*

The three phonological items we recognise we can symbolise as N, Z and R. Each of these generalises over the group of phonetic items listed at 1, 2 and 3 above. So N generalises over m, n, ŋ, ŋ etc. The system of the English verb has N, Z and R as prosodic systems operating at the juncture place between the pronoun and the auxiliary in the BE + ING verbal aspect.

All of these systems involve the articulatory manipulation of consonantal items, and frequently clusters, in the phonetic strings that manifest them. Now, as frequently happens, this child displays many simplifications in consonantal arrangements *vis a vis* the orthodox language patterns, particularly in syllable final position, so at ∧ below:

4   ǎəɓʋɹ‸tǔöˆhĩ‸

the boy strokes him

5   bɛ̠°sə̃ə̃˙ɸ̃t'ã̠ẽ̠β̰‸ã̃ɵ̈
     ɦaek͡ʔdɛ̠ʔ‸

but sometimes I like them

In the case of the BE + ING system the material displays a twofold grammatical distinction (we have no instances in the 8 minute recording of the child producing a first person -ING form). The phonetics relating to these categories has no consonantal complexities in it. Instead the child marshalls other resources, using, for **Z** and **R** check (Q) and zero (0) respectively.

'Check' and 'zero' and the symbols used for them are categories to generalise over and refer abstractly and graphically to the relevant sets of phonetic events in the child's speech. 'Zero' is self-explanatory. 'Check' is used to convey the idea of $\mathcal{I}$ and gemination, both of which have the effect of producing the correct rhythm, but without the consonantal complexity such that

mʌmɪzwɒtʃɹŋ

mummy's watching

or

gɜlzstʌoɷkɹŋ

girl's stroking

entails in the regular language. It will be noticed that in the child's examples here gemination and $\mathcal{I}$ are used in a distributionally stable way. $\mathcal{I}$ occurs before stop articulations, gemination occurs with other articulations. Both of these strategies employ 'non-articulatory' devices. (Likewise, the absence of articulation that is the manifestation of 'zero' in 10 -12 below.)

The presence of **0** to correspond to the standard **R** might be explained by reference to the orthodox speech of the region. Utterances such as

$$ðɪ gɔɑɪnʃʋpɪn$$

$$wɪnɒkkɶmɪn$$

are regular in the non-aberrant speech of West and South Yorkshire. But they are, in fact, still **R** in this accent, though, since ⅄ appears in

$$ðɪʌɑvɪnðədɪnə$$

and the child's speech may be aberrant with respect to utterances of this kind, and hence to the whole system. However, we have no relevant material to check this against. We find for **Q** in the child's aberrant speech

6 $$m̃ʌm̃ễw̥ʋ̥ɒ·tɕɪnd̬ɛm̥̊$$

mummy's watching them

7 $$nɒɶʃᶮɪ̯ʋʋ̯ɣ̓ᶦi̯dɪ̯ᶮɛ̰̄ʔᶜ$$

now she's reading it

8   ꭗ̣ə̣ g̣ɛ̣˙ ⍵̣ꜱ ꓢ̣ṳ̈ö̃ñ̃ ꓲ̣̃

  ꭗə̣˙ ꭡ̌ꭥ̣ꜱ ꓘ̲ɛ̲̣

the girl's stroking the donkey

9   ꭡ̣̌ ꭤ̲ ꭗ̣ḛ̃ꜱ n ꭥ˙ ꜱ ꭤ w ꭥ˙ ɢ ə̃ m ɪ̣

daddy's not watching me

and, for **0**:

10   ꭗ̣ e ꓷ ꭤ̲ ꭥ ĩ ꓲ̃ ə̃ ꜱ

they're having a ...

11   d ë g̣ ö w ĩ̲ ˙ ꭍ ᴼ p̃ᵉ̲ ĩ m̃ ꭍ ᵊ̃

they're going shopping

12   ə̃ n ë ꓷ ꓸᴇ ꭥ b ɪ̣ n ə p ꞌ ɪ k̂ ꜱ̲ n ɪ k̚

and they're having a picnic

The material makes the point that the child's system is organised in the same way as the orthodox model in some respects, and is organised differently in others. We are reminded here of the kinds of relation we found between dialects of the same language. The child keeps the grammatical distinctions, but they are carried by other phonetic means. This means that for her different sets, or better, ranges of phonetic events, or different accumulations of phonetic features will be the subject of generalisations when we refer observed material to abstract categories. The abstract categories here are grammatical ones of 'person' and 'number' within verbal auxiliary.

Since the child retains the grammatical system with the same number of terms and identical terms, but has different phonetics, it follows that at the phonological level, we will have to have different phonological categories making links with the phonetics and the grammar. This we have done. It is worth exploring a little further, though. We notice, for instance that where the orthodox form has a consonant - z , the child's form has a consonantal element too; and where the orthodox form has a vocalic junction in

joəbʌɾygɪn

ðeɪəʌoɑpənɪn

she has a vocalic junction, too. This is what is meant above by saying that the child's system is organised in the same way as the model to some extent. The phonology is not totally different and this is why we have used Q ('check') as the phonological term to relate to the 3rd person singular. 'Check' implies syllable closure, and 'zero' implies lack of syllable closure. So Q is, as it were, a superordinate category to Z (though not to R, and probably not to N). So the phonology becomes less and less differentiated as we make more and more abstract statements.

We note also that all of this is related to the relative simplicity of the child's grammatical system. The orthodox system has gemination to relate to the 'past perfect' aspect, so

hɪbbɪn   ʃɪggɪvən

he'd been   *she'd given*

The child's verbal system does not appear, in any of the material we have (which exceeds the 8 minutes transcribed in detail), to include any uses of this aspect, which may simply not be present in the speech of 5 year-olds, whether orthodox speakers or not. So there may be no question of a partial overlap, for the child, between the phonetics of two systems. The phonetically simpler and quite natural system stands in a different relation to the auxiliary system for this child than for the orthodox speaker.

The relevance of phonetic detail

It is additionally noticed that in a system of the kind used by this child a similar basic resource is used to do a number of jobs. Gemination, or, more appropriately for this use, lengthening, is used, as in the adult system, to carry emphasis or hesitation, so

it goes very fast

But this kind of lengthening is kept apart from the kind that manifests Q in the -ING system or other kinds of linkage, such as the genitival, by the fact that in the latter case the resonance changes throughout the held consonant to divide its length into two, as it were. We have seen this in *now she's reading it* above, where we have ⌄ ⌄ . Another example is

mummy's watching them

In ⌄ ⌄ and ẅ ẅ we see cases of resonance change throughout an articulatory complex that is constant in other respects. This is yet another case, in fact, at quite another level, of the 'partly the same, partly different' principle which is so important in phonology. In the first example resonance moves from central to front and is co-incident with a lip-teeth approximation and voice. The second case is of resonance change from front to back associated with labial-velarity and close approximation. The same thing happens in:

I can't see daddy's head

where the movement in resonance is to be referred to an underlying -CC- shape rather than to -C:-. The situation is parallel to that
above: the movement in resonance is the difference that associates
the phonetic piece - ḣ ḱ - unambiguously with ɿ of ɑ̣ ɑ̣ ɑ̣ ɿ
on the one hand, and ɛ of ʰ ɛ ɑ̣ᶻ on the other. Duration is
again the embodiment of the category gemination, present here to relate phonologically to the grammatical item of genitival link. This
genitival link is, of course, in a different system grammatically to
the phonological Q element of -ING, but is brought in here to show
how similar resources are deployed at different places by the child.
Gemination, or slight lengthening, is often used, for instance, to coincide with pitch prominent elements to produce rhythmic rallentando
effects. This produces a 'jerkiness' in the child's speech, as do the
numerous glottal stops:

It is interesting to note the resonances in this example, where we have
to interpret the ə → ˜ change at ƀ ƀ as purely phonetic, as
opposed to the cases above where we have chosen to interpret similar
changes as relating to the grammar. It seems admissible to us to do
this, at least on an experimental basis, when interpreting material such
as this. This is because we need to respond as sympathetically as possible to what the child might be trying to do. Children such as this one
usually have perfect hearing and a keen sensitivity to the orthodox
speech around them. Given this, a detailed study of their utterances
may bring to light a number of phenomena that parallel the systems of

that model though perhaps only in an indirect fashion. These will be
alongside various other features that are peculiar to the idiolect under
study. In this child's speech, for instance, stretches of nasality occur quite frequently that contain no 'nasals' corresponding to utterances in the orthodox model that would, in careful speech, contain one
or more nasals, eg

13        $d_e e' \hbar \tilde{a} \tilde{\beta} \tilde{\iota} \tilde{\ell} \tilde{a}^{\hbar}$

they're having a ...

14        $b e^{\circ'} s \tilde{\underline{a}}^{\tilde{\circ}} \phi t^{\iota} \tilde{\underline{a}} \tilde{\underline{e}} \tilde{\beta} \tilde{\underline{a}}^{\tilde{e}}{}_{\iota}$

but sometimes I like

15        $\ddot{e}' d_{\jmath} \omega m p' \tilde{\omega} \hbar \tilde{\underline{e}} . \hat{\tilde{e}}' d \tilde{e}$

he jumps up and down

These phonetic effects are integrated into the rhythmic system, it
seems, in that their extent coincides with the accentual piece, and
does not exceed it: so from $'\hbar$ to the beginning of the next accented
syllable in 13, from $'s$ to the corresponding place in 14. If we accept this hypothesis, we would not want to regard $\tilde{e}$ of $d\tilde{e}$
(*down*) as part of the same stretch as the rest in 15. Rather the nasality
here is independent, attaching in its own right to the syllable, as it
does in the 'regular' version of this word.

An approach to variation

It would be wrong to give the impression that all is homogeneity in
the child's speech. There is on the contrary, great variation. Some

cases of -ING verbs include a ə token of *are*, hardly surprising as this is what is in the orthodox model. The child's set of systems is, as it were, on several levels at once. The word *sometimes* exemplified in one form in 14 above, is a good example of variation. Apart from the above form it also turns up as

16   s̜ ɔᵠ m tᶜ ë m̪

17   ƚᶜ ɔ m̪ · ƚᶜ ã̰ ẽ̜ m ᵖ

18   s ã̰ᵊ ᵠ t' a̰ ẽ̜ β̞

19   s̜ ã̰ ᵠ̃ t' a̰ ẽ̜ z̰̃

One thing to speculate on here is that these forms might be seen as falling into two pairs, two 'closed' (17 and 18), two 'open' (16 and 19), where 'open' means a generally open set of articulations, z ᵠ s β , 'closed' means the opposite, so m t . Openness and closeness here seem to be stretch phenomena, and it might be worth hypothesizing that openness and closeness are features of stretches longer than just this lexical item: the contexts are given above to allow this idea to be explored.

20   . . . . ɹ d ᶄ̃ ɔ̃

I don't

21   . . . . jəd

you d. . .

22   jɛʔ . . . . . ɐ dˌᶻəu̞

yes . . . I do

23   bɐ . . . . ãeɭ

but . . . I l. . .

Here is another set of examples:

24   f.ᵚu d fɐhe̠m

food for him

25   w̲ɪg̣ɹ̟g̣ɹ̟ʔ· ɹ̟β̃ɹ̟
          k̓ə̲ɐ̣ɹ̟ə̲tˢ

we gi - give him a carrot

26 ʙ̩ː ʃ̃ẽ n d h ɹ ʒ h ɹ m
ʒ ɹ n · ʈ ə

we send him into ...

27 ʒ ẽ ɲ̃ ẽ· ɛ p ɾ ʋ · d ʈ ɹ m̃ ʒ

and I prod him

These all contain *him*. In 24 and 27 it is final, in the others it is non-final. m appears in the final and pre-stop cases, ʙ̃ in the pre-vocalic case. A lot of cases would be needed if we wanted to put any ideas about openness and closeness to the test: but this material is very suggestive.

Theoretical conclusions

The description and analysis of aberrant speech of the kind manifested by this child is made easier if it is carried out alongside similar work on natural language or languages. This is because many of the phenomena and processes that occur in children's aberrant speech are to be found in natural languages. They are aberrant from the point of view of the language norms of the society the child is growing up in, not in any deeper sense. So, for instance, nasalisation stretches and 'open' versus 'close' stretches are readily found in the world's languages, as is the process whereby a set of phonological consonantal elements are realised by gemination of one phonetic consonantal element. For instance, the suffix -VAL in Hungarian turns up as this only after vowels as in TAXIVAL (*by taxi*). In the case of nouns ending in consonants the ending is CVl, where C is a geminate version of the final C of the nominal stem and V is whatever vowel is produced by the vowel harmony rules, so VONATTAL (*by train*), REPÜLŐGÉPPEL (*by plane*),. GYÜMÖLCSSÖL (*with fruit*). This is a similar situation to that existing in such forms as ʃ ɹ ʋ ɣ ɹ d ɹ n ɹ t and the like. If work is regularly carried out on natural languages it is easier to identify such phenomena, to understand them and to predict various aspects of their further manifestation. In addition, this study shows how important it is to have a detailed and accurate knowledge of the phonological systems of the orthodox model attended to by the child. This provides the only appropriate background for an analysis of what children with such disabilities do. It is inappropriate, to say the least, to compare the child's material with orthodox material that it is not, or rarely exposed to.

Study 2
Dialect and Accent

Introduction

Linguists use the term idiolect to denote the speech of one person. The term is made necessary by virtue of the observation that a language has a manifestation within an individual that is unmatched in all its detail by any other individual. The talk and language of an individual can, of course, vary and change. By 'vary' we mean that a number of observably different forms are present at one time, use of which fluctuates either randomly or according to some system. By 'change' we mean that a form or an item once attested is at a later point in time no longer attested, its place being taken by another form or item. 'Change' is a term of broad applicability and can be used of the individual (between the ages of 20 and 40, for example) or of the community (between the end of the 18th century and the beginning of the twentieth, say). Change and variation can be seen then to operate in two dimensions: over time and, given what was said above about idiolect, over place. 'Place' has a special meaning here, as it has to do with place occupied by a speaker or group of speakers.

Against this panorama of change and variation or variability, which is the potentiality for variation, we have the concepts of community, speaker and language. A speaker is a speaker of something, and normally we have an institutionalised name, or more commonly, set of names to denote what is spoken. Such concepts and labels relate to abstractions which imply a unity. To speak of 'the Rumanian speaking community' in Hungary, or of a 'minority language' or the 'language of secondary education' or even of 'a Koongo speaker' is to have recourse to abstract notions of some complexity. Yet these are basic and essential concepts in linguistic theory in its widest sense.

And they underline work in phonology in a fundamental way just as they underline work at other levels of analysis and statement.

In our introduction, for instance, we talked about the acceptability and representative quality of informants: this is because we want to be able to project from our one informant to the generality of speakers. We also use the notions of variation and variability in making our records and employ a range of graphic devices to show these things. We have no immediate way of knowing what part of such variation or variability is part of the idiosyncracy of the speaker, or whether all of it is: and part of the job of phonology is to separate these strands wherever possible.

The concepts of community, language and the like abstract away from individuals, idiosycracies and observed phenomena of the first order, and, in many of their uses, also abstract away from such other phenomena as variation and variability. In them the emphasis is on oneness, what is the same, much as it is in our statements of syntax and phonology. A monograph on the syntax of Spanish is not usually about any one speaker but purports to have applicability to all speakers, either by operating at such a level of abstraction that all variation and varibility can be referred to it, or by being selective in the range of material that it covers. In these different ways it abstracts away from the totality of the phenomena towards a oneness that is spurious when matched against 'speech facts' but valid when matched against entities and constructs. The term 'Spanish' has meaning in all these spheres. The task of linguistics is to be able to make statements at levels of abstractness appropriate to these meanings. From this point of view all linguistics is sociolinguistics or psycholinguistics; and from what is said above about variation and variability in the individual it will appear that all language description is historical and comparative. With small initial letters, of course. Sociolinguistics and Historical Linguistics are well established as academic disciplines, and had better stay so established: academic disciplines die hard. But practising linguists do well to avoid all such artificial divisions, in relation both to themselves and to their subject matter.

Dialect is talk in places. But the places are held together politically and culturally, and usually the term is used as subordinate to language, where this is an abstraction for an institutionalised nation-state vernacular with a writing-system. This being so, the term dialect is less happily used in situations where this state of events does not hold, as in parts of Africa, for instance. Nor does it apply very happily in situations where the very notion of place is becoming obscured, as in modern technological societies. When a large proportion of the population, even in rural areas, may have moved their homes and places of education and work half a dozen times before they reach their thirties, the applicability of dialect study may be questioned, if by this one means the study of established communities at well-defined geographical locations. Our methodology of phonological analysis and statement should, though, be refined enough to deal with any situation in which variation, variability and change are apparent, regardless of the social and temporal circumstances. An adequate phonological model should enable us to reflect this uniformity and variety in much the same way as we reflect uniformity in our phonological statements for unitary syntactic processes, relegating differences, variations and so on to the realm of exponency.

Representation of sameness and difference

In this study we present an attempt to deal with two kinds of dialectal material, that is, varying over place, by making phonological statements that possess the qualities we think desirable for them. Neither set of examples is in any way exhaustive for the dialects concerned: though the second set of examples is, we think exhaustive, for the portion of the phonology concerned. But in the main they are presented as illustrations of an approach serving to highlight different components of this approach to phonology including an innovatory approach to notation.

The first case is unusual in this book in that the material used is written not spoken and is second-hand rather than first-hand. We include it partly because of this, as an attempt to show that the approach we have developed throughout the book can be used to throw light on material which leaves something to be desired in the matter of presented detail. The focus is on the reinterpretation of broadly transcribed material in terms other than segmental and other than single-layered in the phonemic sense. The material to be examined is unlike most of the remainder of what we have dealt with in that it is published and was, presumably, subjected to a degree of analysis. At the least certain processes of selection have probably been exercised in regard to the form given to the representations. It is dialect material on its own admission, as it were, since it is taken from Joseph Wright's *English Dialect Grammar* of 1905. Wright gives for various the following set of forms for what is orthographically OAK in English.

ēk   ōk   iək   uək   jɛk   wɒk

In this kind of notation, which relates to a particular kind of analysis the forms have one thing in common, the final velar plosive. At a more abstract level we might go on to observe that no vowel is ever opener than half-open, but the kind of notation system used does not allow us to show this.

We have said above that a more acceptable model would be one that allowed us to show both uniformity and variety. The variety is shown, of course, by the kind of array we have taken from Wright. To get at the abstract phonology of this material in its diatopic aspect we need to know what it is that is the same about these items, or, to what extent there can be an abstract same phonological representation that they can all reasonably be representatives of.

The forms are either back or front, where ə can be in either category. Front are ē , iə and jɛ , back are ō , uə and wɒ. The vocalic nucleus is always mid, neither close nor open. The vocalic quality is either constant, ē , ō or changing iə , uə , jɛ , wɒ. And all these vocalic items are candidates for being considered two-place, informally at least, since none is simply a short vowel. All are mono-syllabic as far as we can read the implications of the transcriptions. Two-placeness, which we shall gloss as length, midness of vowel, and centrality are common to all forms. Using characters of the Visible Speech kind, here called phonograms, we shall write this as

Ƴ

The final velar is represented as Ɔ . The formulaic statement for *all* of the forms is, then,

standing for what they have in common. To this *common* formula we add various elements to produce the *general* formula. The general formula is a summation of the phonological elements that relate to the whole range of forms. Front and back are ⌐ Γ respectively. The way in which prominence is distributed over the two-places varies, the possibilities being level, rising and falling. These correspond to, ẽ , jɛ and iə for the category ⌐ . We use = < and > to mark these. The general formula is now

The components of prominence and of front/back are written vertically to show that they are in system, and on a different level to show they belong to a kind of phonological element that has other than punctual relevance. The front and back symbols are placed at the beginning of the formula in accordance with our observation that the main concentration of their phonetic implication and, in these examples, of their diacritic power is at that point.

Particular formulae for the individual items are, for instance

for ᴡ ɒk and so on.

It will be apparent that what has been done here is on a very small array of material, and for a specific and rather narrow purpose. Both of these limitations mean that a certain freedom is available in interpretation and formula making or statement. If more material were to be dealt with, or if the purpose were a different one, the outcome might be different. In the cases we have just dealt with we took no account of the phonological systems of the individual dialects from which the various forms were taken, and within which each must take its place. The kind of formulaic statement that brings together a number of related language forms (dialects) is of a higher level of generality than the statement or series of statements that relate to any one individually and should overarch these and take them into account. In the formulae presented here we have moved straight to the higher level of generalisation; and a great deal of the complexity of joint statement fails to appear.

A second more complicated set of items from Wright's *Grammar* is as follows, for STOVE:

ᴅvn   ɸn   jūn   ūn

ōbn   jɷvn   ōbm   ɷvm

In the case of this array of forms we have a more complex situation. Provisional formulae show C$\bar{V}$C, CVCC, VC, $\bar{V}$C, VCC as possibilities. C1 is limited to j , and CF is always a nasal. We can take bilabiality in this nasal to be part of a stretch feature, shared by �b or v preceding, since bilabiality does not occur in a nasal standing alone; this is always n . The bilabiality is then focussed at CF-1 in such cases as ō bm , ɷvm , and we can regard ō bm and ō bn as close variants. None of the above observations is particularly surprising. We might expect the initial and final consonants to be the same for all forms after all. What is more surprising is that the C1 may be absent, and that the C display can be, at this stage of analysis, CC or C. In the interests of symmetry we might interpret V-beginnings as being the manifestations of a glide type of C item having rounding as a feature plus a rounded vowel: jū - and jɷ - are manifestations of a glide having non-rounding as a feature plus a rounded nucleus. Rounding is a stretch feature in this material as can be seen from the fact that CF-1 when present is �b or v , that is to say, shares the labiality (rounding) of the V. So we might want to interpret the beginning glides as non-segments, giving eg

ʷᴅvn   ʷɸn   ʲūn   ʷūn

ʷōbn   ʲɷvn

and so on. Further we might want to interpret �b and v in a similar way as the manifestation of syllable labiality at CF-1 in -VCC sequences since they alternate with their absence in equivalent forms, and, importantly, can be interpreted in this way. We should not be as ready to look on cases such as u ~ uz in the same way, preferring to see this, perhaps, as a more straightforward case of

consonant loss. We will note here too that the variation is between
ʉ and a sequence of *some opener* vocalic element + ɓ / ʋ :
that is to say that closeness is involved towards the end of the sequence
that constitutes the syllable. Closing is to be associated with labiality
at this point, and ʷ is a useful way of writing closeness + labiality
+ backness (all the vowels except ø are back) so we can now write
eg

jɷʋn ⎫
jūn ⎭   jᵘ̯ɪᵂn

ɷʋm ⎫
wūn ⎭   as   ᵂɪᵂn

ōɓm   ᵂɛᵂn

ɒʋn   ᵂɑᵂn

There are a number of problems with this. One is that if backness
is stated as an exponent of the second ʷ , then ø is not covered.
Another is that it is uneconomical, since in some cases (but some only)
labiality and backness are dealt with twice. It will also be noticed that
we have not dealt with syllabicity yet. Some of these problems arise
from our dealing here with isolated items from different dialects; and
things are not helped by our not having truly detailed records to look at.
But, apart from these two sources of difficulty, we may in fact be
comparing incomparables. It is well known that the definite article before words beginning with a vowel in English is ðɪ . A common
phonetic result of ðɪ + vowel is a j standing between the two, so
we may find:

ðɪjapl̩

the apple

This can then be wrongly divided ð ɪ j a p ḷ , and this form repeated elsewhere:

ə j a p ḷ

is a frequent children's form. The j̊ in j ū n / j ɑ ʋ n
could be of the same provenance. If it were we would be wrong to
try to embrace it within our phonological interpretative processes or in
statement. In these cases we are dealing with the fringes of morphology (in that j̊ - ū n is one morpheme *plus* something else) rather
than with phonology alone, as in the remaining cases.

However the presence of ɸ n in our list provides some base,
on the other hand, for taking j ū n seriously as an integral
phonological form, since it too has an element of frontness in it. Notice that the sparseness of the transcription does not allow us to
know how far the frontness goes. The portion ɸ n has different
implications for us from ɸ ñ , since the latter has backness in it,
the first does not. Also we need to know just how front ɸ is. In the
presence of all these unknowns the analysis is difficult to complete.
This is why we need all the possible information all the time.

In the matter of syllabicity we have no way of knowing, faced
with these representations, how many syllables they are. No syllabicity is marked. English speakers (and this includes native English-speaking linguists, of course) know how many syllables there are in
these words, and we can proceed to discuss matters of syllabicity on
that basis. But when we are working on languages of which we have
no prior knowledge we have only indirect access to a knowledge of
syllable constituency. This is why, up to this point, we have looked at
various possibilities in the interpretation of these forms without taking
syllabicity into account. If we allow ourselves to know that j ɑ ʋ n
is not CVCC, but CVCV, different interpretations may fall out. So,
we shall have to recognise Ṽ at V2 perhaps, and almost immediately
shall have to reinterpret C2 in terms that accord with its alternation
with - u -. SPOON does not, after all, alternate with s p ɑ ʋ n ;
so we shall want to recognise the V at C2 as, again, the manifestation of labiality and closeness as in the previous interpretation. This
time, though, the tactical pattern of syllabicity that is mediating the
basic set of features is different. Instead of CVCC we have CVCV.
In our final phonological formula we shall not want direct representations of either C since the elements manifesting themselves at C are
implicatory for variance, ie for reassembly in other dialects, and

hence fluid in both their phonetic and their phonological relevance. They will be mediated to C at a lower level: but before that the feature bundle closeness + labiality will be mediated through ᵕᵕ to show their relevances. So the route will be

1 Features   Length   ‾

                   Nasality   ~

                   Labiality   ⎫
                             ⎬   ᵕᵕ
                   Closeness ⎭

2   (ʌ) ‾ʌ ᵕ ~ʌ   (ʌ) ‾ʌ ᵕ ~ʌ

3   (c) ∨ c c   (c) ‾∨ c

4   j ɑ ∨ ɯ   j u: n

5   j ~ɷ ~∨ ɯ ?   j u: ᵕn ?

This portrayal of the different interpretative levels omits any detailed account of how the features are organised sequentially: the final formula of the statement makes it clear how this has taken place, but, clearly, some more detailed local statements are necessary to show how 1 relates to 2, for instance. We are concerned here again with phasing. Clearly, too, more is needed. We have bracketted ʌ and

C above because we do not quite know what to do with them, and because they are almost certainly best not treated as ʎ or c . We have not accounted for the difference between ∨ and ɓ in the post -V1 position or for the fact that V is a syllabic nasal and not a nasalised vowel. This last might be regarded as a manifestation of ʷ , but only if other systemic considerations allow. The difference ∨ ~ ɓ might be dealt with in terms of long and short nuclei at V1 for this set of material; any such hypothesis would have to be tested on further comparable material.

A Visible Speech formula for the OVEN set of words might be something like

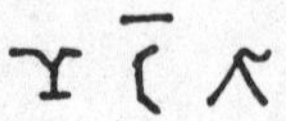

where [is to be interpreted as a back vocalic, ‾ means two-piece (ie either long (+ glide) or short + glide), ʎ means apical nasal, and Υ means either front or back syllable beginning.

Given that we are short of hard phonetic information on these forms, there is not much to be said for going very deeply into their interpretation and analysis. This is additionally true in the light of the probably rather random nature of the set. But they have, we hope, served to represent some of the principles of interpreting written forms so as to provide a set of formulaic statements that serve to bring the forms together, phonologically, and to display systematically their differences at various degrees of generalisation. It will have served, too, to show how results can differ when like elements are viewed and interpreted in the context of their systems. So, for example, the j of jɛk is treated quite differently from the j of jūn . This is in distinction to some phonological approaches which would identify them, giving them the same notational device and the same overall value.

Resonance detail and English Accents

The second portion of this section on comparative work in phonology deals with spoken material, or, more accurately, records deriving from spoken material. The material itself differs from that considered in the first portion in that we now turn to utterances of more than one word and in that there is considerable phonetic detail present in the record. In this material we focus attention on what has earlier been called resonance, here meaning, as often elsewhere, those chracteristics of cavity configuration and corresponding auditory effect that are usually regarded as secondary to some more gross primary articulatory-cum-auditory category. So velarisation of r , m or z , half-clearness of t or ρ , centrality of $\int$ or f would all be resonance features.

The set of resonance features that we recognise is fixed partly by the limitations of our skill, partly by the pragmatics of the language-describing situation. For practical work, seven categories are easily distinguishable, and might in recording work be notated

$$i \quad \iota \quad \vartheta \quad \partial \quad \epsilon \quad \omega \quad \dot{\omega}\dot{\iota}$$

with these symbols written over the consonants they relate to, or, more accurately, to be written where they apply. It is quite common to observe consonantal items that begin with one resonance and end with another, so $^{9}m^{6}$, or, very commonly $^{9}\ell^{w}$. As the two parameters of primary and secondary articulation are, for most practical purposes, independent each of the other, there is nothing at all surprising in this kind of phasing relationship. Accordingly, this method of notation is often in recording work, a desirable alternative to that suggested for the same phemonenon in *Observing*. One place where resonance comes into play in the study of English dialects and accents is with regard to what are sometimes called liquids. We shall use this shorthand term to refer to r and l.

In a number of accents of English that we have examined we have found that a polarity in resonance of liquids occurs. So in accents where l is typically of the dark type, r is clear and *vice versa*. For some of the accents the disposition of clear and dark over the two liquids is different from place to place in structure; for others it remains constant. To avoid this complexity we shall concentrate in our discussion on the intervocalic post-accentual case, as in such words as SHERRY and SHELLEY. In words like these we find a resonance difference throughout all of -VCV. In a clear r / dark l accent, such as some of those of the N.W. Midlands, this resonance will be clear for SHERRY, dark for SHELLEY. Clear and dark here are to be construed to mean, for consonants, having clear resonance, as against dark resonance: for vowels, as having, respectively, fronter or backer articulation. In terms of IPA symbols we should typically find something like $\int \varepsilon \underset{\sim}{u} \underset{\sim}{\iota}$ and $\int \underset{=}{\varepsilon} t \underset{=}{\iota}$ in the records. All of this phonetic difference we would interpret in terms of a pair of phonological diacritics, symbolised here informally by superscript

ᵞ and ᵞ : SHERRY will be, leaving aside the initial consonant,
- ε ʟ ᵞ ʟ   in a N.W. Midlands accent as against - ε ʟ ᵞ ʟ
for SHELLEY. For a Tyneside or Home Counties accent the resonance markers are reversed but the rest of the formula is constant.

Phasing has a role to play here, too. But in this case we are dealing with phasing as extent beyond the phonologically bonded group that corresponds to the lexical unit word. And, in addition we are looking at ranges of extent of two comparable but mutually exclusive elements. The phasing we are concerned with here has implications for the recognition and description of stretches, for the description of varieties, and, possibly, for change. It concerns what happens when words with the phonological pattern $-VC_L V$ such as those above enter into longer sequences.

In our records we have sentences such as

1a   *it's Terry*

1b   *it's Telly*

2a   *let Terry do it*

2b   *let Telly do it*

3a   *Harry came over*

3b   *Sally came over*

recorded as uttered by speakers from Stockport, Haltwhistle and Epsom. The last two have $-VC_L^ᵞ V$ as l, $-VC_L^ᵞ V$ as r, the Stockport speaker has this position reversed. In 1a and b for all speakers there is no difference between the two tokens of *it's*. In the other utterances there are differences between the phonetics of the r and l members of the pair for at least some of the speakers; and these differences are not common to all speakers. So, for example, the Haltwhistle speaker has

⌐——ᵞ——⌐

let Terry do it

┌──── ⌐ ────┐

let Telly do it

where the brackets denote differences, of the ⌐ or ⌐ kind, at all places included within them. So, the final vowel, i of *it* is different in these two utterances for this speaker, as is the ɛ of *let*: all are fronter, in *let Telly do it* than their counterparts in 2a.

For the same speaker a similar bracketing in the represention shows that in 3a the darkness associated with r (*Harry*) has implications for the pronunciation of a , ɪ and the k of *came*, whilst the clearness associated with l results in a stretch with relatively fronter articulations for all these phonetic items. So we find k̟ in 3b as against k in 3a. The Epsom speaker does not do this: the confines of ⌐ and ⌐ extent are different for him, and do not embrace the beginning of the next unaccented syllable, as they do for the Haltwhistle speaker. The rules that govern the junction stretches are different, it seems, for the two accents. An attention to the detail of utterance here enables us to state what appear to be basic and pervasive differences between the phonetics of certain portions of these English accents, differences that various other phonological approaches would bypass or want to treat as immaterial. We have as yet no well-founded experimental information as to just what as listeners we are responding to as listeners when we identify accents, even when these are vestigial. Features such as those described above for $-VC_L V$ structures and others extended from them may be candidates for this job.

It is also worth noting here the relationship between lack of stress accent in English and the extent of resonance features. It is a good example of the intimate tie-up of features of articulation and others from other components of the speech production mechanism, in the construction of phonological accentual system. It should be added here that the state of affairs we have described for the $-VC_L V$ shape is not invariably that obtaining for other shapes. The VC_L shape shows a reversal of resonance polarity for the Epsom speaker, the C ⌐ item being ɛ , whilst the C ⌐ item is ʊ . The question arises here of how we know that these phonetic elements are to be allocated to C_L at all. The answer to this resides in the generality of our analysis. For an analysis of lexical forms only, studied in isolation, we should have only economy of statement together with symmetry as a general goal to guide us. In an analysis of the polysystemic kind that we have outlined here, though, economy is not a paramount consideration, and the appearance of an C_L system at C1 and C2 in C1VC2VC3 does not lead us to expect or posit a similar or identical item at C3. So that we might be prepared to recognise t ɛ ɤ and t ɛ ɹ as members of a diphthong system and do without any C_L item in the consonant inventory. We might be the more pushed to this analysis by the fact that, in order to take ʊ and ɹ as allottable to respectively C_L ɰ and C_L ɰ , we should have to accept the polarity mentioned above.

However, if our analysis is extended to cover junction forms, the link with consonantal versions of the C t ɛ ɭ ɾ ŋ and t ɛ ə ɹ ɾ ŋ are then seen to align themselves with t ɛ ɤ and t ɛ ɹ . So, for purposes of stabilising an invariant formula for the lexical items *tell* and *tear* it becomes necessary to have CVC formulae here, with final C_L, and resonance characteristics which are different from one structural shape to another, more particularly in junctural and non-junctural situations. The two strands of the phonological analysis are then associated each with different faces of the phonology, as it were, one facing towards lexis, the other, in part, towards morphology. The emphasis here is throughout on an interpretation of English as having one basic liquid category, associated with two sets of resonance and articulatory characteristics: the sets themselves are fluid in that they can be assorted differently between different varieties of English, and, within one and the same accent, between different structural shapes.

Our approach has serious implications for the study of linguistic non-uniformity over time and space. The crucial point about non-uniformity has to do with how the non-sameness is encoded, what linguists take to be the unlike elements. It is common to read in the linguistic literature about so-called sound-change or to see such representations as $p > f$ or $a > au$. Again in literature dealing with non-uniformity over space we have such things as $e: > ei$, $p \sim \phi \sim h$. There are implications in the words and graphic devices used: change implies that p is no longer found, for example, whilst variability or variation imply that the elements under discussion are all found. There are close links between non-uniformity over time and over space. The expression 'sound change in progress' implies that various forms scattered over space or over time (in the sense of coexisting for a community) can be construed as moving away from one pole in the scatter towards another. All members are observable at what counts as the same time but for one or a number of reasons a direction is taken as present. These reasons may be general phonetic, social (generation) (prestige), comparative, and the direction may not be only one way. However the nature of the change may appear to be quite different depending on the primes we have established. In comparative linguistics we look at non- uniformity over space without time complications. But how we see relationships and state them will be much affected, again, by the primes we select. And this itself is of necessity influenced by the framework of our earlier observing and recording. We cannot select as a prime what is not there. And if we use segmental elements of the type we have discussed above as the primes for observing, so only these elements or some available distillation of them can serve as primes for statement. This remark holds good for the comparative and historical areas of work as it does for others. So, again, we need all the available material to be present in our records for a just and linguistically sound interpretation to be made. The more phonetic detail we have the clearer it is that we are dealing with the same thing, or different aspects of the same thing. What the same thing is, we get from our phonetic theory, in part; and from phonetician's instinct and experience in part. Instinct and experience usually run ahead of theory; certainly they do where our present phonetic theory and metalanguage is concerned.

Study 3
Creolisation

Preliminaries

This case-study centres on a detailed examination of material taken down from four speakers. It falls into two parts; the first provides an analysis of a part of the V-system of three speakers of British English. The second part extends this examination to an English-based creole. The four informants spoke non-standard varieties ('accents') of English. The accents are those of (i) Hemsby, Norfolk, England (ii) Abertillery, Gwent, Wales (iii) Three Mile Cross, County Antrim, Northern Ireland and (iv) Georgetown, Guyana. The accents of English under discussion are the mother-tongues of all the speakers. For convenience we shall refer to the accents as E1, E2, E3, and E4 as in the order above. Some of the work of observing was carried out face-to-face, some done from tape-recordings.

We restrict our attention here to a corpus of monosyllables containing the vowel counted (for RP English) as No. 9. The material comes from a larger recorded corpus which includes polysyllabic items (eg CUPID, MUSIC, FRUGAL) as well as items containing other vowels (eg PIT, LET, LEAN, NIGHT). The items were read by the speakers from a typed randomised list. Each word was said twice, and a large number of the words were duplicated so as to provide four tokens of it. The speakers were asked to cross off their list any words they did not know. This resulted in a number of place-names (BUDE, LOOE) and a few recondite words (ROOD, GULES) not being said by some of our speakers.

PART ONE

(i) CV configurations

Both of us made, independently, impressionistic records of the speakers. We then jointly produced an agreed version of those records. We give a table below of our (agreed) impressionistic records for some CV items.

Table 1

Lexis	E1	E2	E3
do	dətt	duᵂ	doȳ
dew	dɪ ətt	dɪ ɪu	dzɸȳ
coo	kətt	kᵠuᵂ	koȳ
cue	kjətt	kjɪu	kjɸȳ
moo	mətt	m̃uᵂ	moȳ
mew	mɪətt	mɪɪu	mɪjɸȳ
who	hətt	ħuᵂ	hoȳ
hew	hɪətt	hɪɪu	çɸȳ

What interest us here are the differences between these varieties in terms of syllable resonances. By syllable resonances we mean the resonances, as defined earlier in the book, associated variously with syllable onsets (Co), nuclei and codas (Cco). These resonances can be different from accent to accent in a number of ways

❑ in their number at a particular place in structure

❑ in their nature (ie what they are)

❑ in linkage (ie the relationships between onset and coda, onset and nucleus etc)

For a CoVCco configuration, then, we might have Co with R2 (ie with a system of two resonances types) and Cco with R3 (ie with a system of three resonance types). The members of the R2 set may be two of the members of the R3 set or none of them; and there are other possibilities. Linkage might be total, that is R1 at Co accompanying R1 at Cco and no other linkage possible, or it may be minimal, in that R1 at Co might be accompanied by any of R1-3 at Cco. These differences are, then, of different degrees of complexity: and it is this complexity of resonance associations that will interest us here as we look at this set of English accents. Table 1 shows a number of noteworthy features:

❑ all the speakers have two classes of CV monosyllable containing close rounded vocalic nuclei. One of these classes is made up of items that are generally fronter in resonance, as a set, than those in the other. So, for instance, for

E1:	E3:	(*cue*)

$$k_{+} j \, \vartheta \underset{+}{\#} \qquad k_{+} j \, \phi \, \bar{y}$$

are overall fronter than their counterparts

$$k \, \mathfrak{z} \# \qquad k \, \theta \, \bar{\bar{y}}$$

E1:	E3:	(*coo*)

We distinguish these two classes for the time being, informally, as 'clear' (overall fronter class) versus 'dark' (overall backer class)

◻ all of the items have lip-rounding as part of their make up and this lip-rounding involves most or all of the syllable. (As we indicated earlier our word lists also elicited items with close spread nuclei as well, *lean* and *meat* for instance, in all of which relative front resonance and lip-spreading are a feature of the syllable in its entirety.)

◻ different kinds of lip rounding occur here associated with different lexical items and produced by the different speakers. Thus the lip-rounding produced by E3 is very lax and best described as 'inner rounding'; that is, it is produced with no lateral contraction of the lips. The lip rounding observed for E2 and E3 is can be described as 'outer' lip rounding wherein the lips are laterally contracted and pouted. For all three speakers, however, the lip rounding in items with back overall resonance differs from that observed for items with overall front resonance. This difference can be grossly characterised as 'more' lip rounding in the back resonance items as compared with the front ones. 'More' here means two things: for E3 it simply means that back resonance items have rather closer rounding throughout; for E1 and E2 it means that closer rounding occurs throughout the back resonance items and that in front resonance items not only is the rounding somewhat more open but its onset is gradual.

Now to talk, as we have been doing, of 'two classes of monosyllable' is a generalisation from the mass of our phonetic material and constitutes a categorisation in the realm of phonology. We have treated all the spoken material here in terms of generalised phonetic categories such as roundness, frontness and backness. By 'generalised' here we mean that such labels as these apply to a range of phenomena, which, once used within the purview of phonology must be comparative and relative. So 'relatively front' nuclei are just that; they are not all maximally front: the class of 'relatively front' is, as a class, front with regard to some other class, called for example 'back' where this term is under the same limitations.

As we are here dealing with phonological generalisations these statements cannot be presented in a notation designed to register and represent another kind of generalisation, that is to say phonetic generalisations such as are carried by a graphic device like ᖯ or ⅃ . We shall, then, use here the symbols κ (kappa) and ~κ to stand for front (clear) and back (dark) syllable types (kappa being a mnemonic for 'clear'), and w and ~w to stand for lip-rounded and non lip-rounded syllables. We shall use the Greek iota (ι) to stand for a close vowel, a member of a system which also includes open vowels, as our word list suggests. We shall use Ω to stand for any onset consonants. The English of these speakers includes then syllables that are to be phonologically categorised as wκ and w~κ (together with a class of ~wκ syllables (LICK, MEAT, LATE, LIGHT) that will be of no immediate interest. The iota symbol does not refer to a class of syllables but to a class of vocoids and is a different kind of generalisation. A cumulative generalised phonological representation for the lexical items considered so far can be given as

$$w / \tilde{w}$$
$$\kappa / \tilde{\kappa}$$
$$\Omega \iota$$

In order for such a representation to function it must receive an interpretation; it is necessary that the relationship between its component parts and the sections of the material analysed which each dominates should be given. In the present case these phonetic exponents for each component of the phonology are:

❑ w lip-rounding through some or all of the opening consonant and through the vocalic nucleus of the syllable

❑   ~w lip-spreading throughout the syllable

❑   κ raising of the blade of the tongue towards the front of the hard-palate during consonantal articulations; vocalic articulations in an area from just rear of fully front to central; front on-glides to syllabic nucleus

❑ ˜ĸ raising of the middle or middle-back of the
tongue towards the rear of the hard palate/soft palate
area during consonantal articulations; central or
backish on- glides to syllabic nucleus; vocalic articulations in the area fully back to rear of central

❑ ɪ closeness and vocalicity

(ii) CVC configurations

To this point our material and the phonological abstractions we have
made have been relatively simple and straightforward. However,
when we come to deal with CVC items produced by these speakers
more complex patternings arise. A range of CVC words are given in
Tables 2 and 3.

Table 2

Lexis	E1	E2	E3
cute	kjʉtʃ	kjʉtʃ	kjɤtʃ
newt	nʉtʃ	njʉtʃ	njɤtʃ
nude	nᵊʉd	njᵊʉd	njɤʸd
feud	fᵊʉd	fjᵊʉd	fjɤʸd
dupe	dʉp	djʉp	djɤp
cube	kjᵊʉb	kjᵊʉb	kjɤb
tube	tᵊʉb	tjᵊʉb	tjɤb

Table 2 (cont)

Lexis	E1	E2	E3
duke			
puke			
fugue			
muse			
fume			
prune			
moon			
huge			
crude			

Table 3

Lexis	E1	E2	E3
coot	kəʉt	kuʷt	kot
boot	bəʉt	buʷt	bot
food	fəʉd	fuʷd	fod
rude	ɹəʉd	ɫuʷd	ɹod
hoop	həʉp	ƛuʷp	hop
coop	kəʉp	kuʷp	kop
look	tɒk	tɒk	tɒk̠
book	bɒk	bɒk	bɒk̠
tooth	təʉθ	tɒθ	tʏθ

Table 3 (cont)

Lexis	E1	E2	E3
goose	gɘʉs	guⁿɕ	gʏɕ
pouffe	pɘʉf	puⁿf	pʏɕ
hoof	hɷf	ɦuⁿf	ɦɵɕ
booze	bɘʉz	buⁿz	bɵʏz
soothe	sɘʉð	suⁿð	sɵʏð
soon	sɘʉñ	suⁿñ	sɵn̩
room	ʇɷm̃	ɿuⁿm̃	ɿɵm̩
boon	bɘʉñ	buⁿñ	bɵn̩
doom	dɘʉm̃	ɖuⁿm̃	ɖɵm̩

We can see from Tables 2 and 3 that, as for **CV** items, these speakers have, broadly speaking two classes of **CVC** monsyllables. One class has relatively front overall resonance the other has relatively back overall resonance. Employing the descriptive labels we established for CV syllables we can see that in the 'clear' (ie front resonance) class there are

❏   initial consonantal portions with clear resonance

❏   final consonantal portions with clear resonance

❏   relatively fronter nuclei (when compared with the non-clear class)

In the 'dark' class there are

❏   initial consonantal portions which have dark (either velarized or non-clear eg central) resonance

❏   final consonantal portions with dark resonance

❏   relatively backer nuclei (when compared with the clear class)

However we now have to take account of features which have not appeared before in the analysis:

❏   the range of vocalic qualities especially in E3

❏   a different kind of linkage for resonances

❏   variability between the accents as to (a) what phonological categories they display and (b) how lexical items are distributed across these categories

1 Vocalic quality range

We can see that E3, the Ulster speaker, has a wider range of vocalic qualities in these closed syllable items than do E1 and E2. The occurence of this range of vocalic nuclei is part of a variation in quality and length in syllables which is associated with the nature of coda consonants (usually referred to as Aitken's Law).

In ˜κ syllables E3 has ɷ with final velarity, ɵɤ with final voice and friction and ɵ elsewhere. In κ syllables we find for E3 ɵ with final nasality, ∅ ȳ with final voice and friction and ɤ elsewhere.

For E1 and E2 we find vocalic qualities similar to those observed before for CV syllables with the exception of ɷ with final voicelessness with labiality and friction or velarity and plosion. For **E1** and **E2** where ⌒ occurs in ˜κ CVC syllables the nucleus is noticeably shorter than in other ˜κ CVC syllables.

2 Resonance linkage and cohesion

As well as exhibiting a wide range of vocalic variation the material for **E3** confronts us with the need to recognise that the phonological primes κ and ˜κ can enter into complex relationships. We can see, for instance, that unlike the earlier **CV** cases where words were either κ or ˜κ throughout, some **CVC** words in **E3** may have an onset associated with one resonance type (˜κ) and a coda which is associated with another (κ). In such cases the final consonantal articulation is the locus for the second resonance category. At first sight the items which exhibit this more complex pattern of resonance linkage look random. However closer inspection reveals that they are grouped together by having either final nasality: *boom, boon, doom, room* . . . final labiality and plosion: *coop, soup, sloop, hoop* . . . or final friction: *hoof, pouffe, move, goose, booze, lose, hooch, mooch, tooth* . . . . It would appear that for **E3** we have to recognise that certain articulatory events are routinely accompanied in word-final position by a specific kind of resonance ('clear') and that this resonance is independent of other resonances in the same item.

This, of course, distinguishes **E3** from **E1** and **E2** which do not show such an 'unlinked' association of resonance. **E1** and **E2** display resonance cohesion. The relationship of resonance with articulatory activity under consideration here cannot be dismissed as 'simply phonetic'. It has do do with certain kinds of articulatory activity occuring in syllable coda position. In syllable initial position for **E3** articulatory complexes of nasality with labiality/alveolarity, or labiality and plosion, or friction, exhibit differing resonance characteristics depending on whether the lexical item they begin is associated, as a whole with the κ or ˜κ category.

The different resonance characteristics of initial consonants do not necessarily show resonance linkage with different vocalic nuclei. They are not 'predictable' in any straightforward way on the basis of some kind of, say, some 'universal rule' of 'co-articulation'. Thus we find, for example:

230   Creolisation

E1

nude

rude

E3

prude

prune

loom

loose

boon

moon

That is we find front (in articulation and/or resonance) consonants before back nuclei and different articulatory and resonance features before and after what is impressionistically the same vocoid.

3. Lexical association of resonance categories

All the accents here also display differences in the ways in which words and resonance categories associate. For instance, *prune* and *lute* are ˜κ items for E1 but κ items for E2 and E3; *noon* and *loot* are ˜κ items for E1 and E2 but κ items for E3. This state of affairs is highly reminiscent of that dealt with by the so-called 'lexical diffusion' hypothesis. Although lexical diffusion is classically construed as having (trivially) to do with segmental-type units in phonology it would seem entirely appropriate that higher order phonological categories (eg resonance categories) should be considered within this hypothesis.

In the context of these observations it is legitimate to ask why the resonance features we have identified are not systematically discussed in the phonological literature on English. It is not, for instance, the case that we have stumbled across some extraordinarily exotic varieties of English. Effects like these are common, widespread, and readily observable. We suspect that their absence from phonological analysis is due either to an inadequate attention to observable detail or, given other phonologists' obsessions with punctual segmental contrasts, if such features *are* recorded in impressionistic work they are not deemed important for phonological analysis and are duly omitted.

As we noted earlier the resonance categories we are concerned with (when associated with consonantal items) are of the type usually dealt with under 'secondary articulations' in the phonetics text books. Secondary articulations are so called because they are different in stricture type (having a more open stricture) from the 'primary' articulation. However, there seem to be two other implications in the literature: one is that they are secondary in phonetic and phonological status and the other that they are worth mentioning mainly, if not only, when they can be dealt with in the 'simple' (segmental) and biunique way.

In phonological treatments of English reference to resonance characteristics of consonants, if made at all, is almost always restricted to those associated with alveolar lateral articulations. (Sporadic reference in the literature on the phonetics of English is made to the resonance features of post-alveolar approximant articulations and to those of nasals; but this reference is typically made within the context of teaching pronunciation to non-native speakers.) However, it is obvious that all consonants have resonance characteristics and if one listens at all carefully these are audible and stateable. One can only presume that the lack of reference to this in the phonological literature for English rests on the assumption that the resonances of consonants other than 'l' are 'neutral' and are 'conditioned' by the environing nuclei in some fashion, and in any case of only phonetic interest. On the basis of the present material alone there are no good grounds for any of these assumptions. Therefore, we argue, it is essential that such resonance features be systematically recorded in impressionistic work. Failure to do so simply prejudges which bits of the articulatory-acoustic information can be considered relevant for phonological statement.

Table 4 below shows some of the correspondences and non-correspondences amongst lexical items in terms of association with resonance categories across the accents.

Table 4

E1	E2	E3
˜κ ˜κ	˜κ κ	˜κ κ
prude = prune	prude ≠ prune	prude ≠ prune
˜κ ˜κ	κ ˜κ	κ ˜κ
rule = spool	rule ≠ spool	rule ≠ spool
˜κ ˜κ	˜κ κ	˜κ κ
rude = crude	rude ≠ crude	rude = crude
˜κ̆ ˜κ̄	˜κ̆ ˜κ̄	˜κ κ
book = boom	book = boom	book ≠ boom
κ ˜κ	κ ˜κ	κ ˜κ
plume ≠ sloop	plume ≠ sloop	plume ≠ sloop
˜κ ˜κ	˜κ κ	κ κ
loot = lute	loot ≠ lute	loot = lute

A number of generalisations can be drawn from this table which shows, for instance, that maximum lexical differentiation occurs here in the **E2** (the Welsh accent). But since the table is restricted in what it includes both in terms of accents and in terms of items, a small number of additions could change the picture considerably. For this reason we prefer that it should be regarded as illustrative only.

More interesting is the phonological and phonetic complexity of **E3** (the Ulster accent), a complexity which shows up in other places, as in the quantity-quality systems already referred to. **E3** is reminiscent of Irish in that different prosodic features can appear at beginnings and ends of syllables. However we do not have the detailed extensive information which would allow us to explore the intricacies of such a possible relationship. Even allowing for the possibility of a complex phonological system here influenced by Irish, this accent shows up some commonalities with the other two. So, for instance, *sloop* and *spool* are ˜κ in all three, but *loot* is not. This might well have something to do with the histories of these words; *sloop* and *spool* being of Dutch origin, *loot* not. (The *Oxford English Dictionary* gives Hindi as the origin of this last.) Certainly the items, whether **CV** or **CVC**, considered in this study have different sources. Those in -**ew** are from what were -**VC** patterns in English originally, those in -**oo**- from an earlier 'long o'. That is, the one has a front source, the other a back source. They reveal these sources still, in that one class (-ew) is κ, the other (-oo-) is ˜κ. In the case of **E1** and **E2** this affects the whole syllable, in the case of **E3** the first part of the syllable.

One class of items, those in **u( )e** is to be regarded differently. These, in one sense, have no phonology being English accomodations of French loans. The French vocalic item(s), having no exact counterpart in English, have been adapted to the English system by putting them into that part of it which most models the French and in which they do not fall together with many English words. As these words presumably had closeness, frontness and roundedness as part of their vocalic makeup in French they are accomodated by allocating them to the κ class (ie closeness, frontness and roundness but differently allocated with respect to syllable structure) - j u in many, but as we have seen, not all, accents.

This portion of the English vowel system has traditionally caused problems for phonological description within both phonemic and generative type approaches. There are differences of opinion, for instance, as to whether j u should be treated as a unit (phoneme) or as a **CV** sequence. Both of these 'solutions' run into trouble. In the first if j u is treated as some kind of complex vocalic unit then there is the problem that it is the only diphthong of English which has second element prominence. In the second the problem which confronts analysts is that of defective distribution. If words such as DEW and NEW are treated as **CCV** or STEW and SPEW as **CCCV** then the analyst has to deal *ad hoc* with the constraints on which vowels can follow d j (ie only ʊ and ɔ ə). In the treatment presented here no problem of this kind arises. All the fronting and backing elements are assigned to phonological units whose domain is the syllable leaving only punctual features such as apicality and plosion, say, to be stated for the syllable initial in such words as DEW, DO, and TWO.

The type of phonology pursued in this study assigns all of what is different over these three accents to the syllable domain of phonological structures, leaving the punctual elements constant in all cases. By doing this it accomodates one of the central intuitive facts about accents in a formal way, namely that accents of the same language are in some respects the same in some respects different. By paying attention to detailed matters of resonance we are able to show similarities of system and of categorisation over these accents. The fact that resonance categories appear to be distributed over words in ways that are not always easily explicable on either synchronic or historical grounds (if these are indeed different) is not as distressing as it was once made to appear. A good deal of evidence has been coming to light recently to suggest that phonological systems are considerably richer and more heterogeneous than sixty years of phonemic analysis has brainwashed us into believing.

PART 2

(i) CV configurations

We now extend our examination to take in material from a fourth kind of English, **E4**, which is that spoken by an inhabitant of Georgetown, Guyana. We have noted above that in E3 there is a kind of loosening of the simple and rigid relationship between resonance categories and other syllable onset and syllable coda events that holds in E1 and E2. This loosening in the linkage goes much further in this Guyanese English: and although semi-systematic relationships are present, they are complex and not immediately apparent. There are more resonance types in operation, too, and a very wide range of vocalic types exhibited in the various subsets of the lexicon. In all it is necessary to deal here with fifteen distinct vocalic nuclei, most of which are in fact diphthongal in nature. Correspondences between one or other of these vowel types and the nature and/or resonance of the consonantal tokens that accompany them are at the centre of the phonological complexity thrown up by this accent.

Clear CV configurations

We start with the NEW, PEW class of lexical items. All items here have initial clearness of consonantal articulation followed by a palatal glide, either fricative or non-fricative. The overall cCV group falls into three classes by virtue of the vocalic nuclei:

cCV	mew	view	pew	spew	$(\,j\,) \; \vartheta \; \overset{+}{\text{u}}$
	new	dew	chew	hew	$(\,j\,) \; \underset{\smile}{\overset{+}{\vartheta}} \; \overset{+}{\text{u}}$
	cue	skew	stew		$(\,j\,) \; \vartheta \; \overset{+}{\text{u}}$

Brackets around $\dot{j}$ indicate that in some cases (*chew, stew*) there is a $\int$ -glide, not a $\dot{j}$ one.

It will be seen that the vocalic nuclei can be grouped as front, central, and back types in phonetic terms. Certain phonetic links exist between them and the consonantal elements of the relevant syllables. So, the back, velar, articulation in *skew, cue* is accompanied by the backest of the three nuclear types, and the frontest nuclear vocalic type accompanies a labial set. There are apparent asymmetries here in that *chew* and *stew*, for instance, do not have the same vowel class. The interpretation of this as an asymmetry depends, of course, on any expectations for symmetry and on such notions of classification as we have from the IPA alphabet and similar sources, which in themselves inform our expectations. But the possibility is worth considering that more 'real-life' factors than phonetic symmetry rule the present-day disposition of these phonetic complexes in Guyanese. Such factors may be the sources of the words, their mode of transmission into the language, the time of such transmission and so on. In addition we have again the possibility, as in the case of E3, of some admixture, into the English accents, of features from an at one time co-existing set of phonetic couplings, characteristics of some other language.

Dark CV configurations

In the case of CV items with initial dark resonance we have again three vocalic nuclei possible, falling again into a front, central and back set. A number of words of **dCV** type appear in the cumulative table above; but, whilst that table shows exhaustively the kinds of phonetic quality associated with **dCV** syllables in **E1 - 3**, more detail is needed for a closer specification of **E4**:

dCV	*two*	*do*	*sue*	*zoo*	*rue*	ə ö̈ ʷ
	coo					ɔ ʷ
	goo					u ʷ

More detail is required, too, when we consider items of CC_LV type (where C_L is a 'liquid'). With these last there is still a two-way resonance opposition, but this time it is mid (resonance) versus clear. For this CC_LV configuration we might want to regard mid as the equivalent of dark, as there is no dark to contrast with here. But mid will recur as a category in systems where dark is present. We will discuss this situation later. For the time being the CCV table will show the two resonances as **d** and **m**. Vocalic nuclei fall into only two types for each resonance class this time, a front and a back for each class. Though, since the front of one class is phonetically identical with the back of the other, we have, over both resonance classes, three types of vowel. They could be front, central and back again, though this might be misleading as the relationship between these categories and the resonance classes would not be the same as for CV structures for which the labels were previously used.

In this array of material there is overlap, for the first time in our survey, between resonance classes in terms of associated nuclear vocalic qualities, as follows

dCC_LV *glue*   *grew*   *crew*

clue

mCC_LV *brew*

blew   *slew*   *flew*   *true*

It is striking here that all velar beginnings are dark, whilst all anterior articulations correlate with medium resonance; in this part of the system medium resonance is the clearest resonance available. 'This part of the system' is the 'liquid cluster' part. Both 'liquid' and 'cluster' are phonological terms, and assignment of items to this class is a matter of choice for the analyst. For these reasons it is not at all odd to find this rather complex set of phonetic material assignable to the phonological categories since these are of necessity abstract.

In the same way 'dark' is a phonological category which is phonetically variable and restateable for each phonological configuration that it appears in. In the material we have been considering different realisations are to be stated for **d** in CV and in CCV configurations. It is noteworthy that the back vocoid for dCC_LV is marginally fronter ( ) than for **dCV** ( ); we might want here to make an assessment of the phonology of these items in terms of their spelling, -oo- on the one hand as against -ew- on the other. As we pointed out above, E4 may have a phonology that acts as a repository of historical, social and other signals. From this point of view it is not at all odd that *grew* should be phonologically different in all ways from *goo*.

(ii) CVC configurations
Clear CVC configurations
Some aspects of the phonology of the classes of lexical items dis-

cussed above reappear when we move on to CVC and CVCV configurations. We know from the inspection above of E1 and E2 that their relatively simple phonology entails what we there call cohesion which names the relation whereby the resonance of syllable onset is shared by syllable coda. In E4 cohesion does not apply, but the relevant vowel qualities reappear, so that the phonetics of *due* are found again in the CV-portions of *dupe*, *duke*, and *dune*, and those of *cue* in the CV-portions of *cute* and *cube*. This extends to CVCV, so that *cue* reoccurs in *cupid*, *stew* in *stupid*, and *pew* in *pewter*. In dCVCV(C) too, we have the phonetics of *two* in *toucan*, of *coo* in *cookie* and of *boo* in *booty*. None of this is predictable, of course, given the complexity and looseness of fit amongst the resonances, vocalic nuclei and the other articulatory complexes in this material. In fact cCVC and dCVC both fail to show cohesion in E4, which is reminiscent of E3 in this respect. Final -C in these classes can have any of three resonance categories c, m, and d, exemplified by:

c	*muse*	*fume*	*fuse*
m	*mute*	*puke*	*cute*
d	*feud*	*cube*	

There is some agreement here inside the categories with orthodox articulatory types: m associates with voiceless final plosives, d with voiced ones. By virtue of this association others are not found. So bilabials are found in different resonance categories. This is the reverse side of the coin from the C- initial resonances, where, looking for correspondences of this kind, such as we found were with place of articulation, in a broad sense, rather than with glottal features. What we sometimes have here is a violent disruption between the CV- and the -C parts of CVC. We find, for instance, relatively front vowels, as in *cube*, being followed by a velarised plosive, which may be a rephasing of an earlier - ｂ ｕ .

Dark CVC configuations

The situation with regard to dCVC and dCCVC is even more complicated. Not only is cohesion absent, but there is no regular co-occurrence of syllable nucleus with syllable onset consonant or consonant cluster type. It is necessary to recognise six vocalic types and two resonance categories, **d** and **m**. Partial lists of resonances for initial consonants and consonant clusters are:

m   st   sp   br   tr   l

d   kr   gr   m   n   hg

but, for instance, initial gr - is not always associated with the same nuclear vocoid. We number the vocoids from 1 to 6 as follows:

1 əu   2 ətt   3 ü   4 u

5 ö   6 əu

Lack of uniformity between initial consonant and nuclear vocalic types is shown by the words *groom* and *group*: the first has 6, the second has 5. In the same way we have:

> *cruise* 5   *broom* 6
>
> *croup* 4   *brute* 2
>
> *Bruce* 5

Nor do identical vowels accompany identical resonance sets:

> m m   m m
> *spool* 4   *spoof* 5
>
> d d   d d
> *room* 3   *goon* 6

and overall lack of cohesion is shown by:

m d	d m	d m	d	d	m d
stoop	*hoot*	*goose*	*mousse*		*lewd*

But some sets of co-occurrences can be shown. So, for example, the distribution of some of the vowel types can be stated in relation to other characteristics, though not in a very direct way. Such co-occurrences include

- ❑ if either C_0 or C_{c0} has voice, nasality, and labiality vowel 3 occurs. Nasality is audible throughout the syllable eg

$$\widetilde{noon} \quad \widetilde{prove} \quad \widetilde{room}$$

- ❑ if finals are labial and voiceless, vowel 5 occurs eg

$$loop \quad soup \quad swoop$$

- ❑ all items with final laterality have vowel 4 eg

$$fool \quad spool \quad tool$$

- ❑ all items with vowel 6 are $C \ldots \widetilde{C}$ eg

$$boom \quad doom \quad goon \quad tomb$$

Conclusion

The observations made here are not easily interpretable in phonological terms for a number of reasons. One is that we are dealing with monosyllables only, uttered in isolative style (citation form). The sets of oppositions set up to handle these forms may not operate over longer pieces. In longer pieces, as we have seen in other material, it is often the case that features play hierarchical roles, appearing over longer stretches to the exclusion of other features that characterise 'basic' elements, such as monosyllables in isolation. Secondly, as the material is restricted to one small corner of the vocalic repertoire, we are not in a position to generalise over the vocalic qualities or the resonances that operate at the syllable initial and final places.

What we do have is a set of detailed observations on this limited material which show that the phonetic parameters that interact to constitute it are combined in ways that appears to be quite other than that found in other accents. We have confidence in the validity of the observations for two reasons. One is that the word-list was recorded twice by the speaker without time for prior rehearsal. Impressionistic records were made of both lists and showed remarkable uniformity. The second reason is that a check on the reliability of the observations is provided by the observations on the other accents, **E1 - E3**, which were attended to with equal care, but did not reveal such complexity.

The kind of English described under **E4** is typically called a creole. In such language varieties it is common to find portions of systems from two or more genetically unrelated sources contributing to a complex whole, in lexis, morphology, syntax and, as here, phonology. Tracing the sources of the elements in such an amalgam is a difficult business and falls beyond the scope of this study.

In languages that are not creoles we are used to finding a considerable number of systems, so this point is not one of qualitative difference. However in such non-creoles the area of unification is found, to a large extent, in the phonetics. So that even when the phonology of auxiliaries, say, is different from that of possessives, the detailed phonetic material that relates to both may show a unity in various general characteristics of organisation, sequencing, piecing that transcends categorisation at other levels. In this creole material such phonetic unity is not found. The language seems not to have, as it were, settled down phonetically in the way displayed by languages with a tighter more cohesive and genetically fixed unified central core and a longer history of establishment.

Study 4
Child Language

Introduction

Phonological studies of children's language are dominated by simplistic and, on the whole, uninspired and unrevealing segment-by-segment analyses. Most phonological treatments of children's language are constrained by theories which are monosystemic in orientation and which pay rather little attention to phonetics. In this study we explore some of the implications of not pursuing phonological analysis on a segment-by-segment basis and of taking seriously the notion that in order to do phonology properly we should aim to include all the phonetic data which is relevant to the phonological statement.

We have argued in earlier sections of the book that it is important to pay close attention to phonetic detail. Failure to do so can result in a misrepresentation or misunderstanding of the material. So, for instance, in the domain of children's language development, if phonological treatments fail to take adequate account of the phonic variation there is simply no way of assessing the validity of the frequent claims in the child language literature that often in children's speech there is considerable collapsing or merging of (adult) phonological contrasts. It may well be that the claims made in the literature are valid but the illustrative material and descriptions which accompany them are in general so crass, phonetically, as to render such judgements highly questionable. Clearly all forms of rendering speech into written symbols are data reducing. This is not in question. The point is that some phonological treatments of children's speech reduce the primary phonic data inappropriately.

It is the issue of homonymy, of putative collapsing of contrasts in children's speech, that we take as our starting point here. We will argue that

- ❑ for at least one child the question of whether (adult) phonological contrasts are collapsed or not can be resolved by close attention to the phonic data

- ❑ for at least the part of the child's speech under consideration here there is no compelling reason to make the phonological analysis exclusively in terms of punctual, catenative phonological units

- ❑ an adequate phonological analysis of this child's speech must take account of syllable-resonance linkage features and must recognise 'resonance pieces' of different kinds

- ❑ the phonological analysis must be made in terms of a number of systems

The data we want to consider derive from tape recordings and face-to-face observation of the speech of a Yorkshire girl, Manda. Manda's speech was studied over a period of seven months from 5;4 years to 5;11 years by ourselves and an undergraduate, Kate Brown. Tape recordings and face-to-face impressionistic records were made at regular intervals over this period and one of us (KB) had regular contact five-days a week with Manda.

Labial glides

The focus of analysis here will be 'labial glides' in Manda's speech. In Manda's speech labial glides are of two main kinds. These will be designated Type 1 and Type 2. Type 1 glides are generally characterised by bilabiality or labio-dentality with open approximation and neutral or front resonance. Type 2 glides are characterised by labial-velarity and open approximation. These two articulation types occur as the initials of words such as (1) RED, RICH, ROPE, and (2) WET, WITCH, WOKE repectively; and as components of the initials of (1) TRIP, PRINCE, SCRATCH and (2) TWICE, DWARF and SQUASH respectively.

When the study of Manda's speech began it was clear that in many respects she was like the ' r/w children' often discussed in the child language literature. Many of the initial labial glides in words such as RED and RICH, on first hearing, closely resembled those in words such as WET and WITCH. We say 'closely' because in spite of these labial glides being similar in terms of lip rounding (and in some cases place of labial approximation) on careful listening and observation it was clear that Manda was systematically keeping the glides in these words distinct in a variety of ways. While Type 2 glides in Manda's speech show little variability in articulatory terms throughout the period studied, Type 1 glides exhibit a wide range of variation. Word initial Type 2 glides are characterised by voice, outer lip-rounding, bilabiality, velarity and open approximation. They are also consistently longer (when word initial) than Type 1 glides.

Charateristics of Type 1 glides

The following possibilities for Type 1 glides occur

- ▢ voice, bilabiality with open approximation, symbolised ß̞

- ▢ voice, labio-dentality with open approximation. The labio-dentality here is of two main kinds: endo-labiality (where the top teeth form a stricture with the inside of the bottom lip) and exo-labiality (where the top teeth form a stricture with the top or outside of the bottom lip) Endo-labial glides are symbolised ʋ̝ exo-labial glides are symbolised ʋ̟ . Exo-labial glides are restricted in occurrence to intervocalic position and to certain kinds of initials (see below)

- ▢ voice, bilabiality with co-ordinate endo-labiality with open approximation. These glides are restricted to the earliest stage of Manda's speech which was studied, and to initials of utterances preceded by silence

Manda is not unusual in the range of Type 1 glides which appear in her speech. Other children in the same school exhibit similar ranges of Type 1 glides. Manda's mother, like many of the adults in the area has slightly velarized and rounded endo-labial glides as the initials of words such as RED, RUN, etc. Her father, however, has slightly velarized and rounded post-alveolar approximants at the same place in structure.

Differences between Type 1 and Type 2 glides

All the Type 1 glides in Manda's speech can occur with lip-rounding and lip-spreading. In word-initial position, however, those of them which occur are never velarized. Thus even those Type 1 glides in Manda's speech which are characterised by bilabiality, lip rounding and open approximation are distinct from her Type 2 glides by virtue of being shorter in duration and by not admitting the possibility of velarization. In addition to this certain other characteristics of Type 1 glides mark them as being distinct from Type 2. The earliest impressionistic records made of Manda's speech indicate that her Type 1 glides were strongly lip rounded irrespective of the roundedness of the following vowel. Thus, for instance, we find all with lip rounded initials:

ring   rang

real   room

Even here, however, there appears to be some phonological constraint on the occurrence of certain of the Type 1 glides. Lip rounded bilabial approximants occur very infrequently before tokens of back vowels. (It may be that it is in this environment that bilabial Type 1 glides and Type 2 glides are most susceptible to confusion and that this distributional preference represents some kind of differentiation strategy on the part of the child.) Moreover all the words we have in which Manda employs this initial bilabial Type 1 glide share the characteristic of having non-glottalised endings. (Manda regularly produces final voiceless stops and affricates with preceding glottal stop and creaky voice during the preceding vocalic nucleus. Occasionally there are ejectives in this position.) Thus bilabial Type 1 glides occur in words such as ROW, RASH, REAL, ROAR(S), ROOF and ROSE (=*rosie*). Although there is not enough data for other parts of her language for this early stage these distributional facts suggest that some kind of syllabic phonological

constraints are operating in delimiting the possible range of Type 1
glides which can occur.

As we have indicated Type 1 and Type 2 labial glides are kept distinct in Manda's speech in a number of ways. In addition to the
phonetic characteristics already noted the possible presence or absence
of weak friction associated with certain of these glides serves further to
distinguish the two types. While word-initial Type 2 glides are characterised in part by the absence of audible friction this is not the case for
Type 1 glides. Type 1 glides with labio-dentality are often accompanied
by a very marked eversion of the lower lip and also by weak friction.
When both of these features are present the glides are almost always
longer than other Type 1 glides. These fricated Type 1 glides have some
kind of 'emphatic' function in Manda's speech, being stylistically or
'discourse' conditioned. The fricated glides occur in two contexts

- □   as a response to clarification requests

- □   in elicitation or 'minimal pair' style

The first of these contexts emerges most clearly from recordings of
Manda in conversation with KB. There are thirty-five instances of fricated Type 1 glides as responses to clarification requests. In thirty-one
of these thirty-five instances the original glide was a lip-rounded variant. The second context for fricated Type 1 glides arises out of one of
the techniques used to elicit labial glides from Manda. As a stimulus
for elicitation we assembled a picture book. In using this book with
Manda we found that where we had fortuitously placed pictures close
together which gave 'minimal pairs' (eg *rail ~ whale*; *ring ~ wing*)
Manda regularly produced fricated Type 1 glides. There are some hundred and twenty of these cases in the data.

Variability and distribution of Type 1 glides

The phonetic variability of Type 1 glides in terms of presence or absence of friction and endo or exo-labiality turns out to play an interesting and unexpected role in other parts of Manda's speech.

To illustrate this claim we now direct attention to the characteristics of intervocalic Type 1 glides in Manda's speech. We begin with a
consideration of intervocalic Type 1 labial glides which are word-
internal.

Intervocalic Type 1 glides

These glides exhibit three recurrent characteristics. (1) they are never characterised by friction, (2) they are never rounded (whatever vocalic nuclei flank them) and (3) they are variably endo- or exo-labially articulated. Clearly these glides do not have the same range of possibilities as do the initial Type 1 glides described above. This clearly suggests that any attempt to make one overall statement about the behaviour even of Type 1 labial glides in Manda's speech is doomed to failure. In order to make sense of the phonic data it is necessary to recognise a number of systems within which the labial glides function in rather different ways.

The words *giraffe* and *fairy* and the phrase *here it is* will serve as examples of the behaviour of these word-internal intervocalic Type 1 glides. Labial glides in words such as GIRAFFE where they initiate accented syllables are characterised by voice, endo-labiality and open approximation. Those in words such as FAIRY where they do not initiate an accented syllable are characterised by voice, observably lax exo-labiality, and open approximation. In linking juncture such as *here it is*, *tearing off*, Type 1 glides have the same characteristics as those in words like FAIRY. The important feature here is that endo-labiality occurs only where the glides initiate an accented syllable. The other word-internal Type 1 glides are characterised by exo-labiality. Word-internal Type 2 glides also vary depending on whether or not they initiate accented syllables. Those which do are characterised by a tenser, closer lip-rounding and greater duration than those which do not.

Turning now to intervocalic Type 1 glides in Manda's pronunciation of words such as a ROUNDABOUT and AROUND, we find that the first of these most frequently has a Type 1 glide which is weakly fricated. In the second the glide is never accompanied by friction. Manda's pronunciation of *a house*, *a hexagon* (the name given to tables of that shape in her classroom at school) and *an apple* is also interesting in this respect. In casual running speech these nouns are often pronounced with a Type 1 glide between the indefinite article and the noun thus:

ə'ʮæösʲ   ə'ʮa̱ɓ̩ʲ

a house   *an apple*

ə'ʮɛ̱ʔksəgəm

a hexagon

Under 'emphatic' conditions Manda frequently produces a glottal stop rather than a labial glide. For example:

ʔəʔˑæɷsʲ   ʔəʔà̱ɓəʲ

a house   *an apple*

The obvious conclusion to be drawn here is that from a phonological point of view endo-labiality with weak friction is associated with the beginning of accented syllables and hence can be said to be one of the exponents of accent. However, friction with labio-dentality is only an exponent of accent when the syllable which it begins is word initial. Thus the absence of (the possibility of) friction with the Type 1 glides in *a house* etc can be taken as marking the fact that these glides are not phonologically syllable initial items. They are linking items and therefore have a different status in the child's speech.

Although cursory listening and investigation might suggest that Manda's r/w contrasts are collapsed this is clearly not the case. The Type 1 and Type 2 glides have different ranges of phonetic possibilities even though some of their features do overlap.

Glide types and whole-syllable differences

To this point we have been considering such words as RUN and WON only in terms of the differences in word-initial glides. The following words taken from Manda's speech direct attention towards further characteristics which must be recognised in phonological statement:

rope

woke

ring

wings

rich

witch

room

whoosh

(In order to achieve comparability the only words admitted for consideration here are prepausal.) These records reveal that not only are there differences between the labial glides but also that there are properties of whole syllables which serve to distinguish words with Type 1 glides from those with Type 2 glides. Words with initial Type 1 glides (henceforth Class 1 words) and those with Type 2 glides (henceforth Class 2 words) have different kinds of resonance associated with identical patterns of syllabic cohesion and integration. These integrative features, which characterise the V's and C's in these words, are not systematically present in the same way at other points in the child's speech. Class 1 words show a syllable resonance wherein there is a generally front articulation at V and front resonance at C. Class 2 words, in contrast, have a syllable resonance characterised by a generally back articulation of vocalic nuclei and back resonance in the final consonantal portions. What we have here then is two kinds of 'resonance piece'. From a phonological view point these resonance and articulatory features must be treated together. As Class 1 words are defined as having a Type 1 labial glide as their initial and Class 2 words are defined as having a Type 2 glide as their initial, these glides too are best treated together with the syllable resonance features. Thus the initial glides and the articulatory and resonance features of these words are to be treated as exponents of single units being focussed at the onset of the accented syllable.

Long-domain resonance characteristics

Class 1 words can now be characterised as LDFR items (long-domain front resonance) and Class 2 words as LDBR items (long-domain back resonance). The principal exponents of these long-domain resonances can be stated for three-place structures of the kind illustrated above:

LDFR

- ☐ syllable onset: endo-labiality with non-velarity, voice and open approximation

- ☐ syllable nucleus: vocalic articulation in Zone 1 (even where the vocoid may ultimately be referred to a 'back' category). (See Table 1 below)

- ☐ syllable coda: the final consonantal portion(s) always has a 'clear' (palatalized) resonance, and may have a relatively front articulation

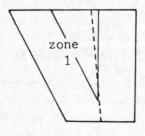

Table 1

LDBR

- ☐ syllable onset: bilabiality with velarity, voice and

open approximation accompanied by appreciable duration

❑ syllable nucleus: vocalic articulation in Zone 2 (even where the vocoid may ultimately be referred to a 'front' category) (See Table 2 below)

❑ syllable coda: the final consonantal portion(s) always has a 'non-clear' (centralised or velarized) resonance, and may have a relatively back articulation

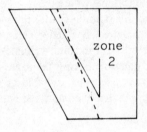

Table 2

For three-place structures where the coda is realised by voice, alveolarity and laterality LDBR items show clear rather than non-clear resonance at the coda. Two place structures (CV open syllables such as RAY, ROW, WHY, WAY) show the same exponents at syllable onset and nucleus as do three place structures.

The treatment of these initial glides as exponents (along with other features) of units having at least a syllable domain effectively 'removes' them from the phonological inventory of punctually stated consonants. These initial glides do, of course, function as consonants with respect, for instance, to their behaviour with preceding definite and indefinite articles.

To those more acquainted with segmental, phonemic types of analysis the present treatment might look rather odd. It is, however, well motivated in two important ways. First, though a detailed analysis will not be presented here, the behaviour of other, non-glide, initial consonants is rather different. Other consonantal types (eg plosives and fricatives) do not enter into syllable integration as do these labial glides (eg with resonance integration between Co and Cco). Second, other glides (having alveolarity and laterality on one hand or palatality on the other) do enter into both syllable cohesion and integration similar to those discussed here. All of which suggests that the glides, as a set, are rather different in their phonological status from other members of the phonetic consonantal inventory and hence require rather different treatment in the analysis.

Polysyllabic domain of resonance

Although the long-domain resonances are stated here for accented syllables which are co-extensive with word pieces they do, in fact, have extent beyond the immediate syllable where they are focussed. The examples that we have cited to this point have all been monosyllables. In polysyllabic words of the structure 'accented syllable-unaccented syllable'. (where a labial glide initiates the first syllable) the same long-domain resonances can be stated as having the same implications but extending here to include the unaccented syllable as well. This is so whether the words are morphologically complex or not. Thus

robin

rabbit

robot

reading

washing

woken

The following polysyllabic pieces show that the long-domain resonances also have extent beyond the word. There are noticeable differences in the realisation of the items *he*, *it* and the indefinite article depending on whether they occur in an LDF or LDB resonance piece:

$$ʔe̦ˈʉ̈i̦·d̦ʒ̦ï̈ʔ̥ʶ°$$

he reads it

$$ʔ̈ε̈ˈwɒ̫ʄ̫ɛ̣ˈε̃̈ʔʰ$$

he washed it

$$ï̈ˈʉ̈ïʔțʂˈm̦æ̃·n$$

a rich man

$$ʔəˈw·ɪʔ·t̫ʃ$$

a witch

$$ʔə̲ˈwə̲·ɐ̃n̫ï̈ˈʉ̈ʔ$$

a 'w' and a 'r'

Rhythmic domains of resonance

The examples above show that long-domain resonances can have extent over the unaccented syllable immediately preceding and following the accented syllable where they are focussed. Our impressionistic records provide some evidence to suggest that the extension of domain of the resonances to preceding unaccented syllables requires that such syllables be rhythmically short. Thus there is no noticeable difference in quality in the vocoids in the unaccented syllables of the following pairs, which occur in the recordings: *turning round, getting wet; baby frog, baby one; better run, under what; very red, very wet*. The resonances seem here to be functioning, in part, to integrate larger rhythmical pieces. The domain of the resonances then encompasses the rhythmical foot in which they occur but never extends to accented syllables in preceding or following feet.

Having seen some of the implications of long-domain resonances it is instructive to reconsider some aspects of Manda's speech dealt with earlier: words where a Type 1 glide occurs in an unaccented place (including its occurrence in linking juncture) and, related to this, Manda's versions of such utterances as *a house*, *a hexagon* (which have a labial glide linking the article to the noun). In none of these cases is there any evidence to suggest that we need to treat the material in terms of long domain resonance. Where a Type 1 glide occurs at these unaccented places the surrounding nuclei and consonantal portions do not exhibit the systematic phonic features of LDFR which was statable for accented places. Indeed the vocalic and consonantal portions here vary considerably in their resonance and articulatory characteristics. Moreover the glide items themselves in such positions exhibit different resonance characteristics (ranging from clear, through central to back). These facts offer confirming evidence that those Type 1 glides which initiate accented syllables are different phonological entities from those phonetically similar glides occuring elsewhere and must be treated as such. It makes no sense to treat this phonic material in a monosystemic fashion. Indeed it is not possible to account coherently for the observable phonetic facts if a monosystemic approach is adopted.

Emphatic speech and resonance variation

Although the statement of long-domain resonance accounts for a great deal of the phonic matter under consideration, a number of other phonetic facts about these items require comment. A look back to the words cited earlier reveals that there are variations in the ways in which Class 1 and Class 2 words begin which have not yet been treated. That is, we find Class 1 items beginning with both 'plain' and palatalized labiodental approximation. We also find Class 2 items beginning with both 'plain' labial-velar approximation and with noticeable increased duration in the glide and/or vocalic onset to the glide. Close consideration of the circumstances under which these realisations occur shows that such variation is not random. It has to do with the realisation of a system of word initial emphasis to which we alluded earlier. These alternations are therefore most effectively treated as exponents of an emphasis system in which there are two terms F and ˜F (front and non-front) articulations. F-onsets are exponents of non-emphasis while ˜F-onsets are exponents of emphasis. We have already discussed some of the phonetic features which characterise the beginnings of emphatic Class 1 words (friction, marked endo-labiality and increased length). In addition to these features emphatic versions are not palatalized at the onset; rather they have central resonance. Emphatic Class 2 words in their turn are characterised by increased length at their onset and/or by noticeably back vocalic onsets to the initial bilabial articulation.

So far we have suggested that a considerable amount of the phonic substance of words such as RING and WING in Manda's speech is to be accounted for not in punctual segmental terms but in terms of phonological units having a long domain. For the purposes of this study we have not and will not address the issue of identifying and stating other systems of units which are 'placed' in these words. However when we come to state the organisation of words such as TRIP and TWIST in Manda's speech some consideration of this matter is necessary. This is because the initial 'clusters' in these words are best regarded as single phonological items with complex phonetic exponents. One obvious reason for adopting this course is that certain labial gestures and resonances are observable in the initial occlusion as well as in the strictures of open approximation which follows it.

Resonance features of initial clusters

Words of the kind TRIP, FROG, GROW and SCRATCH will be referred to as Class 1a items. Words such as TWIST, TWICE, DWARF and SWIM will be referred to as Class 2a items.

In the discussion above of items from Class 1 certain labial gestures (endo/exo-labial) were identified as being related to the realisation of a particular phonological unit at accented or unaccented places. At accented places, in words such as RUN, an endo-labial articulation was found. In words such as VERY an exo-labial articulation was found. However as words of Class 1a show both of these articulation types can occur. This phonetic alternation is thus not associated with a system of accented or unaccented places. However the co-occurrence of endo- or exo-labial articulation with particular places of occlusion is severely limited. Endo-labial articulation in Class 1a items is restricted to occurrence with initial alveolarity and occlusion. Exo-labial articulation is found with initial labio-dentality, labiality, velarity, and occlusion (eg in FROG, PRINCE, SPRING, CRACK, SCRATCH, GROUND) but never with alveolarity and occlusion. Moreover, unlike the labial glides in Class 1 items, discussed earlier, some of the glides in Class 1a items can occur with velarization. We find for instance:

$$ꬵ^ɑ \underset{w}{ʋ} \underset{+}{\overset{ə}{ʋ}} ü \overset{ʔ}{\underset{w}{}} t^c \qquad \underset{+}{ʋ} g \underset{+}{ʋ} a̱ ̃ũ n d^{ʔ}_o$$

fruit   *ground*

$$ɓ^ʔ \underset{+}{ʋ} ḻ ʔ k^h$$

brick

That is, velarization can occur in words of Class la where the preceding occlusive is labial or velar. Labiodental approximants in words such as CRISP, CRACKLE (where the initial occlusion is at the velum) are only rarely velarized and, at the latest period studied, never occur with velarization.

Why should this be so? A consideration of the patterning of English word beginnings suggests that this distribution of velarized/non-velarized labio-dental approximants in items of Class 1 may well be of some phonological interest. While English has no native words which begin **bw, pw, fw, gw** it does have words beginning with **tw** and **dw** as well as **tr** and **dr**. Thus while there might be some premium for speakers to keep **tr/tw** words distinct by non-velarization of the initial **tr** it is of little consequence, from a phonological point of view, whether the **pr, r, gr, fr** initials are velarized or not. (The sporadic occurrence of velarization in **dr** words in Manda's vocabulary can be plausibly related to the existence of apparently only one **dw** word in her vocabulary (DWARF) - a word she had probably acquired from KB during the course of this study.) Evidence for the phonological importance of clear or dark resonance with labial glides in words of Class la can be seen if we consider such items as CRISPS, CREAM, CROAK and CRAB for instance. In impressionistic records made at the beginning of the period of study these words appear with word initial configurations such as

$$k \underset{\underset{+}{ʋ}}{\overset{ə}{ʋ}}_o \qquad k \underset{+}{\overset{ʋ}{ʋ}}_o \qquad k^ə \underset{\underset{+}{ʋ}}{ʋ}_o$$

That is, we find an exo-labial glide occurring with or without dark resonance. Some three and a half months later the same words are only ever produced with the following initials

$$K \, \overset{\partial}{\underset{\underset{+}{\upsilon}}{\upsilon}} \underset{o}{+} \qquad K \underset{\underset{+}{\upsilon}}{\upsilon} \underset{o}{+}$$

that is with an exo-labial glide having either central or clear resonance but never one having dark resonance. At the latest stage studied (in the last month of recording), Manda produces these words with the following initials

$$K \, \overset{\partial}{\underset{\underset{+}{\upsilon}}{\upsilon}} \underset{o}{+} \qquad K \, \overset{\partial}{\underset{\underset{-}{\upsilon}}{\upsilon}} \qquad K \underset{\underset{-}{\upsilon}}{\upsilon}$$

Some words at this latest stage (eg CROAK, CROOKED, CRUMB, CRUST, CRAWL and CROW), all of which have non-front vocalic nuclei, are always realised with an endo-labial glide in their initial configuration. (Compare the earlier observations concerning the infrequent occurrence of non-velarised lip-rounded glides before tokens of non-front vowels.) We can plausibly argue that these changes in the ranges of pronunciation relate to a reassorting of lexical categories: kr-initial words (because there are also kw-initial words) are being aligned with **tr** and **dr**-initial words. Further support for this interpretation is provided by the fact that there is no reassorting of articulatory and resonance type with words which have **gr**-initial (where there are no **gw** congeners - at least not in Manda's speech).

Those words in which there is a possibility of velarized labiodental glides differ from those in which there is not, both in the class of possible initial occlusives which occur (labials and velars) and also in that they admit the possibility of vocoid between the occlusive and the glide. Thus we find the following variants:

frog   *pram*

grape

Class la items then do not form a simple group. The phonological

analysis must distinguish between those words with initial alveolarity
and closure and the others in this 'class'. For the present purposes we
can do this simply by recognising a sub-class (Class la(ii)) which is
identified by the presence of certain initial occlusives (labials and
velars).

A brief consideration of items from Class la and Class 2a shows
that long domain resonance statements of the kind proposed for Class 1
and 2 items are again applicable:

frog   *squash*

crack   *quack*

cream   *queen*

drink   *swim*

Here again we see that certain words (Class la) have the general
characteristics of relatively fronter nuclei and consonantal portions and
a tendency to clear resonance in their codas. On the other hand items
from Class 2a have generally backer realisations and a darker resonance in their codas.

The exponents of the LDF resonance for Class la items are statable
thus:

LDFR Class la (i)

- ❏ syllable onset: initial occlusion has co-ordinate endo-labialization with clear (central or palatalized) resonance which continues with open approximation until onset of the syllable nucleus

- ❏ syllable nucleus: as stated above for LDF resonance Class 1 items

- ❏ syllable coda: the final consonantal portion(s) has non-dark resonance and may be fronted in articulation

LDBR Class la (ii)

- ❏ syllable onset: either (a) the initial occlusion has co-ordinate exo-labialization with clear (central or palatalized) resonance which continues with open approximation until the onset of the syllable central nucleus; or the initial occlusion may have co-ordinate exo-labialization. In both cases it always has dark resonance. It may be followed by a period of openness + orality + voice + relatively back resonance which continues with velarized exo-labialization and voice until the onset of the syllable nucleus

- ❏ syllable nucleus: as stated above for Class la items

- ❏ syllable coda: the final consonant(s) has non-dark resonance. If the initial is dark, final non-darkness is realised as centralised resonance unless the final is a nasal in which case there is clear resonance. If the initial is dark any onglide to a final consonant is less peripheral than if the initial has clear resonance

It should be noted that for Class la certain features of the syllable initials which for Class 1 items were stated as F/ ̄F exponents of emphasis are here accounted for by recognising a sub-class of items Class la (ii).

The reason for this is that the front/back variations observed in the Class la words are properties of word phonology and not exponents of an emphasis system. Whereas with Class 1 words emphasis was realised, in part, by relatively back resonance associated with initial labiodentality with words of Class la we find both front and back resonances being realised in emphatic styles. Thus we find:

brown   *grass*

freeze

occurring as emphatic realisations of these items. (The realisation of emphasis in words of Class la appears to be realised solely by increased length in the initial.)

The exponents of the LDB resonance for Class 2a items are statable as follows:

LDBR Class 2a

- ☐ syllable onset: initial occlusion has dark resonance (centralised or velarized) and is noticeably labialized. This labialization with velarity and open approximation continues until the onset of the syllable nucleus

- ☐ syllable nucleus: as stated above for LDBR Class 1 items

- ☐ syllable coda: the final consonantal portion(s) has dark (centralized or velarized) resonance and may also be retracted

As with Class 1 and 2 items for items from Class la and 2a the LDFR and LDBR have extent beyond the syllable on which they are focussed.

The resonance pieces which result include, as with Class 1 and 2 items, immediately preceding and following unstressed syllables, thus

scratching

swimming

grubby

twenty

a *train*

a *twist*

a *crisp*

a *twin*

it's *tripped*

it's *twisted*

The differences in vocalic quality and consonant resonance, at the places indicated in bold in the glosses, are, as with Class 1 and 2 items, more or less front, clearer or darker, depending on the resonance category focussed at the accented syllable.

Conclusion

In presenting this brief sketch of a small part of one child's speech we have tried to draw attention to a number of features which seem to us to be crucial if we are to come to an understanding of the phonic aspect of language development

❑   it is necessary to begin with observations which are
    as finely detailed as we can possibly make them.
    The great bulk of so-called phonological treatments
    of children's language are vitiated because they do
    nothing more than simply elevate an impoverished,
    broad transcription to phonological status. Such ap-
    proaches can only obstruct the research process

❑   in making phonological statements there is no rea-
    son to expect to find 'contrast' organised on a
    segment-to-segment basis, ie realised at one place in
    structure only

❑   there is no reason to expect that the most felicitous
    phonological statement will treat phonic details
    which are punctually and segmentally represented in
    impressionistic records in a punctual, segmental way
    in statement. Indeed by looking at such features as
    'resonance pieces' we may get much more interest-
    ing insights into the way the child's language is or-
    ganised

❑   there are compelling reasons to recognise the need
    for polysystemic statement. Monosystemic ap-
    proaches are, by their very nature, insensitive to the
    systematically variable properties of language

We have attempted to show that if phonological treatments of
children's speech free themselves from restricting (and rather unin-
teresting) segmental phonemic concerns it is possible to account for the
phonetic variation we find rather than throwing it away. (As phonologists, we are not, after all, interested in producing writing systems for
children's speech which is really all that phonemic-type analyses are
useful for.)

   Some of the aspects of Manda's speech which we have discussed
may seem rather 'exotic'. If this is so, we suspect it is because the usual descriptions of children's speech in the literature tend to grossly sim-
plify the phonic data. If in our representation of children's speech we
diligently try to respond to as much of the phonic data as possible quite
a different picture of the systems and structure of children's speech emerges when we come to do our phonology.

Study 5

Intonation and Interaction

Preliminaries

This study sketches an approach to the phonological analysis of intonational contrast and function, in one localised variety of British English. It attempts to show how a close consideration of the content and structure of conversational talk can contribute to the identification and elaboration of relevant functional categories for phonological analysis. It is therefore rather different from most current approaches to the study of intonation systems in three theoretically important respects

- ❏ the material considered derives entirely from naturally occurring face-to-face conversational interaction.

- ❏ the analysis attempts to prejudge as little as possible the salience of phonetic features.

- ❏ the analysis seeks explicitly to motivate and warrant the functional categories employed by reference to the observable behaviour of the conversational participants.

Thus, no invented or hypothesised material is allowed to contribute to the analysis; although pitch features are examined in the analysis, they are not assumed to have any *a priori* functional primacy; the analysis does not simply rest on or trade on the unexamined and unexplicated intuitions of the analyst concerning function and functional distinctiveness.

Material

The material considered here comes from tape-recordings made during the course of a large-scale sociolinguistic survey of urban Tyneside (the Tyneside Linguistic Survey [TLS]). The particular fragments of interaction which will be the focus of attention here are taken from freewheeling, informal interviews with six adult localised Tyneside speakers. At the end of interviews carried out as part of the TLS research, the interviewer (a localised Tyneside speaker - McN) was required to ask the interviewees whether or not they recognised and used certain putative local dialect words. These test words were presented orally to the interviewee, prefaced by a version of the following statement:

> 'I'm going to read out a list of words and for each one I'd like to know if you know what it means and if you use it yourself. They're all local words.'

We will concentrate on the interviewees' responses to the presentation of these test words. In particular we will deal with the ways in which interviewees, on occasions 'repeat' these words. We will show that a careful consideration of the interactive aspects of this material yields fruitful insights for an understanding of intonational systems.

Examining the interaction

We begin the analysis with a consideration of some interactive aspects of the talk. We do this in order to motivate the functional categories we will map the phonetic material onto. The primary aim here will be to try and identify and describe the kinds of interactional tasks that are being attended to and accomplished in the interviewer/interviewee talk.

Simple displays of recognition

Fragments 1 - 6 give some initial impression of the unproblematic ways in which this dialect-word-test part of the interviews can run off:

1

    McN: erm bait
                  (.)
    JoH: aye
    McN: aye=
    JoH: =scam
    McN: aha (.) yes (.) aye

2

    McN: er (0.2) fettle
                  (.)
    GSh: ye:s
    McN: like to fettle somebody
    GSh: ⌊ yes aha

3

    McN: er: stot
                  (0.5)
    EiR: er:: (.) no
    McN: you wouldn't use it now
    EiR: no

4

    McN: erm (.) parky
                  (.)
    DWi: yes:
    McN: bout your food
    DWi: mhm

5

    McN: er (.) clamming
                  (.)
    LPh: yes
    McN: mhm: you would use it
    LPh: ⌊ clamming
                  (.)
    LPh: I might do (.) yeah

6

    McN: bullets (.) for sweets
                (0.3)
    EiR: n:o:
    McN: no

(The appendix at the end of the study gives details of the transcription conventions.)

In fragments 1 - 6 following the presentation of the test word, the interviewees respond with a *yes* or *no* (or equivalent). These straightforward positive or negative responses appear to be displaying recognition of the word and claiming its use or otherwise. Occasionally McN pursues the second aspect and, as in fragment 5, asks further *you would use it*. The following fragments illustrate various other ways in which the 'recognition task' can be unproblematically accomplished:

7

    McN: er: parky
              (.)
→ JoH: I've often said that ha ha ha
    McN: ⌊d'you use
    McN: aye (.) parky about your food
    JoH: ⌊why aye (.) aha

8

    McN: h:owk
              (0.2)
→ LPh: eh (.) no I don't use that one
    McN: ⌊no:

9

    McN: er (0.2) beck (.) meaning a stream
              (0.4)
→ LPh: well I don't hear it (.) here very much=
    McN: =no

10

        McN: er what about knooled (.) be knooled
                  (0.2)
→ DWi: oh aha I've used that (* *) definitely
        McN: ⌊ yes ⌊yes

11

        McN: bullets
                  (0.2)
→ GSh: no: (.) I don't use that (.) no: sweets
        McN: ⌊ no   ⌊mhm no
                  (.)
        McN: yeah yeah
        GSh: I used to when I was a kid mind you (.) aha
        McN: ⌊ uh yeah

We will refer to the interviewee's turns (at the places arrowed in the
margin) as **recognition displays**.

Understanding checks

On other occasions, however, problems can be seen to arise in the suc-
cessful management of this word recognition task. This is exemplified
by the following fragments:

12

        McN: er (0.2) varnigh
                  (3.5)
        EiR: varnigh
                  (0.4)
        McN: aye (1.5) you know for nearly
                  (1.5)
        EiR: w I've never heard it but I've heard me
                ⌊mother use it

13

    McN: m er (0.5) what about er (0.3) knooled
              (0.2) you know (.) to be knoo:led
              (0.6)
    JoH: h be knooled
              (0.5)
    McN: wh (.) er (0.2) aye like
    McN: er
    JoH: uh I've often said it yes
    McN: aye (0.4) mhm

14

    McN: boody (1.0) boody
              (0.7)
    JoH: boody
              (0.2)
    McN: aye
              (0.5)
    JoH: oh no (.) no I'd not say that ...

15

    McN: e: (1.0) mel
              (2.8)
    JoH: mel
              (.)
    McN: mel (1.2) aye (1.4) know (0.5) not
              (0.5) for a hammer
              (2.3)
    JoH: don't think I've ever heard it now: n:
    McN: [no

16

     McN: ... er: (0.5) aside (0.4) for beside
                (1.0)
     DWi: aside
                (0.2)
     McN: yeah its just aside the fire (2.2)
             ⌊could you say that
                (1.5)
     DWi: aside
                (.)
     McN: or would you rather say beside
                (0.5)
     DWi: beside
                (.)
     McN: mm

17

     McN: er (0.2) varnigh
                (3.5)
     DWi: varnigh
                (0.3)
     McN: aye (1.5) you know for nearly
     DWi: I've never heard it but I've heard me
             mother (.) use it

18

     McN: er: (1.5) hoy
                (1.2)
     DWi: hoy
     McN: hoy it across: (.) uhu
                (0.7)
     DWi: uhum

19

```
McN:   er (0.8) mel
              (0.9)
ApC:   what
              (.)
McN:   mel
              (0.4)
ApC:   mel:=
McN:   =mhm (0.6) ha- ha- (.) ha- h I
              think it's only men that know it
HuC:   hammer
              (.)
ApC:   no: I don't have that
```

20

```
McN:   aside h (0.4) meaning beside
              (1.5)
LPh:   aside=
McN:   =aside (.) do you say (.) it's
              just aside the fire
              (0.4)
LPh:   on:o hh I don't
              (.)
McN:   no (0.3) but you do hear people saying
              it=
LPh:   =I've heard it said
```

In fragments 12 - 20 we find that following the production of a test word by McN there is a noticeable pause before the interviewee responds. (These pauses range from 0.5 seconds to 3.5 seconds.) Then, rather than producing a simple recognition display, the interviewee responds with what looks like a repetition of the test word itself.

Common to all these interchanges is that McN's turn after the repetition contains some kind of acknowledging or confirmatory token. In addition it may also contain some kind of synonymous construction for the test word or an exemplification of its meaning. This suggests that McN is taking the repeat as a turn which is designed to get him to clarify some aspect of his previous utterance.

Supporting evidence for this claim, that in producing these repeats interviewees and signalling that they have got a problem, can also be found in the sequential placement of their subsequent talk.

Notice that the interviewee makes no attempt to produce any further talk until McN has done this post-repeat turn. This is not happenstance. There is no evidence that the interviewees had begun speaking, had paused, and intended to speak on but that McN cut in on their turn at talk. They do not, for instance, attempt to do talk in overlap with McN which could indicate that they had wished to go on speaking when McN interrupted, that their turn was not complete (despite the pause) and that it had been cut short. These repeat turns are designed to be just one word long.

A further point to observe is the rapidity with which McN's turn begins after the repeat. Any intervening silent pause is never more than 0.5 seconds. This can be taken to indicate that whatever the problem is that has occasioned the repeat turn it is one which needs fairly rapid resolution before the interchange can proceed. In the light of these analytic observations consider the following, somewhat more intricate exchange:

```
21
McN:   erm (1.3) bray
          (1.8)
LPh:   brere
McN:   b:ray
          (0.3)
LPh:   bray (2.0) wha- what do you mean a-uh horse (0.7)
McN:                              ⌊ for to hit
LPh:   hhh (.) ⌈oh: ye- a- ye- hh hh er y:es I haven't heard it for
McN:           ⌊no: for to hit
LPh:   a long⌈time  though
McN:          ⌊ m:
McN:   nm: you don't use it- (.) these days m=
LPh:   = I've never used that
McN:                      ⌈ no
LPh:   no
```

Here, after a malproduction by the interviewee and a repetition by McN of the test word, the interviewee repeats the word and then there follows a pause of two seconds. This is further followed by an overt question from the interviewee which seeks to elicit from McN an appropriate frame of meaning for the test word. That is, when McN does not do any talk which treats her repeat as requiring a confirmatory or clarifying response from him she goes on to reformulate her talk explicitly in question form. Notice that McN's talk in overlap with this turn shows a responsiveness to this evolving question in that he now offers a framing gloss for the test word. In this sequence we find rather nice confirming evidence that LPh's repeat was designed as a check on understanding and was required to be treated as such.

In these fragments then the interviewees do not offer any explicit sign of recognition, or otherwise, of the test item until after McN's turn which confirms that they have produced the correct word. We will refer to these kinds of repeat as **understanding checks** - they are designed to check that a preceding utterance has been heard or understood correctly and they require a response before proceeding with any further talk.

Repeats as displays of recognition and of mulling over

(a) Alternative designs for recognition displays

Now consider another set of interchanges found in this corpus. In these we find the test-word repeated before a *yes* or *no* recognition token is produced.

22

        McN: er (1.0) bonny
                    (1.3)
        GSh: bonny aha
                    (0.4)
        McN: aye
        GSh: I use bonny

23

        McN: er (0.5) bait
                    (0.5)
        EiR: bait (.) yes
                    (.)
        McN: yes

24

      McN: er (0.7) knooled
                  (1.0)
      LPh: knooled (.) aha
                  (0.2)
      McN: aye
                    (.)
      LPh: I use that-

25

      McN: er: (.) bait
                  (1.2)
      DWi: bait (.) mhm m
                  (0.2)
      McN: yes:

The following fragments, 26 - 29, in addition to re-doing the test-word, all contain laughter particles of various kinds. This suggests that as well as displaying recognition these turns carry some additional interactional import such as, say, displaying surprise at being presented with that particular word.

26

  McN: bray
        (.)
  GSh: yes I do I bray aha youhous bray hay hh hh ha ha huh huh huh
  McN: [yeah you bray thehehm yeah (* * *) bray yeah

27

  McN: er (1.0) howk
        (0.4)
  DWi: hh (.) howk huh huh (.) he- heh heh
  McN: [hah hah hah hah
  DWi: heh yehes: heh huh=
  McN: yeah (.) er (.) d'you use that meaning like to poke out
  DWi: [cough]
  McN: or- (.) to give somebody a good howking
        (0.3)
  DWi: hah he- (.) give somebody a good howking

28
   McN: bray (1.0) for to hit
   ApC: [b:ray: (1.0) hhh -a ha-ha-ha-ha hhhh
                (0.7)
   ApC: not really I'm very familiar with - (.) I have used it
   McN: [yes
               (.)
   McN: yes (0.2) but you wouldn't use it now (.) no

29
             McN: er (0.8) varnigh
                     (0.9)
             GSh: varnigh (1.0) oh yes I've sometimes
                    said varnigh
             McN: aye (.) uh (.) yeah

30
             McN: erm (0.6) cree
                     (2.6)
             EiR: cree: (1.9) I've heard it but'd not
                    use it
                       (0.2)
             McN: yeh
             EiR: mhm (.) cree

31
   McN: er (0.5) cree
          (1.2)
   GSh: c:ree: (0.4) no::
          (2.0)
   McN: uh- um (0.2) pigeon cree or a-
   GSh: no: m:
          (0.2)
   GSh: cree oh yes: pigeon cree ducket (.) or: ho-ho-ho-ho-
   McN: [aye yes (.) yes mhm   [yeah

32

McN: ... e: (0.5) aside (0.4) for beside
    (1.0)
DWi: aside
    (0.2)
McN: yeah its just aside the fire (2.2)
   could you say that
    (1.5)
DWi: aside
    (0.8)
McN: or would you rather say beside
    (0.5)
DWi: beside

33

McN: er (.) hh (.) ken (.) for to know
    (0.4)
ApC: hh I dinna ke:n: (.) oh no I leave that
McN: ⌊ mm
ApC: to me s: (.) cousin from Glasgow ...

34

McN: er (1.1) clarts
    (0.3)
ApC: clarts (.) clarty (0.4) we:ll: might do=
McN: =yeh

35

McN: howk
    (.)
GSh: how:k it out m::
McN: or give someone a good howking
GSh: ⌊ no   ⌊ no
GSh: no: I wouldn't u
McN: ⌊ no aye

36

McN: uh (.) er (.) bullets
    (0.8)
LPh: bla:ck bullets (0.3) mn: (.) no:
McN: ⌊ no mm

37
```
        McN:   er (.) fettle
                       (0.2)
        EiR:   fine fettle (.) yes I might say Oh I'm
        McN:                 [ yeah
        EiR:   in fine fettle this morning
        McN:            [ yeah
```

In all of these fragments (22 - 37) we again find that the interviewee repeats the test word. However it is clear from the interviewees' subsequent talk and from the placing of McN's talk relative to these repeat-turns that they are rather different from the understanding checks we have just looked at. In all of these fragments we find that the interviewees' turns which contain the repeat of the test word also contain a form of *yes* or *no* (or extended equivalent formulation). They are designed as **recognition displays**. McN certainly treats them as such. Notice, for instance, that even where the interviewee leaves a noticeable pause after the repeated item (eg in fragments 28, 29 and 30) McN makes no attempt to come in. Rather he delays his next turn at talk until the interviewee has produced speech which explicitly displays recognition of the test word. That is, these repeats, at the moment of their production as not heard by McN as displaying problems in the way that the repeats in fragments 12 - 20 are. (Recollect the speed with which McN's confirmatory/clarifying turn was done in those examples.)

(b) Recognition and mulling over

Closer inspection of fragments 22 - 39 above, however, reveals that although there are similarities in the recognition turns they do not actually form a unitary group. Even though McN does not respond to the repeats as exhibiting problems which require speedy resolution, in fragments 12 - 20 something other than simple recognition and confirmation/denial of use is going on.

In fragments 29 - 37 the issue for the interviewee at the point of repeating the test word is not one of 'have I heard the word correctly' (as in the case of the understanding checks) but rather 'let me think about this, let me try the word out before I give you a response'. These repeats are displays of **mulling over** [the word]. We can see that recognition is not a problem here, for in a number of cases the interviewee is able to employ the word appropriately - in itself a display of recognition. So, for example, in fragments 33 and 35 the test words are built into utterances to try them out. In 36 the word is appropriately collocated (meaning 'mint humbugs'), and in 34 the interviewee does not simply repeat the word but does it again in its adjectival form. It is only after such talk that the interviewees venture an opinion as to use. None of these cases are treated as checks by McN. He does not, for instance, come in with the kinds of confirming, appropriacy/clarifying turn that we have seen earlier. In all these cases the interviewees frame their answers in terms of use (eg in fragment 30 EiR asserts hearing, rather than using, and in 29 GSh claims occasional but not regular use of the words in question). The issue of use, rather than recognition (or any of the other things implicated by an understanding check) is the one that is seen as salient here by the interviewer too.

Phonetic correlates of repeat turns

We will begin examination of the phonetic aspects of the repeat turns by looking first at those we have designated **understanding checks**. The main reason for beginning with these forms is that apparently similar phenomena have received consideration in the linguistics literature - but not, however, in relationship to the other kinds of repeat turns represented here. Repeated utterances such as those in fragments 12 - 20 are conventionally referred to as **echo questions** and usually glossed as 'requests for the repetition of something unheard, forgotten, or disbelieved'. Standard linguistic discussions of these forms observe that interrogative echoes bear some of the marks of question classification, in that they can be divided into **yes-no** and **wh-** types, where the former typically has 'rising question intonation'. Some discussions further distinguish between **recapitulatory echo questions** (which repeat prior talk as a way of having its content confirmed) **and explicatory echo questions** (which ask for clarification, rather than the repetition of something just said). We prefer to use the term **understanding check** here because it more transparently characterises the material at hand than **echo question** does (notice that McN does not systematically distinguish in his responses to these checks between recapitulatory or explicatory echoes). One reason for adopting **understanding check** rather than **echo question** emerges when we consider the following fragments:

40

    McN: erm (0.6) bairn
             (0.6)
    ApC: ben
             (0.4)
    McN: bairn
    ApC: bai::rn
             (0.2)
    McN: yes little bairn
    ApC: hh oh sometime I say bairn (.) yes

41

    McN: er (1.0) howk (1.8) howk
             (0.5)
    JoH: hous:e
             (.)
    McN: no howk (.) you know for:
    JoH: aye I-
             (.)
    JoH: oh haye howk definitely definitely aye aye
    McN: yeah

42

    McN: er (0.6) cree
              (1.2)
    DWi: crib=
    McN: =cree:=
    DWi: =cree: (0.5) ye:s:
              (0.3)
    McN: yes

43

    McN: er (2.2) gully
             (0.5)
    EiR: knife
             (.)
    McN: aye=
    EiR: =yes=
    McN: =you use that
    EiR: [I use gully (.) yes

Again in these exchanges the interviewee's first turn appears to be doing work to elicit a clarification of what has been said. In these fragments, however, we do not find a repeat of the test word. In 40 - 42 the interviewee's utterance is a malproduction of the test word, while in 43 at the same place we find a lexical item which is similar in meaning but not similar in sound to the test item. Nonetheless the responses of McN in the next turn show similarities to those at this point in fragments 12 - 20. He responds in a way appropriate to the interviewee having done an understanding check which treats the prior utterance as problematic and requires clarification of what was said. That the interviewee's turns in these fragments represent similar phenomena can also be seen by considering their talk subsequent to the understanding check. In all these cases the check is done with a single word and the interviewee produces no further talk until after the interviewer's next turn. Again as in the case of the checks considered earlier, McN responds rapidly to confirm/disconfirm the interviewee's version of the test word, always repeating the word where there has been a malproduction. It is only after McN has done this that the interviewee offers any sign of recognition or otherwise of the test item.

(a) Understanding checks

All the understanding checks in this corpus are characterised by a falling pitch contour (not the rising contour suggested by conventional treatments). The pitch fall is one which starts high in the speaker's range and quickly falls to low. There is a marked crescendo-descrescendo coincident with the pitch peak and the whole word is louder than the interviewee's usual talk and louder than the interviewer's preceding turn. We do find pitch falls co-occurring with other of the repeated words in this corpus but they differ from those which characterise checks in a number of ways:

- ❑ either they do not end low or
- ❑ they do not start high and the fall is not rapidly executed and/or
- ❑ they co-occur with breathy voice quality and/or
- ❑ they are quieter than the interviewee's usual talk and quieter than the interviewer's preceding talk.

We will now examine some of these other pitch falls which co-occur with repeats.

(b) Prefaces to checks

Consider the following fragments in all of which we find a pitch fall occurring with a repeated test word.

44

        McN: er (2.4) cree
                  (1.7)
        JoH: cre:e:: (0.2) for hut
                  (0.2)
        McN: aye
                 (0.6)
        JoH: I say hut (.) ha ha

45

McN: erm (0.3) bait
         (2.5)
LPh: ba:i:t (.) you mean putting lunch uh- lunch up an that
McN: ⌈mhm aye
         (0.9)
LPh: we:ll (1.5) wl I don't use it (.) I (.) I've really got
McN: ⌈ you wouldn't use it ⌈ no
LPh: no:: reason to use it
McN: ⌊mm:
LPh: but
         (.)
McN: yeah
LPh: me mother used to use it=
McN: =yeah=
LPh: =I know that:

46

        McN: em: (1.0) gully
                 (0.6)
        ApC: gully (.) s that a knife
                 (.)
        McN: mhm (0.2) yeah
        ApC: ⌈ a gully (.) might do
        McN: yea:h

The pitch contour which occurs here with the interviewee's repeats of the test word is one which falls to mid or just below mid. Notice that in each case after repeating this word there is a micropause and then more talk from the interviewee in which they propose a gloss for the test item. In fragments 44, 45 and 46 the final word in the gloss is realised with the quickly executed high to low fall described earlier. In fragment 45 this same high to low fall is located on the word *lunch*. In each of these exchanges McN does not attempt to come in with confirmation, disconfirmation or clarification directly after the repeated test word with the high to mid fall. His receipting turn is only done after the production of the high to low fall. From the design of the turns in which they occur and from the way they are treated by McN it appears that the talk produced at these places in these fragments is different from that 12 - 20. Here there is indication in the interviewee's subsequent talk that they have heard what was said (there is not a hearing problem) but they are uncertain as to the meaning of what was said. In these cases, then, it is specifically the meaning problem which is being presented for resolution. Thus the pitch movement co-occurrent with the repeated test word is not hearable as a simple check but as a preface to a check. Certainly McN's behaviour can be taken to support such an analysis. Such behaviour on the part of the McN, significantly, points to the interactional salience of the mid pitch ending to the fall. This suggests that we can profitably treat end-point of fall as having relevance for a system of delimitation in which falls to low implicate finality while falls to non-low are implicative of non-finality.

(c) Mulling over

In fragments 29 - 39 which exemplify **mulling over** or **try-outs** we find that the repeats are done with falling pitch which ends low in the speaker's range. But here, unlike the pitch falls with check-repeats, the falls never begin above mid. In addition they are not rapidly executed, and they are characterised by longer duration. This means that we find rather flat, narrow falling pitch contours with a gradual quietening of loudness throughout the word - occassionally moving into whisper phonation. All of these repeats are noticeably quiet and frequently realised with breathy voice (sporadic we find overall nasalisation of the repeated word). Thus mulling over is characterised by a cluster of phonetic events quite different from that associated with understanding checks.

It may be that the features of loudness and voice quality referred to here are crucially involved in the production and recognition of mulling over for these interactants. In some cases we find a repeat (or malproduced near repeat) done with a high to low falling pitch. In each such case, however, the overall volume of the repeat is noticeably below the norm for the interviewee and much quieter than McN's preceding talk; the falls are long in duration with the loudness contour getting quieter throughout the word ; all are accompanied by breathy voice; and none are treated by McN as understanding checks.

(d) Recognition displays

The cluster of phonetic events which characterise repeats as recognition displays is very different from those considered so far. All these recognition displays we find a rising pitch contour. Unlike checks and mulling over the pitch of the start of the rise may be high or low. Thus fragments 24 and 24 both start relatively high in the speaker's range unlike the other cases. There may also be variability in the loudness features associated with these repeats. They may be very loud (eg fragments 27 and 28), or at around the speaker's norm for volume. They may have have an overall loudness increase (eg fragments 27 and 28), or they may have a gradual diminishing of loudness throughout the repeat (the rest). They are not, however, produced with loudness below the speaker's norm.

Understanding checks with different grammatical structures

The material considered so far demonstrates that repeats of words can function distinctively for localised Tynesiders as **understanding checks, recognition displays** or **mulling over.** We have shown that one of the phonetic correlates of these functions is pitch. In contrast to many varieties of English, these Tynesiders accomplish understanding checks not with rising contour but with falling ones. However, the following fragments suggest that it would be premature to conclude that all utterances functioning as understanding checks have the same pitch exponents.

47

```
McN:   e: (.) never mind I'll mangage but
                        (.)
ApC:   never mind I'll mangage what
                        (.)
McN:   I'll manage but
                      (0.4)
ApC:   but (.) yes that's fine
```

48

```
McN:   could you give us em the (.) opposite
                 of (0.8) I'll be going  there  this week

                       (1.9)
DWi:   give you what
McN:   the opposite
```

49

```
McN:   would you mind stop talking
                       (2.5)
LPh:   would you mind st stop what
McN:   talking
LPh:     talking
McN:      [ yeah
                     (0.2)
LPh:   n no I wouldn't
```

50

```
McN:   e:: (.) when did it happen you
                     (0.5)
GSh:   when did it happen what
                       (.)
McN:   when did it happen you
                     (0.7)
GSh:   happen you
                  (.)
McN:   yeah
                    (0.5)
GSh:   oh no (.) I don't think I would say that (.) n:o
```

51

    McN: er (.) I'm gann to stay with the son
             for the holidays
                  (1.0)
    JoH: uh you gannin where
    McN: I'm going to stay with the son for the holidays
                  (0.9)
    JoH: aha I say that (.) I don't ever stop with him th=
    McN: =don't you (0.2) do you call him the son
                  (0.5)
    JoH: aye the son (.) aye

52

    McN: Jack didn't think much to the race
                  (1.1)
    JoH: Jack (0.3) didn't think much to the what
                  (0.4)
    McN: to the race
                  (0.4)
    JoH: to the rain
                  (0.5)
    McN: the race
                  (0.3)
    JoH: h oh no (.) no (.) I never say that

These interchanges, which involve the same speakers considered previously, come from a part of the TLS interviews where attention focussed on grammatical acceptibility. Interviewees were presented orally with a number of syntactic constructions and were required to say whether or not they found them acceptable and could produce them, in appropriate circumstances, themselves. We see in each of the fragments here that after a presentation of the construction by McN, the interviewee partially repeats the utterance but explicitly questions (by use of *what, where*) a further part of the presented construction. In all these cases McN's next turn is only minimally delayed and is formulated as a (rapid) whole or partial repeat of his initial turn. Unlike the cases of understanding checks considered earlier, however, these checks are not done with a falling pitch contour. Instead where an understanding check is done containing a wh-word for the item (or items) being checked the pitch contour used (as in non-localised English) is a rising one. (We also find the straightforward (high to low fall) contour with increased loudness in fragments 49, 50 and 52. In 49 it co-occurs with LPh's utterance (*talking*) which checks again what the last word of McN's first utterance. In 50 it co-occurs with the word *you* in GSh's turn *happen you* which again seeks to check the last, apparently problematic, word in the test-sentence. In 52 the high to low fall contour co-occurring with H's malproduction *rain*. Here, as in the other cases McN responds quickly to correct or confirm the item so checked.

This difference in pitch exponents between word-repeat and wh-checks serves to remind us that it is not the case that all functionally similar entities have the same exponents and points to the need to formulate our phonological statement in poly-, rather than mono-systemic terms. These same interchanges also contain instances of the kinds of phonetic events which were earlier identified as characterising understanding checks. This difference also serves to alert us to problems in attempting to describe different varieties of English in terms say of an inventory of 'tones' whose 'meanings' are stated *a priori*. It is no use trying to import functional categories (such as tones) arising from an analytic statement of one variety into the description of another variety. If we are to get to grips with intonational meaning and the relationship of intonational exponents to categories/function then, we must clearly pay close attention to phonetic, general linguistic and interactive detail.

Appendix

Notation conventions

The notation employed in this study derives in the most part from that designed by Gail Jefferson. Conventional orthography is used with minor modifications to suggest pronunciation features. In addition the following conventions are employed:

:   as in IPA conventions this symbol indicates sustention of sound. The more colons the longer the sound.

(0.4)   pause within or between turns, given in tenths of a second.

(.)   pause of one tenth of a second or less; referred to as a 'micro-pause'.

=   marked at the end of one speaker's turn and at the beginning of the next indicates that the end of the first turn and the beginning of the next are almost, but not quite, simultaneous.

[square brackets represent the point at which simultaneous speech begins

(**)   where asterisks appear in parentheses, we have been unable to assign any representation to the enclosed portion. The number of asterisks corresponds to the number of syllables we hear the speaker as having produced.

hhh   audible outbreaths or breathiness in words. The number of 'h's' corresponds to the duration of the outbreath(s) measured in tenths of a second.

˙hh   audible inbreaths. The number of 'h's' following the raised point corresponds to the duration of the inbreath measured in tenths of a second.